# THE DRAMATISTS GUILD RESOURCE DIRECTORY™

# 2011

## The Writer's Guide to the Theatrical Marketplace™

## 17th Edition

*Focus* Publishing
R. Pullins Company
PO Box 369
Newburyport, MA 01950
www.pullins.com

ISBN 13: 978-1-58510-403-1
ISBN 10: 1-58510-403-5

The Dramatists Guild Resource Directory and The Writer's Guide to the Theatrical Marketplace are trademarks of The Dramatists Guild.

Cover image © istockphoto / THEPALMER

This book is published with permission by Focus Publishing/R. Pullins Company, PO Box 369, Newburyport MA 01950 www.pullins.com, with the expertise of Joshua Faigen of Folio Publishing Services.

10 9 8 7 6 5 4 3 2 1

1110BB

# Table of Contents

# Preface

Welcome to the 17th printed edition of The Dramatists Guild Resource Directory. Each year we add features that we think our members will find important to their lives as dramatists; this year is no exception. In addition to the standard submission opportunities and resources, you'll notice that we've added the following:

- An extended discussion/dissection on synopsis writing
- Updated ten-minute/short play submission opportunities
- Volunteering opportunities for dramatists across the country
- Submission opportunities for our LGBT dramatists
- An updated bibliography of books on playwriting and musical theatre writing

We're continuing to post the Dramatists Bill of Rights (so you'll always know your rights and protections in whatever situation you find yourself in), our statement of submission fees and still provide you a variety of resources if you are looking for further education.

A strong word of advice about this Resource Directory: by the time we go to press, a number of the opportunities listed within these pages will no longer exist, will not have the same staff listed or will not have the same deadline date as printed. It is essential that you verify the information we provide either by going to the Member's Lounge at www.dramatistsguild.com and double-checking the information on our website, or, by going directly to the website of the theatre, contest, festival, etc.

The organizations listed in the Resource Directory receive hundreds of inquiries, so please be responsible with your submissions.

1. When submitting to a particular program within a contest, theatre, sponsoring organization, etc. name the specific program you're submitting to, since many groups sponsor multiple programs.

2. Include a self-addressed stamped envelope (SASE) with sufficient postage. Most organizations won't return material without one, while some organizations don't return material at all. You may also include a self-addressed stamped postcard (SASP) to be notified when the organization has received your material – or if they are interested in reading your script. It's always a smart (and economically sound) choice to discover if the organization takes electronic submissions.

3. Many opportunities accept submissions electronically now. It might be wise (not to mention cheaper) to do your research and determine if this

is the case with a theatre you're interested in. If electronic submissions are not noted on their website, it's worth an inquiry directly to the theatre.

4.  Include your contact information in a query letter, since some organizations prefer blind submissions, with no identification on the script itself.

Please review each organization's policies carefully to ensure that all authorial rights are upheld. If you find a listing you believe is inaccurate or misleading, or if you have questions about any listing, write to us here at the Guild. Remember, though, listings by their nature are never complete, and any listing or omission doesn't necessarily constitute approval or disapproval by the Guild, its Council, officers, employees, agents, or affiliates.

Finally, much thanks to Prerna Bhatia, Stephen Brown, Emma DeGrand, Steven Hajar, Tari Stratton, Roland Tec and Angel Zeas for their invaluable contributions to this resource.


Rebecca Stump                                      Gary Garrison
Editor                                          Executive Director,
                                                  Creative Affairs

# The Dramatist Bill of Rights

The Dramatists Guild is America's professional association of playwrights, librettists, lyricists and composers, with over 6,000 members around the world. The Guild is governed by our country's leading dramatists, with a fifty-five member Council that includes such dramatists as Edward Albee, Stephen Sondheim, John Patrick Shanley, Tony Kushner, Marsha Norman, Lynn Nottage, Emily Mann and Christopher Durang.

Long before playwrights or musical theatre writers join the Dramatists Guild, they often struggle professionally in small to medium-sized theatres throughout the country. It is essential, therefore, that dramatists know their rights, which the Dramatists Guild has defended for nearly one hundred years. In order to protect the dramatist's unique vision, which has always been the strength of the theatre, s/he needs to understand this fundamental principle: dramatists own and control their work.

The Guild recommends that any production involving a dramatist incorporate a written agreement in which both theatres/producers and writers acknowledge certain key rights with each other.

## In Process and Production

1. ARTISTIC INTEGRITY. No one (e.g., directors, actors, dramaturgs) can make changes, alterations, and/or omissions to your script— including the text, title, and stage directions—without your consent. This is called "script approval."
2. APPROVAL OF PRODUCTION ELEMENTS. You have the right to approve the cast, director, and designers (and, for a musical, the choreographer, orchestrator, arranger, and musical director, as well), including their replacements. This is called "artistic approval."
3. RIGHT TO BE PRESENT. You always have the right to attend casting, rehearsals, previews and performances.

## Compensations

4. ROYALTIES. You are generally entitled to receive a royalty. While it is possible that the amount an author receives may be minimal for a small- to medium-sized production, *some* compensation should always be paid if *any* other artistic collaborator in the production is being paid, or if any admission is being charged. If you are a member of the Guild, you can always call our business office to discuss the standard industry royalties for various levels of production.

5. BILLING CREDIT. You should receive billing (typographical credit) on all publicity, programs, and advertising distributed or authorized by the theatre. Billing is part of your compensation and the failure to provide it properly is a breach of your rights.

## Ownership

6. OWNERSHIP OF INTELLECTUAL PROPERTY. You own the copyright of your dramatic work. Authors in the theatre business do not assign (i.e., give away or sell in entirety) their copyrights, nor do they ever engage in "work-for-hire." When a university, producer or theatre wants to mount a production of your play, you actually license (or lease) the public performance rights to your dramatic property to that entity for a finite period of time.

7. OWNERSHIP OF INCIDENTAL CONTRIBUTIONS. You own all approved revisions, suggestions, and contributions to the script made by other collaborators in the production, including actors, directors, and dramaturgs. You do not owe anyone any money for these contributions.

   If a theatre uses *dramaturgs*, you are not obligated to make use of any ideas the dramaturg might have. Even when the input of a dramaturg or director is helpful to the playwright, dramaturgs and directors are still employees of the theatre, not the author, and they are paid for their work *by the theatre/producer*. It has been well-established in case law, beginning with "the Rent Case" (*Thompson v. Larson*) that neither dramaturgs nor directors (nor any other contributors) may be considered a co-author of a play, unless (i) they've collaborated with you from the play's inception, (ii) they've made a copyrightable contribution to the play, and (iii) you have agreed in writing that they are a co-author.

8. SUBSIDIARY RIGHTS. After the small- or medium-sized production, you not only own your script, but also the rights to market and sell it to all different media (e.g., television, radio, film, internet) in any commercial market in the world. You are not obligated to sign over any portion of your project's future revenues to any third party (fellow artist, advisor, director, producer) as a result of a production, unless that production is a professional (i.e., Actor's Equity) premiere production (including sets, costumes and lighting), of no less than 21 consecutive paid public performances for which the author has received appropriate billing, compensation, and artistic approvals.

9, FUTURE OPTIONS. Rather than granting the theatre the right to share in future proceeds, you may choose to grant a non-exclusive option to present another production of your work within six months or one year of the close of the initial production. No option should be assignable without your prior written consent.

10. AUTHOR'S CONTRACT: The only way to ensure that you get the benefit of the rights listed above is through a written contract with the producer, no matter how large or small the entity. The Guild's Department of Business Affairs offers a model "production contract" and is available to review any contracts offered to you, and advise as to how those contracts compare to industry standards.

We realize that making demands of a small theatre is a difficult task. However, you should feel confident in presenting this Bill of Rights to the Artistic Director, Producer, Literary Manager, or university administrator as a starting point for discussion. At the very least, any professional in the dramatic arts should realize that it is important for writers to understand the nature of their work—not just the artistic aspects, but the business side, as well—and that they stand together as a community, for their mutual benefit and survival, and for the survival of theatre as a viable art form in the 21st century.

# Suggested Formatting for Plays and Musicals

Included in this document are suggested formats for plays and musicals drawn from suggestions of distinguished dramatists, literary managers, teachers of dramatic writing, producers, professional theatres and publishers. It is the Guild's belief that these formats present a standard that will work for most professional opportunities. A few additional elements to consider:

1.  Formatting works towards two purposes: easy reading and the ability to approximate the performance time of the written story. For plays, we've given you a traditional and a more modern format to choose from. Admittedly, not all stories or styles of writing will work within a standard format. Therefore, use your better judgment in deciding the architecture of the page.

2.  There is an industry standard (though some may say old-fashioned) of using the 12-point Courier-New font; we've also noted that Times New Roman is used in more modern formatting. With the proliferation of computers and word-processing programs, there are literally hundreds of fonts to choose from. Whatever your choice, we recommend that you maintain a font size of 12 points – thereby assuring some reliable approximation of performance time.

3.  Though you wrote the story, someone has to read it before anyone sees it. Therefore, make your manuscript easy to read by employing a standard format with clearly delineated page numbers, scene citations and act citations. Headers and footers are optional.

4.  If you're using a software program, such as Final Draft, to format your work, be aware that you have the ability to create your own format in these programs that can be uniquely named, saved and applied to all of your manuscripts.

5.  Usually, between the title page and the first page of the story and/or dialogue, there is a page devoted to a character break-down. What's important to note on this page is the age, gender and name of each character. Some dramatists write brief character descriptions beside each name.

6.  While it is cost-effective for both xeroxing and mailing, realize that some institutions prefer that you don't send double-sided documents. We recommend that you inquire about preference.

7. There is no right or wrong way to signify the end of a scene or act. Some writers do nothing but end the scene; others write "black out", "lights fade down", "End Act 1" or some other signifier that the scene or act has concluded.

8. The binding margin should be 1.5 inches from the edge. All other margins (top, bottom, right) should be 1.0 inch from the edge.

## Sample Title Page

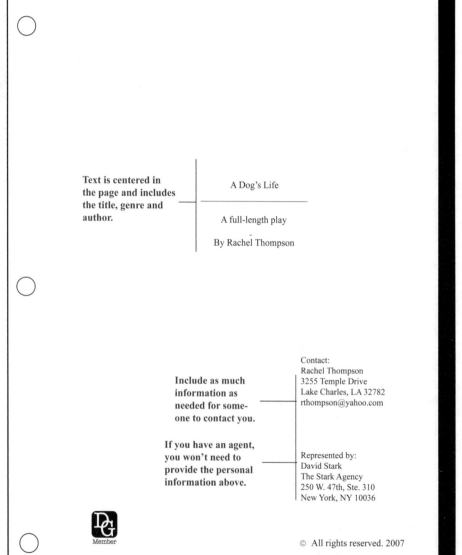

**Text is centered in the page and includes the title, genre and author.**

A Dog's Life

A full-length play

By Rachel Thompson

Contact:
Rachel Thompson
3255 Temple Drive
Lake Charles, LA 32782
rthompson@yahoo.com

**Include as much information as needed for someone to contact you.**

**If you have an agent, you won't need to provide the personal information above.**

Represented by:
David Stark
The Stark Agency
250 W. 47th, Ste. 310
New York, NY 10036

Member

## Traditional Play Format

From Tennessee Williams' *Not About Nightingales*

Essential page
numbering**
16.

BOSS
(removes cover from basket)
Speak of biscuits and what turns up but a nice batch of
homemade cookies! Have one young lady - Jim boy!

(Jim takes two.)

BOSS
Uh-huh, you've got an awful big paw, Jimmy!
(laughs)
Show the new Arky-what's-it to Miss Daily news - or is it
the Morning Star? Have a chair! I'll be right with you -
(vanishes for a moment)
Sweat, sweat, sweat's all I do these hot breezy days!

JIM
(sotto voce)
He thinks you're a newspaper woman.

BOSS
Turn on that fan.
(emerging)
Well, now, let's see -

EVA
To begin with I'm not -

BOSS
You've probably come here to question me about that ex-
convicts story in that damned yellow sheet down there in
Wilkes county - That stuff about getting Pellagra in here
- Jimmy, hand me that sample menu!

JIM
She's not a reporter.

BOSS
Aw. - What is your business, young lady?

(She opens her purse and spills
contents on floor.)

Dialogue begins
1.5 inches from
left side to
account for
binding. Dialogue
is single-spaced.

Stage action is
indented 3 inches
from left; put in
parenthesis. A blank
line is inserted
before and after.

Dialogue extends
to 1.0 inch from
right margin

Stage action reliant
on the proceeding
dialogue is indent-
ed to the left of the
character name.

Character name
in all caps; in the
center of the page.

Standard font for
this formatting is
12.0 point,
Courier New.

Stage action is
indented 3.0 inches
from left margin
and enclosed in
parentheses.

**There are many ways to paginate your play, from the straightforward numerical
sequence of 1, 2, 3 to an older format of 1-2-16, (meaning Act 1, Scene 2, Page 16).

## Modern Play Format

### From Tennessee Williams' *Not About Nightingales*

Essential page
numbering
16.

Dialogue begins
1.5 inches from
left side to
account for
binding. Dialogue
is single-spaced.

Character name
in all caps; in the
center of the page.

Dialogue extends
to 1.0 inch from
right margin

Stage action begins
in the center of the
page and scans to
the right margin. A
blank line is inserted
before and after.

Standard font for
this formatting is
12.0 point, New
Times Roman.

Stage action reliant
on the proceeding
dialogue is indented
to the left of the
character name.

BOSS

You've probably come here to question me about that ex-convicts story in that damned
yellow sheet down there in Wilkes county – That stuff about getting Pellagra in here
– Jimmy, hand me that sample menu!

JIM

She's not a reporter.

BOSS

Aw. – What is your business, young lady?

EVA

I understand there's a vacancy here. Mr. McBurney, my landlady's brother-in-law,
told her that you were needing a new stenographer and I'm sure that I can qualify
for the position. I'm a college graduate, Mr. Whalen, I've had three years of business
experience – references with me – but, oh – I've – I've had such abominable luck
these last six months. – the last place I worked – the business recession set in they
had to cut down on their sales-force – they gave me a wonderful letter – I've got in
with me.

She opens her purse and spills contents
on floor.

BOSS

Anybody outside?

JIM

Yes. That woman.

BOSS

What woman?

JIM

The one from Wisconsin. She's still waiting –

BOSS

I told you I don't want to see her.
                    (talking into phone)
How's the track, Bert? Fast? Okay.

Sailor Jack's mother, MRS. BRISTOL, has
quietly entered. She carries a blanket.

MRS. BRISTOL

I beg your pardon, I – You see I'm Jack Bristol's mother, and I've been wanting to
have a talk with you so long about – about my boy!

## Musical Format

From *APPLAUSE*, Book by Betty Comden, Adolph Green.
Music by Charles Strouse, Lyrics by Lee Adams

Essential page
numbering**
56.

Dialogue begins
1.5 inches from left
side to account for
binding. Dialogue
is single-spaced.

KAREN
(to Margo)
Margo, you've been kicking us all around long enough. Someone ought to give *you*
a good swift one for a change!

(She leaves.)

Stage action is indented
3 inches from left; put
in parentheses. A blank
line is inserted before
and after.

EVE
Miss Channing . . . if I ever dreamed that anything I did could possibly cause you any
unhappiness, or come between you and your friends . . . please believe me.

Dialogue extends
to 1.0 inch from
right margin

Character name
in all caps; in the
center of the page.

MARGO
(in a low, weary voice)
Oh, I do. And I'm full of admiration for you.
(stands, approaches Eve)
If you can handle yourself on the stage with the same artistry you display off the
stage . . . well, my dear, you are in the right place.

Stage action reliant
on the proceeding
dialogue is indented
to the left of the
character name.

(She speaks the following lines as the music
of WELCOME TO THE THEATRE begins.)

Welcome to the theater, to the magic, to the fun!

(She sings.)

WHERE PAINTED TREES AND FLOWERS GROW
AND LAUGHTER RINGS FORTISSIMO,
AND TREACHERY'S SWEETLY DONE!

Lyric are in all
CAPS, separated
line to line by either
musical phrasing
and/or the rhyming
scheme and clearly
indented from the
left margin.

NOW YOU'VE ENTERED THE ASYLUM,
THIS PROFESSION UNIQUE
ACTORS ARE CHILDREN
PLAYING HIDE-AND-EGO-SEEK . . .

Stanzas are separated
by a blank line and
distinguish themselves
by dramatic thought
and/or changes from
verse to chorus to
bridges, etc.

SO WELCOME, MISS EVE HARRINGTON,
TO THIS BUSINESS WE CALL SHOW,
YOU'RE ON YOUR WAY
TO WEALTH AND FAME,
UNSHEATH YOUR CLAWS,
ENJOY THE GAME!
YOU'LL BE A BITCH
BUT THEY'LL KNOW YOUR NAME
FROM NEW YORK . . . TO KOKOMO

For duets, or
characters singing
counter-point,
create two columns
side by side, following
the same format here.

WELCOME TO THEATRE,
MY DEAR, YOU'LL LOVE IT SO!

**There are many ways to paginate your play, from the straight forward numerical
sequence of 1, 2, 3 to an older format of 1-2-16, (meaning Act 1, Scene 2, Page 16).

## The Submission Letter and Production Resume

Though there is no right or wrong way to write a letter of introduction to your work, realize an effective submission letter should be short, professional and with just enough information so the reader knows you've submitted exactly what was called for in the solicitation. And while it's tempting to entice the reader to want to read the script with an overly expressive narrative in your submission letter, consider that this is the first exposure to your writing (of any kind) that will be read by someone in the producing organization . Be mindful, then, how you represent yourself on paper, and allow your play or musical to speak for itself.

A common question is often asked when writers construct a production resume: what do you do if you don't have a lot of readings or productions to list on your resume? Whatever you do, don't misrepresent yourself; don't say you've had a reading or a production of a play at a theatre that you haven't had. You'll eventually be found out and look worse than someone who has a thin resume. If you don't have a lot of production experience with your writing, write a brief synopsis of each of the plays you've written, cite any classes or workshops you've taken as a playwright and detail any other experience you have in the theatre (as stage manager, director, actress, dramaturg, etc.). People are more likely to be sympathetic to you being young in the theatre than they are to you being someone who misrepresents themselves.

A more accomplished playwright's resume should list the productions or readings of plays (by theatre and date), awards, grants, writers colonies attended, workshops, festivals invited to and any special recognition received as a writer. Give the reader a sense of the whole of your writing career, including memberships in theatre groups, professional organizations and related writing work. Include your address and phone number at the top or bottom of your resume, cover sheet of your play and obviously on the return envelope. Again, there are any number of variations on how to construct a writer's resume, but a template to inspire your thinking can be found on the following page.

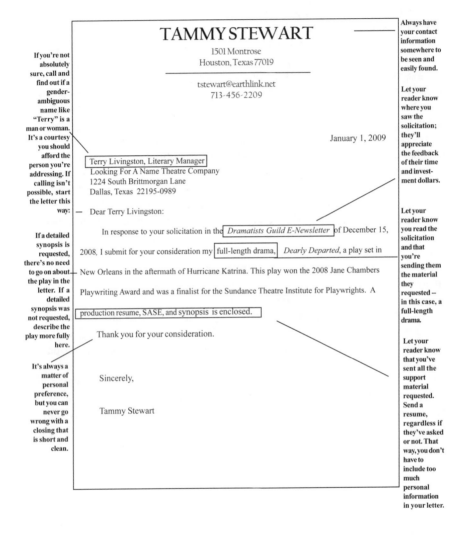

# TAMMY STEWART

1501 Montrose
Houston, Texas 77019

tstewart@earthlink.net
713-456-2209

January 1, 2009

Terry Livingston, Literary Manager
Looking For A Name Theatre Company
1224 South Brittmorgan Lane
Dallas, Texas 22195-0989

Dear Terry Livingston:

In response to your solicitation in the *Dramatists Guild E-Newsletter* of December 15, 2008, I submit for your consideration my full-length drama, *Dearly Departed*, a play set in New Orleans in the aftermath of Hurricane Katrina. This play won the 2008 Jane Chambers Playwriting Award and was a finalist for the Sundance Theatre Institute for Playwrights. A production resume, SASE, and synopsis is enclosed.

Thank you for your consideration.

Sincerely,

Tammy Stewart

If you're not absolutely sure, call and find out if a gender-ambiguous name like "Terry" is a man or woman. It's a courtesy you should afford the person you're addressing. If calling isn't possible, start the letter this way:

If a detailed synopsis is requested, there's no need to go on about the play in the letter. If a detailed synopsis was not requested, describe the play more fully here.

It's always a matter of personal preference, but you can never go wrong with a closing that is short and clean.

Always have your contact information somewhere to be seen and easily found.

Let your reader know where you saw the solicitation; they'll appreciate the feedback of their time and investment dollars.

Let your reader know you read the solicitation and that you're sending them the material they requested – in this case, a full-length drama.

Let your reader know that you've sent all the support material requested. Send a resume, regardless if they've asked or not. That way, you don't have to include too much personal information in your letter.

14

# Tammy Stewart

tstewart@earthlink.net
713-456-2209
1501 Montrose
Houston, Texas 77019

Note your most current address, phone number and email address. If they want to contact you, you want to make it easy for them.

## PRODUCTION HISTORY

Cite the name of the play and genre.

***Dearly Departed*** (full-length drama)

| | |
|---|---|
| Winner, Jane Chambers Playwriting Award | July 2008 |
| Finalist, 2008 Sundance Theatre Institute for Playwrights | May 2008 |
| Early scenes published in *The Best Stage Scenes of 2008*, Smith & Krause, Inc. | April 2008 |

Cite the name of the theatre that produced the play and where it was produced. You may want to list the kind of production presented.

***Forty-Love, Roger*** (full-length comedy)

| | |
|---|---|
| Winner, Arthur W. Stone New Play Award | September 2007 |
| Hedgerow Theatre Company, Summer Showcase Series, Staged Reading | June 2007 |
| Miranda Theatre, New York City, Off-Off Broadway Equity Showcase | May 2007 |

***Maddie Makes a Madness*** (10-minute play)

| | |
|---|---|
| Finalist, Actors Theatre of Louisville, National Ten Minute Play Contest | December 2007 |

***Daily Puppy Dot Com*** (10-minute play)

| | |
|---|---|
| Summer Shorts Festival, Miami, Florida | May 2006 |
| Turnip Theatre Festival, New York City, Equity showcase | January 2006 |
| Published in *Ten On Ten: The Best Ten Minute Plays of 2006*, Focus Publishing | |

Cite publications as if they were productions. Why not let whoever know that your work's been published?

Because a lot of theatres are specific about the kind of second production they'll provide, note the nature of the production.

Date your events from the most recent to the least recent.

## AWARDS

| | |
|---|---|
| Residency, MacDowell Colony | January 2003 |
| Texas State Foundation for the Arts, Artist Grant | January 2002 |
| The Young Playwrights Award, Texas Education Theatre Association | May 1998 |

## MEMBER/ASSOCIATIONS

Dramatists Guild of America, Associate Member
Minneapolis Playwrights Center
Writers Focusing Writers, Houston, Texas
Scriptwriters, Houston, Texas

Professional memberships, education, writers groups you belong to and the like should be noted.

## EDUCATION

| | |
|---|---|
| MFA in Playwriting, University of Houston (with Edward Albee, Lanford Wilson) | May 2002 |
| BFA in Acting, The University of Michigan | May 2000 |

# Art of the Synopsis II

*Whether we love writing a synopsis or hate writing a synopsis of our most recent work (and most of us belong to the latter group), one thing has become abundantly clear: we have to do it and it must be done extremely well. Why? The number of theatres requesting a synopsis as an introduction to our work has increased dramatically over the last decade and there is nothing to suggest that trend will reverse itself.*

*To help our members understand the purpose, craft and pitfalls of writing a synopsis (after all, there is no real instruction to speak of anywhere), we've included liberally edited highlights from the second Art of the Synopsis panel, held in New York on April 27, 2010 at the Cherry Lane Theatre. Panelists included:* **Morgan Jenness** *(Abrams Artists Agency),* **Linda Chapman** *(Associate Artistic Director, New York Theatre Workshop),* **Jeni Mahoney** *(Artistic Director, Seven Devils Playwrights Conference). The panel was first conceived and moderated by Guild Director of Membership,* **Roland Tec.**

\*\*\*\*

**ROLAND TEC:** A month ago I was having lunch with two friends. And one of them referenced some play of mine from ancient history. And the third person at the table said, "Oh, I don't know that play. What is it about?" And I instantly turned into a blubbering idiot. I couldn't believe what was coming out of my mouth. I was just saying all sorts of gobbledygook, like, "Oh, it's a play. It's about the people's relationships to their body and blah, blah, blah." I mean, it just meant nothing. It was not dramatic. It had no action. And it was boring. And you could see their eyes glossing over, you know?

So, this is something that we all struggle with. And I think if there's one lesson that we can take away from these sessions, it's that the most important thing we can do for ourselves when we try summarizing, describing, synopsizing our work is to lean heavily on trusted colleagues and friends. Because they have a perspective that we don't; we're too close to the work, and we have to open ourselves to that help.

\*\*\*\*

**MORGAN JENNESS:** I spent ten years at the Public Theatre with Joe Papp in the literary office, and then about three years went back with George C. Wolfe. I also, like Linda, looked at thousands and thousands of scripts and synopses.

Now in my current position at the agency, I help writers do blurbs. And I do call them blurbs. It's interesting because when it says synopsis, generally I think

16

it has two meanings. It either means a summary, which really is a much more blow-by-blow plot summary, or a blurb, which is a kind of a tease. I do what I call fly-fishing, which is a similar thing. I don't have to generally send ten pages, but, you know, I'll drop an e-mail or write a letter, or say, "Here's this play. It's about this. It deals with this theme. It might be of interest to you because of this."

**ROLAND TEC:** And is that language coming from your head? Or is it coming from a conversation?

**MORGAN JENNESS:** Generally, I ask the writers to do it themselves, which a lot of times it's like, "Oh, no, I can't do that." I find having to do it for a writer is fantastic. Because basically they really have to think about what is my play about? If I had to describe it in five, six, sentences, what is it? What is at the essence of it? What's the DNA of it?

And sometimes for the writer it's, "Oh, no, it's about this." And then I'm able to say, then, "What is the central action?" I just went through something interesting with a writer recently, and this writer's been writing for years. And he said, "Oh my God, I should've done this before they did the marketing." Because he had described his play in a way that it set up a false expectation, I think, for the audience.

It takes a while. It's not easy to do. It's like, "What are the adjectives?" What's one or two adjectives that you can add onto the first line where you describe a character's main action and circumstance and you add a couple of adjectives that are absolutely the right kind of evocative wording that can really nail it. It takes time.

But I do think it's a terrific exercise for the writer. And it's just something I still feel I'm learning how to do. Every time I approach a new work, I think, "Oh my God, how do we distill this down?" And it really takes a while.

**JENI MAHONEY:** For me usually when I'm dealing with a synopsis, once we've selected a playwright to come work with us in Idaho, we'll start working with the playwright on the synopsis for their play or what we actually call a blurb. Synopsis sort of is right in the middle of two separate things. It doesn't really quite say one thing or the other.

**ROLAND TEC:** Next year we'll offer the Art of the Blurb.

**JENI MAHONEY:** Exactly. But really what we're doing at that point is trying to put together a blurb that's going to be for marketing, yes, but it marks the beginning of the development process because we're taking scripts that aren't totally finished yet and refining them. They're still in process. Blurb or synopsis writing becomes a conversation between myself and the playwright because it is a work in development. So I feel it would be really wrong of me to try and define what somebody else's play is before they're really finished writing it.

And then it becomes a discussion about exactly what the play's about. And it actually turns out to be a really great tool for the playwright to realize where they need to put some attention and what the action of the play really is.

**ROLAND TEC:** I want to talk about some of these synopses that were submitted to us for discussion. We asked that members submit either a synopsis of a new, original work, or, a synopsis of a play most likely familiar to all of us, like *A Streetcar Named Desire*. Let's talk about a new, original work: *Veils*. It is really informative for us to see four very developing versions of the same piece.

### *Synopsis for VEILS* by Thomas Coash

*1)     Inspired by a ban on women wearing burkas on their campus, Intisar, an African-American Muslim girl studying at the American University in Cairo, and Samar, her Egyptian roommate, embark on a project to create a short video exploring the controversy surrounding the Muslim practice of women wearing veils...or not. Along the way they discover that cross cultural friendships in a post 9/11 world require courage and understanding.*

*2)     When Intisar left her home in the U.S. and enrolled in the American University in Cairo, she thought she'd finally fit in. But when a ban on women wearing burkas on campus causes a riot, Intisar and her Eygptian roommate Samar are surprised to find themselves of opposite sides of the cultural divide and wondering if their friendship can survive.*

*3)     When Intisar left her home in the U.S. and enrolled in the American University in Cairo, she thought she'd finally fit in. But when a campus-wide ban on wearing burkas causes a riot, Intisar and her Eygptian roommate Samar are surprised to find themselves of opposite sides of the cultural divide. Will their video project, exploring the controversial practice of wearing veils... or not, help them heal their bruised friendship, or will if force them further apart?*

*4)     Intisar, an African-American Muslim student, thought she might finally fit in when she enrolled for a year abroad at the American University in Cairo. But when a campus-wide ban on wearing burkas causes a riot, Intisar*

*and her Eygptian roommate, Samar, are surprised to find*
*themselves on opposite sides of a bitter cultural divide. Will*
*their video project, exploring the controversial practice of*
*wearing veils… or not, salvage their friendship or shatter it?*

**JENI MAHONEY:** This is a really interesting synopsis or blurb. Tom
Coash, the playwright, was fantastic to work with on this because he's a literary-
minded sort of guy, and he really got into this process. I think that he was also
looking for the form of his play and this process really informed that. Take a
look at the first synopsis. "Inspired by a ban on women wearing …"

And basically, to some extent, that's what the play is about, although there's
a whole lot of action in the play that isn't really conveyed in this particular
synopsis. I think it does convey what inspired the playwright to take this story
on. And it gives us a sense of who the characters are. I felt we need to find a
way to kind of get into the action of the piece; the play itself encompasses the
time period during which Inistar is in Cairo. So I used that as a beginning point
in our discussion. Then, I tried all different angles on the action. We'd go back
and forth, and he'd eventually say, "Oh, okay, on this one I think we're getting
closer." And that became the second synopsis on the list.

"When Intisar left her home in the US…"

**ROLAND TEC:** Right away I'm struck with the difference between the
word 'controversy' in the first one and the word 'riot' in the second one.

**JENI MAHONEY:** Yes! Well, it's actually what does happen; the action of
the riot is significant. So, it's not just a controversy. Tom liked that blurb, but I
felt it was still missing a huge element, which was the video that they're making
(and that's a lot of the action of the play).

So he worked on finding a way to make the making of this video, and the
conflict that comes around that, more active. What we came to was, "When
Intisar left her home in the US and enrolled in the American University in
Cairo" —which, by the way, launches us into this new place,—"she thought
she finally fit in." I think it helps to contextualize what her struggle is as an
individual. "But when a campus-wide ban on wearing burkas causes a riot…"

I took that and we actually worked it for a long while to incorporate the
video project that would cause such conflict. We loved playing with the different
word choices of what that conflict was going to be. And when we got to the last
line here, we were both so excited that it worked out. I mean, we were just giddy.

As we kept refining, we ended up with, "Intisar, an African American," and
that's the other thing we worked in – the fact that Intisar was African American,
which is a huge part of her struggle of trying to fit in. In America she was
considered within her African American community to be Muslim, not quite
fitting in. Then she goes to this other far-away place where she also doesn't fit in.

That, I think, is really important. So we finally end up with: "Intisar, an African American Muslim student..."

**ROLAND TEC:** And how long did that take, that process?

**JENI MAHONEY:** We probably went back and forth for a week and a half.

**ROLAND TEC:** And again just to keep reminding ourselves, it's always really important to know: "What is our purpose?" In this case the purpose is to get people—correct me if I'm wrong—to get people in McCall, Idaho to be curious to come to a reading of this play, right? That's what this language is for.

**JENI MAHONEY:** Yes, and also hopefully to get people elsewhere interested and perhaps looking at the play. I think it's really always helpful to know, "Am I writing a grant proposal? Or am I selling tickets to a show?" Those are two completely different things, so you sort of want to have an idea of that.

****

**JENI MAHONEY:** Shall we look at *Colony Collapse*? I'll read the first one that Jim sent me.

### Synopsis of *COLONY COLLAPSE* by James Price

*1)     Something is killing Boyd Clinch's honeybees, and he has a suspicion that his brother Morgan knows what it is. If Boyd doesn't figure it out soon (and his brother's not telling), he will lose his bees, his farm, and most importantly, his wife. Frustrated and out of answers, Boyd befriends an unlikely ally (through a chance meeting in the forest), and his new friend not only helps him solve the mystery, but changes the way he looks at the world, forever.*

*2)     Boyd's bee colonies are dying just as his brother's company clandestinely develops an experimental pollination process which promises to make bees obsolete. Boyd knows he's facing the battle of a lifetime, and just when it seems that he might lose it all – his bees, his farm, even his wife – a chance encounter with an unlikely ally promises to change Boyd's luck, and the world's, forever.*

Again, I think this lays out some aspect of what the story is. We see in the second version of it that the brother isn't only being quiet, he's actually actively developing an experimental pollination process which will make bee colonies obsolete. That's an extremely active, really aggressive thing to be doing when your brother is actually a bee farmer. I suspect that the playwright was trying to not get too far into this whole thing about the clandestine experiments of this company, which is rather convoluted.

**ROLAND TEC:** That actually does raise one common pitfall: it's often a trap to attempt to cram every detail of plot into your synopsis. It just becomes this unwieldy thing. If you're going to give somebody a road map of everything that happens on stage, then you're actually giving them an excuse not to go see the play. Right?

**JENI MAHONEY:** Right. It's definitely a challenge to know what to put in here so that you're hopefully not ruining it for anybody. For example here, the actual "ally" that he meets in the forest is something that the playwright did not want to give away.

**ROLAND TEC:** You mean, who the ally was?

**JENI MAHONEY:** Yes. Because the ally is a six foot tall bee. So we didn't want to give that away but at the same time we're trying to figure out how to enlarge the scale of the synopsis so that we get the importance of him meeting this giant bee; a meeting that potentially changes the world. It's the core conflict. But, you do have secrets you want to keep. I decided that the secret of the brother's clandestine efforts to get rid of bee colonies was not a secret worth keeping. There was a secret worth keeping, and that was the bee.
To keep the synopsis focused on the conflict, we added in the second version, "Boyd's bee colonies are dying ..." Similarly, we suggested the love story between the husband and the wife by adding the loss of the wife in as the final blow in the beekeeper's life.

**ROLAND TEC:** In the first version, it's "changes the way he looks at the world forever." And then in the second version it's "changes the world," right? I mean, that's just so much bigger.

**JENI MAHONEY:** Yeah, major.

****

**ROLAND TEC:** Wendy, could you read your *Streetcar* synopsis for us?

**WENDY YONDORF:** Blanche Dubois, an aging Southern belle with social pretensions moves in with her sister Stella and Stella's husband in their sweaty, tiny, blue-collar New Orleans apartment. Blanche spins webs of lies and drinks in order to conceal the steamy and sordid details of her past. Even toward the final scenes, Blanche's piteous story of a millionaire who will carry her off in her yacht are savagely proved nothing more than another attempt to hide herself from the harsh light of reality. Blanche's tragedy is of the woman who grew up in one set of circumstances, and when things are no longer valid, she doesn't have the strength to change with the times. Her descent into mental collapse is inevitable and complete.

**ROLAND TEC:** One thing I found immediately striking in this synopsis is that this is Blanche's play in this version. And that's always such an interesting directorial question when you're doing *Streetcar*. Is it Blanche's play? Is it Stella's play?

**LINDA CHAPMAN:** The first thing that jumps out to me is "social pretensions." It feels like a real judgment—a kind of an alarm or hitting my thumb with a hammer. I don't know that she has social pretensions. I think she was brought up in a certain way. And I don't think she's pretentious; her behavior is pretty inbred. Again, this demonstrates the power of how our adjectives and descriptions are used.

**MORGAN JENNESS:** I think a lot of the adjectives here—"the sweaty, tiny, blue-collar . . ." are really evocative and put us in the setting; great. One thing I picked up on referred to the final scene or the end of the play. How to do this kind of writing and not give it all away is the challenge. A synopsis really tells you how you're angling what the play is. And with a play that we've seen done by so many different directors, choosing so many different angles on it, a blurb or a synopsis really angles the play in a certain way. So, if you're the playwright, you should know that your blurb or synopsis is giving a very specific take on your work

**LINDA CHAPMAN:** I think you have to find out what's compelling about the form, and maybe the actual conflict is between the form and the content. If you can dramatize that for me in your blurb, that would intrigue me. Again, if you look at the background of the theatre before you approach them with your work, you'd see that New York Theatre Workshop, for example, has eclectic taste and looks at all kinds of material. And because we have worked with people who use video, dance and music in non-traditional ways, you'd want to dangle a few of those kinds of things that you know we're already interested in front of us. I think there are no holds barred in terms of making your approach to a particular organization specific.

Now, if you were going to a more traditional theatre, and you think, "Well, they might really like this play if they really got into it," you might want to soft-sell the more non-traditional elements of it and show them that there is actually a narrative thread here that you can follow and that it is accessible. So, again, it's really the primary question: who are you talking to?

****

**ROLAND TEC:** Mark, could you share your *Sweeney Todd* blurb? Here's an example of an excellent log line because it captures the tone of *Sweeney Todd* and some thematic content. It's just one line.

**MARK SNYDER:** Barber takes revenge on the corrupt society that incarcerated him, one shave at a time.

**ROLAND TEC:** Beautiful. So, if you're in an elevator and you've just written *Sweeney Todd*, that's what you're going to say. But does everybody understand why that's so strong? It's got humor, but it also has the thematic content in it too, which to do in one sentence is not easy.

**JENI MAHONEY:** It made me think of something that Roland said at the beginning of this discussion, which is the fact that our objective in helping writers write a synopsis is to get the person you're working with to have that "A-ha" moment. I think it's kind of impossible to sit in a room and write by yourself. So the only way to make them fun is to really engage in a discussion about them, you know?

**ROLAND TEC:** The first time you gather your actor friends to read the script, keep them for ten minutes and ask them what that play is about that they just read. It's amazing what you'll learn just asking that simple question. It may not be what you thought at all, but it will teach you something about your own work.

# The DG Statement on Submission Fees

The Dramatists Guild of America denounces the practice by festivals, play contests and educational events of charging excessive fees to dramatists who submit their work. Any request for submission fees should be accompanied by a complete explanation of how those fees are to be spent. The Guild also insists that contests and festivals announce the names of all finalists and winners to all participants.

It is important that members understand that submission fees are not the norm and, when required, the festival should offer something significant in return for the writer's investment, such as a large cash prize, a residency or a production. Reading fees are in no case acceptable, as most festivals receive that money from other grant sources. In no case should playwrights have to pay to simply have their work read.

The Guild also strongly disapproves of a festival's placing any encumbrances on the work as a result of the play being chosen a finalist or a participant. Any future participation in the life of the play must be earned by the festival by producing the work, and should never be granted by the writer without consultation with the Guild. If the festival expects any subsidiary income from the plays, that information should be stated clearly in all of the organization's printed and electronic materials related to the event.

The Council of the Guild feels that its members should be made aware of all legitimate opportunities available to them, and so we have listed in this section those particular contests and festivals that charge fees and have provided explanations regarding how their submission fees are spent, as well as full disclosure of any encumbrances they place on a selected writer's work, when offered by the sponsor.

# Career Development Professionals

## Accountants

**Kimerling and Wisdom**
29 Broadway, #1412,
    New York, NY 10006
Ross Wisdom
Tel: (212) 986-0892
rwisdom@kwllc.us
www.kwllc.us
    Est. 1970.

**Marks Paneth & Shron LLP**
622 3rd Ave., New York, NY 10017
David R. Marcus, Partner
Tel: (212) 503-8833
Fax:(212) 503-8834
dmarcus@markspaneth.com
www.markspaneth.com
    Est. 1907. Nationally ranked, full-
    service public acconting firm for
    individuals and companies in the
    entertainment industry.

## AGENCY
### *From the Desk of Gary Garrison*

On the average, I get three to four phone calls or emails a day that go something like this: *"I need an agent. I know everyone needs an agent, but I **really need** an agent. Why can't the Guild help get me an agent or a director or anyone who can help promote my work? And why can't the Guild get more theatres to respond to play-wrights and new plays? We need more opportunities!"* Look, I just want to get square with you once and for all: we are a member-service and advocacy organization. And while I don't want to downplay the importance for some of you to be professionally represented by an agent (or your work placed in a theatre), it is not one of the man-dates of this organization to help you secure representation or production.

It doesn't matter what anyone has to say about writers and agents, the truth is hav-ing an agent is perceived — right or wrong — as a benchmark of success that comes with certain positive opportunities and a healthy amount of validation. The desire in most of us, then, is never likely to go away. But if you really want to pursue the agent thing, I want you to take a good, honest look at simple facts and figures to help you make sense of what's ahead of you.

- The numbers: talking to my colleagues here at the Guild, and then making a few phone calls around town to some very respectable agents, to our best estimation there are approximately thirty-five agents dedicated to promoting dramatic writing for the theatre. That's thirty-five agents total — throughout the whole country — that represent every playwright you know by name, and then the many hundreds you don't know (yet). The simple numbers alone show the odds are against most of us having an agent.

- Most agents that I've spoken with are rarely interested in representing a single piece of work and are far more interested in representing (and helping you grow) a body of work. To approach an agent to represent a single play or musical is not likely to get you anywhere. Agents, like all theatre business people, are as interested in the present as they are the future.

- Twenty years ago, maybe even ten years ago, a hit production of a play or a musical and a good New York Times review (or any major newspaper review) would almost ensure that you'd have an agency knocking at your door. That's not true any longer; there's a glut of material and writers out there that remain unrepresented. Theatre, like most arms of the entertainment industry, is ageist.

Jeeeeeez, Gary, did you have to be so . . . honest? In a word, yes, because so many of us are singularly obsessed about getting an agent. Are there exceptions to any of the points above? Of course there are exceptions; that's what makes this life interesting. Can you have a productive, successful career in the theatre without professional repre-sentation? You bet, and a heck of a lot of people do.

*Please understand that we provide a list of working literary agents as a convenience for you — nothing more. By listing these agents (which is not a comprehensive list), we do not intend to suggest that they are seeking new clients or that we are particu-larly endorsing them as agents. Unless indicated otherwise, send a query and synopsis to one agent at a time.*

## Agents & Attorneys

**Abrams Artists Agency**
275 Seventh Avenue 26 Floor, New York,
NY 10001
Robert Alterman
Tel: (646) 486-4600
Fax:(646) 486-0100
www.abramsartists.com/literary.html
  Agents: Sarah L. Douglas, Charles
  Kopelman, Beth Blickers, Morgan
  Jenness, Maura Teitelbaum, Kate
  Navin, Ron Gwiazda. Professional
  recommendation. Submission
  Materials: Query letter, synopsis and
  S.A.S.E..

**Ann Wright Representatives**
165 West 46th Street Ste #1105, New
York, NY 10036
Ann Wright
Tel: (212) 764-6770
Fax:(212) 764-5125
  Est. 1961. Response Time: 5/15/10
  Preferred Genre(s): All genres.

**Barbara Hogenson Agency, Inc.**
165 West End Avenue #19C, New York,
NY 10023
Barbara Hogenson, Owner
Tel: (212) 874-8084
Bhogenson@aol.com
  Est. 1994. Response time: 2 mos.
  Preferred Genre(s): All genres.
  Preferred Length: One-act or Full-
  length. Submission Materials: Query
  and synopsis only.

**Beigelman, Feiner & Feldman, P.C.**
100 Wall Street, 23rd Floor, New York,
NY 10005
Ronald Feiner, Esq., Senior Partner
Bfflaw.com

**Bret Adams Ltd.**
448 West 44th St, New York, NY 10036
Ben Coleman
Tel: (212) 765-5630
Fax:(212) 265-2212
becoleman@bretadamsltd.net
www.bretadamsltd.net
  Est. 1953. Staff: Bruce Ostler, Mark
  Orsini; Natasha Sinha (literary); Margi
  Rountree, Ken Melamed, Michael

Golden (acting). Query must include
professional recommendation. Preferred
Genre(s): All genres. Submission
Materials: Query letter only.

**Brooks & Distler**
110 E. 59th St., Fl. 23, New York, NY
10022
Marsha Brooks, Esq., Partner
Tel: (212) 486-1400
Fax:(212) 486-2266
brookslaw@aol.com

**Cowan, DeBaets, Abrahams &
Sheppard LLP**
41 Madison Ave., Fl. 34, New York, NY
10010
Frederick P. Bimbler, Esq., Partner
Tel: (212) 974-7474
Fax:(212) 974-8474
fbimbler@cdas.com
www.cdas.com

**David H. Friedlander, Esq.**
81 Park Dr., Mount Kisco, NY 10549
David H. Friedlander
Tel: (914) 241-1277
Fax:(914) 470-2244
david@dfriedlander.com
www.dfriedlander.com

**Farber Literary Agency Inc.**
14 East 75th Street, New York, NY
10021
Don C. Farber
Tel: (212) 861-7075
Fax:(212) 861-7076
www.donaldfarber.com
  Est.1990. Response: 1 mo. Preferred
  Genre(s): All genres. Preferred Length:
  Any length. Submission Materials:
  Query, synopsis, full script, SASE.

**Fifi Oscard Agency, Inc.**
110 West 40 Street, Suite 2100, New
York, NY 10018
Carolyn French
Tel: (212) 764-1100
Fax:(212) 840-5019
www.fifioscard.com

Est. 1956. Preferred Genre(s): All genres. Preferred Length: Any length. Submission Materials: See website.

**Fitelson, Lasky, Aslan, Couture and Garmise**
551 5th Ave., #605, New York, NY 10176
Jerold Couture, Attorney
Tel: (212) 586-4700
Fax:(212) 949-6746
dramalex@aol.com

**Frankfurt Kurnit Klein & Seiz**
Frankfurt Kurnit Klein & Seiz, 488 Madison Avenue, New York, NY 10022
S. Jean Ward, Esq.
Tel: (212) 826-5584
sjward@fkks.com
www.fkks.com

**Franklin, Weinrib, Rudell & Vassallo PC**
488 Madison Ave., New York, NY 10022
Eric Brown
Tel: (212) 935-5500
Fax:(212) 308-0642
ehb@fwrv.com
www.fwrv.com

**Gage Group Inc.**
14724 Ventura Blvd, Sherman Oaks, CA 91403
Martin Gage
Tel: (818) 905-3800
Fax:(310) 859-8166
Est. 1975. Submissions not returned. Response: 3 mos. Submission Materials: Professional referral only.

**Gersh Agency Inc. [NY]**
41 Madison Ave, 33rd Floor, New York, NY 10010
Susan Cohen
Tel: (212) 634-8126
Fax:(212) 391-8459
Must be submitted through professional recommendation.

**Gordon P. Firemark, Esq.**
Law Offices of Gordon P. Firemark,

10940 Wilshire Blvd, 16th Floor, Los Angeles, CA 90024
Gordon P. Firemark
Tel: (310) 443-4185
Fax:(310) 477-7676
gfiremark@firemark.com
www.firemark.com /
www.theatrelawyer.com

**Graubart. Law Offices of Jeffrey L. Graubart, P.C.**
350 W. Colorado Blvd., #200, Pasadena, CA 91105
Jeffrey Glaubart
Tel: (626) 304-2800
Fax:(626) 304-2807
info@jlgraubart.com
www.entertainmentlaw.la
Est. 1970.

**Harden Curtis Associates**
850 7th Ave, #903, New York, NY 10019
Mary Harden, President
Tel: (212) 977-8502
Fax:(212) 975-8420
www.hardencurtis.com
Est. 1995. Response: 2 mos. Preferred Genre(s): All genres. Preferred Length: Any length. Submission Materials: Professional referral only.

**International Creative Management (ICM) [CA]**
10250 Constellation Blvd., Los Angeles, CA 90067
Tel: (310) 550-4000
books@icmtalent.com
www.icmtalent.com/lit/lit.html
Talent & lit agency. Preferred Genre(s): All genres. Preferred Length: Any length. Submission Materials: See website.

**International Creative Management (ICM) [NY]**
825 8th Ave., New York, NY 10019
Tel: (212) 556-5600
Fax:(212) 556-5665
books@icmtalent.com
Talent & lit agency. Preferred Genre(s): All genres. Preferred Length: Any length. Submission Materials: See website.

**International Creative Management (ICM) [UK]**
4-6 Soho Sq., London, W1D 3PZ United
   Kingdom
Tel: (442) 074-3208 Ext 00
books@icmtalent.com
www.icmtalent.com/lit/lit.html
   Talent & lit agency. Preferred Genre(s):
   All genres. Preferred Length: Any
   length. Submission Materials: See
   website.

**Judy Boals Inc.**
307 W. 38th St., #812, New York, NY
   10018
Judy Boals, President
Tel: (212) 500-1424
Fax:(212) 500-1426
info@judyboals.com
www.judyboals.com
   Submit via personal recommendation.
   Response : 1 mo. Submission
   Materials: Query letter and S.A.S.E..

**Law Office of Gary N. DaSilva**
111 N. Sepulveda Blvd., #250, Manhattan
   Beach, CA 90266
Tel: (310) 318-5665
Fax:(310) 318-2114
mail@garydasilva.com
   Response: 1 mo. Submission Materials:
   Query letter only.

**Law Office of John J. Tormey III, Esq.**
217 East 86th Street, PMB 221, New
   York, NY 10028
John L. Tormey, PLLC
Tel: (212) 410-4142
Fax:(212) 410-2380
brightline@att.net
www.tormey.org
   Entertainment Transactional and
   General Practice.

**Paradigm**
360 Park Ave. South, 16th Floor, New
   York, NY 10010
Tel: (212) 897-6400
Fax:(212) 575-6397
www.paradigmagency.com
   Agents: William Craver, Lucy Stille,
   Jack Tantleff. Response: 6 mos.
   Submission Materials: Query letter and
   S.A.S.E..

**Paul, Weiss, Rifkind, Wharton & Garrison**
Att: C.Googe, 1285 Avenue of the
   Americas, New York, NY 10019-6064
Peter Felcher
Tel: (212) 373-2391
jbreglio@paulweiss.com
www.paulweiss.com

**Peregrine Whittlesey Agency**
279 Central Park West, New York, NY
   10024
Peregrine Whittlesey, Agent
Tel: (212) 787-1802
Fax:(212) 787-4985
pwwagy@aol.com
   Submission Materials: Query letter &
   SASE.

**Peter S. Cane, Esq.**
230 Park Avenue, Suite 1000, New York,
   NY 10169
Peter S. Cane, Attorney
Tel: (212) 922-9800
Fax:(212) 922-9822
peter@canelaw.com

**Robert A. Freedman Dramatic Agency, Inc.**
1501 Broadway, #2310, New York, NY
   10036
Marta Praeger, Agent
Tel: (212) 840-5760
Fax:(212) 840-5776
   Est. 1917. Response: 4 mos.
   Submission Materials: Query letter and
   S.A.S.E..

**Robert S. Perlstein, Esq.**
1501 Broadway, Suite 703, New York,
   NY 10036
Robert S. Perlstein, Attorney
Tel: (212) 832-9951
Fax:(212) 831-9906
rspesq@judgedee.net
   Clients: major performers, conductors,
   singers, actors, musicians, arrangers,
   orchestrators, screenwriters, television
   producers, authors; emphasis in
   classical music.

**Robinson, Brog, Leinwand, Greene, Genovese & Gluck**
875 Third Avenue, 9th Floor, New York, NY 10022
Richard M. Ticktin, Partner
Tel: (212) 603-6308
Fax:(212) 581-5981
rmt@robinsonbrog.com
www.robinsonbrog.com
   Submit through professional recommendation. Submission Materials: Query letter and S.A.S.E..

**Ronald A. Lachman**
468 N. Camden Dr. #200, Beverly Hills, CA 90210
Ronald Lachman, Attorney
Tel: (323) 655-6020
Fax:(323) 655-6099
ron@ronaldlachman.com

**Soiree Fair Inc.**
133 Midland Ave., #10, Montclair, NJ 07042
Karen Gunn, President
Tel: (973) 783-9051
Fax:(973) 746-0426
Soireefair@yahoo.com
www.soireefair.com
   Est. 1995. Material must be unoptioned, unpublished, unproduced and be submitted with professional recommendation. Preferred Genre(s): Plays. Preferred Length: Full-length. Submission Materials: Query and synopsis only.

**Steiger. Law Office of Susan J. Steiger, Esq.**
60 East 42nd Street, 47th floor, New York, NY 10165
Susan J. Steiger, Attorney
Tel: (212) 880-0865
Fax:(212) 682-1965
   Est. 1982.

**Susan Gurman Agency, LLC**
245 West 99th Street, Suite 24A, New York, NY 10025
Tel: (212) 749-4618
Fax:(212) 864-5055
assistant@gurmanagency.com
www.gurmanagency.com

Est. 1993. Response: 1 mo. Submission Materials: letter and resume only.

**Susan Schulman, A Literary Agency**
454 W. 44th St., New York, NY 10036
Susan F. Schulman, Agent
Tel: (212) 713-1633
Fax:(212) 581-8830
schulman@aol.com
www.susanschulmanagency.com
   Preferred Genre(s): All genres.
   Preferred Length: Full-length.
   Submission Materials: See website.

**The Marton Agency, Inc.**
1 Union Sq. W., #815, New York, NY 10003
Tonda Marton, Agent
Tel: (212) 255-1908
Fax:(212) 691-9061
info@martonagency.com
   Specializes in brokering foreign-language rights to US theater works. Promotes plays to associates abroad, generally after a production has been mounted in the US.

**The Shukat Company Ltd.**
340 W. 55th St., #1A, New York, NY 10019
Tel: (212) 582-7614
Fax:(212) 315-3752
staff@shukat.com
   Preferred Genre(s): All genres.
   Preferred Length: Full-length.
   Submission Materials: Query, sample, SASE.

**Volunteer Lawyers for the Arts (VLA)**
1 E. 53rd St., Fl. 6, New York, NY 10022
Elena M. Paul, Esq., Executive Director
Tel: (212) 319-2787
Fax:(212) 752-6575
vlany@vlany.org
www.vlany.org
   Est. 1969. Provider of pro bono legal and mediation services, educational programs and publications & advocacy to the arts community in NYC. Fees: based on client's finances.

**William Morris Endeavor**
1325 Avenue of the Americas, New York,
   NY 10019
Donald Aslan
Tel: (212) 586-5100
   Staff: Val Day, Peter Franklin, Biff Liff,
   Roland Scahill, Jack Tantleff, Susan
   Weaving. Submission Materials:
   Professional referral only.

**Writers & Artists Agency [CA]**
8383 Wilshire Blvd., #550, Beverly Hills,
   CA 90211
Tel: (323) 866-0900
Fax:(323) 866-1899
info@wriart.com
   Submission Materials: See website.

# Commercial Producers

**Araca Group**
545 W. 45th Street, 10th floor, New York,
   NY 10036
Amanda Guettel, Development Associate
Tel: (212) 869-0070
Fax:(212) 869-0210
creative@araca.com
www.araca.com
   Est. 1997. Broadway/off Broadway
   productions. Preferred Genre(s): Plays
   or Musicals. Preferred Length:
   Full-length. Submission Materials:
   Agent only submissions.

**Arielle Tepper Productions**
1501 Broadway, #1301, New York, NY
   10036
Tel: (212) 944-9696
Fax:(212) 944-8999
info@atpnyc.com
www.atpnyc.com

**Boyett Ostar Productions**
268 West 44th Street, 4th Floor, New
   York, NY 10036
Tel: (212) 702-9779
Fax:(212) 702-0899

**Cameron Mackintosh Inc.**
1650 Broadway, #800, New York, NY
   10019
Shidan Majidi, Production Associate
Tel: (212) 921-9290
Fax:(212) 921-9271
smajidi@camack.com
www.cameronmackintosh.com
   Mary Poppins, Les Miserables, The
   Phantom of the Opera, Oliver!,
   Oklahoma!, My Fair Lady, The

Witches of Eastwick, Miss Saigon,
   CATS. Preferred Genre(s): Musical
   theatre. Preferred Length: Full-length.
   Submission Materials: Agent only
   submissions.

**Dodger Properties**
311 W. 43rd St., #602, New York, NY
   10036
Tel: (212) 575-9710
info@dodger.com
www.dodger.com
   Est. 1978. Jersey Boys. Preferred
   Genre(s): All genres. Preferred Length:
   Full-length. Submission Materials:
   Agent only submissions.

**Jane Harmon Associates**
One Lincoln Plaza, #280, 20 W. 64th St.,
   New York, NY 10023
Jane Harmon
Tel: (212) 362-6836
Fax:(212) 362-8572
harmonjane@aol.com
   Est. 1979. Production: drama/comedy.
   Submit via email. Response: 4-6 wks.
   Preferred Genre(s): Plays. Preferred
   Length: One-act or Full-length.
   Submission Materials: Synopsis, SASE.

**Margery Klain**
2107 Locust St., Philadelphia, PA 19103
Margery Klain, Producer
Tel: (215) 567-1512
Fax:(215) 567-2049
mklain1011@aol.com
   Est. 1985. Material must be
   unoptioned. Response: 2 mos.
   Preferred Genre(s): Plays. Preferred

Length: Full-length. Submission
Materials: Professional referral only.

**Margo Lion Ltd.**
246 W. 44th St., Fl. 8, New York, NY
10036
Rick Hayashi
Tel: (212) 869-1112
Fax:(212) 730-0381
office@margolionltd.com
www.margolionltd.com
  Email submissions preferred. Response:
  1 yr. Preferred Genre(s): All genres.
  Preferred Length: Full-length.
  Submission Materials: Agent only
  submissions.

**Nederlander Organization**
1450 Broadway, Fl. 6, New York, NY
10018
Charlene Nederlander, VP, Corporate
  Development
Tel: (212) 840-5577
Fax:(212) 840-3326
www.nederlander.com

Est. 1912. Preferred Genre(s): All
genres. Preferred Length: Full-length.
Submission Materials: Agent only
submissions.

**Shubert Organization**
234 W. 44th St., New York, NY 10036
D.S. Moynihan, VP, Creative Projects
Tel: (212) 944-3700
www.shubertorg.com
  Est. 1900. Preferred Genre(s): All
  genres. Preferred Length: Full-length.
  Submission Materials: Agent only
  submissions.

# Publishers

**Anchorage Press Plays Inc.**
617 Baxter Ave., Louisville, KY 40204-
1105
Marilee Hebert Miller, Publisher
Tel: (502) 583-2288
Fax:(502) 583-2288
applays@bellsouth.net
www.applays.com
  Est. 1935. Educational, professional
  and amateur venues. Response Time: 6
  -9 mos. Preferred Genre(s): All genres.
  Special Interest: Theatre for Young
  Audiences. Preferred Length: Any
  length. Submission Materials:
  Complete script.

**Asian Theatre Journal**
2840 Kolowalu St., Honolulu, HI 96822
Tel: (888) 847-7377
Fax:(800) 650-7811
uhpjourn@hawaii.edu
www.uhpress.hawaii.edu/journals

Dedicated to performing arts of Asia,
traditional and modern, incl. original
and translated plays. Special Interest:
Asian-American. Submission Materials:
Query letter only.

**Baker's Plays**
45 W. 25th Street #9, New York, NY
10010
Roxane Heinze-Bradshaw, Associate
  Editor
Tel: (212) 255-8085
Fax:(212) 627-7753
publications@bakersplays.com
www.bakersplays.com
  Submit via website. Response time: 8
  mos. Preferred Genre(s): All genres.
  Submission Materials: Online only.

**Big Dog Publishing**
P.O. Box 1400, Tallevast, FL 34270
Dawn Remsing, Editor
Fax:(941) 358-7606
info@bigdogplays.com
www.bigdogplays.com
  Est. 2005. Plays for family and school
  audiences (K-12). Publishes 25-40
  plays/year. Response time: 2-3 mos.
  Prefer produced/award-winning work.
  No email. Preferred Genre(s): Plays or
  Musicals. Special Interest: Theatre for
  Young Audiences. Preferred Length:
  One-act or Full-length. Submission
  Materials: See website.

**Broadway Play Publishing Inc. (BPPI)**
56 East 81 Street, New York, NY 10028-0202
Christopher Gould, President
www.broadwayplaypubl.com
  Est. 1982. Response time: 2 mos query,
  4 mos script. Preferred Genre(s): All
  genres. Preferred Length: Any length.
  Submission Materials: Query letter
  only.

**Callaloo**
4212 TAMU, Texas A&M University,
  College Station, TX 77843
Charles H. Rowell, Editor
Tel: (979) 458-3108
Fax:(979) 458-3275
callaloo@tamu.edu
callaloo.tamu.edu
  Quarterly journal devoted to creative
  work by and critical studies of the
  work of African-Americans and
  peoples of African descent throughout
  the African Diaspora. Response time: 6
  mos. Preferred Genre(s): All genres.
  Special Interest: African-American.
  Preferred Length: Any length.
  Submission Materials: Query, 3 copies
  of work, SASE.

**Capilano Review TCR**
2055 Purcell Way, N. Vancouver, BC V7J
  3H5 Canada
Tamara Lee, Managing Editor
Tel: (604) 984-1712
Fax:(604) 990-7837
contact@thecapilanoreview.ca
www.thecapilanoreview.ca

Est. 1972. Unpublished poetry, drama,
visual arts. Response time: 4 mos.
Please use Canadian postage for SASE.
Preferred Genre(s): Verse. Preferred
Length: Any length. Submission
Materials: See website.

**Confrontation**
CW Post Campus English Dept.,
  Brookville, NY 11548
Martin Tucker, Editor
Tel: (516) 299-2720
  (516) 299-2720
Fax:(516) 299-2735
mtucker@liu.edu
www.cwpost.liu.edu/cwis/cwp/culture
  Material submitted must be
  unpublished. Preferred Genre(s): Plays.
  Preferred Length: 10 min and one-acts.
  Submission Materials: Complete script,
  SASE.

**Contemporary Drama Service**
885 Elkton Dr., Colorado Springs, CO
  80907
Mark Zapel
Tel: (719) 594-4422
Fax:(719) 594-9916
editor@contemporarydrama.com
www.contemporarydrama.com
  Est. 1970. Material for school, college,
  church and amateur venues.
  Production: age 12-30, cast limit 20.
  Response: 1 mo. Preferred Genre(s):
  No translation. Preferred Length: Any
  length. Submission Materials: Query
  letter and S.A.S.E..

**Currency Press**
Box 2287, STRAWBERRY HILLS, 2012
  Australia
Victoria Chance, Publisher
Tel: (029) 319-5877
Fax:(029) 319-3649
enquiries@currency.com.au
www.currency.com.au
  Publisher/distributor of performing arts
  books on Australian drama, film, music
  (incl. play and film scripts) in Australia
  & New Zealand. Preferred Genre(s):
  Plays. Preferred Length: One-Act.
  Submission Materials: Complete script,
  SASE.

**Dramatic Publishing Company**
311 Washington St., Woodstock, IL 60098
Linda Habjan, Submissions Editor
Tel: (800) 448-7469
Fax:(800) 334-5302
plays@dramaticpublishing.com
www.dramaticpublishing.com
  Est. 1885. Response: 8 mos. Preferred
  Genre(s): All genres. Preferred Length:
  Any length. Submission Materials:
  Complete script, SASE.

**Dramatics Magazine**
2343 Auburn Ave., Cincinnati, OH 45219
Don Corathers, Editor
Tel: (513) 421-3900
Fax:(513) 421-7077
dcorathers@edta.org
www.edta.org/publications/dramatics.asp
  Est. 1929. Natl. monthly magazine for
  HS theater students & teachers,
  printing 7 one-acts and full-lengths/yr.
  Response: 5 mos Preferred Genre(s):
  Plays. Preferred Length: Any length.
  Submission Materials: Complete script.

**Dramatists Play Service, Inc.**
Attn: Michael Fellmeth, 440 Park Avenue
  South, New York, NY 10016
Michael Q. Fellmeth, VP, Publications
Tel: (212) 683-8960
www.dramatists.com
  Performances licensed. All venues
  except commercial. Response: 6 mos
  Preferred Genre(s): Plays or Musicals.
  Preferred Length: Full-length.
  Submission Materials: Query and
  synopsis only.

**Eldridge Publishing Company Inc.**
Box 14367, Tallahassee, FL 32317
Nancy S. Vorhis, Senior Editor
Tel: (850) 385-2463
Fax:(850) 385-2463
editorial@histage.com
www.histage.com
  Est. 1906. Performances licensed, all
  venues. Material for junior/senior high
  school & community theatre. Email
  work to newworks@histage.com
  Response: 2 mos. Preferred Genre(s):
  Plays or Musicals. Special Interest:
  Theatre for Young Audiences. Preferred

Length: One-act or Full-length.
Submission Materials: query, full
script, audio, SASE.

**Empire Publishing Service**
Box 1344, Studio City, CA 91614
Joseph W. Witt
Tel: (818) 784-8918
empirepubsvc@att.net
www.ppeps.com
  Est. 1960. Publishes performing arts
  books, incl. sheet music. Work must
  have been produced. Response: from 3
  days to 1 yr. Preferred Genre(s): All
  genres. Preferred Length: Any length.
  Submission Materials: Query letter and
  S.A.S.E..

**Meriwether Publishing Ltd.**
885 Elkton Drive, Colorado Springs, CO
  80907
Mark L. Zapel
Tel: (719) 594-4422
Fax:(719) 594-9916
editor@meriwether.com
www.meriwetherpublishing.com
  Theatre arts books written by drama
  educators and professionals, plus
  DVDs, CDs and videos for classroom
  use. Submit by US mail. Preferred
  Genre(s): Plays. Preferred Length: Any
  length. Submission Materials: See
  website.

**Moose Hide Books**
684 Walls Rd., Sault Ste. Marie, ON
  P6A-5K6 Canada
Richard Mousseau, Publisher
Tel: (705) 779-3331
Fax:(707) 779-3331
rmousseau@moosehidebooks.com
www.moosehidebooks.com
  Response: 1 month. Submission
  Materials: Query letter and S.A.S.E..

**NewMusicals.com**
22 Grenhart Street, West Hartford, CT
  06117
R. J. Chiarappa, Submissions Editor
Tel: (860) 236-0592
Fax:(860) 236-5762
info@newmusicals.com
www.newmusicals.com

Internet site to promote new
unoptioned/unpublished musicals.
Contact via email. Response: 1 mo.
Preferred Genre(s): Musical theatre.
Preferred Length: One-act or Full-
length. Submission Materials: Full
Script, audio.

**Norman Maine Publishing**
Box 1400, Tallevast, FL 34270
Dawn Remsing, Editor
Fax:(941) 358-7606
info@normanmaineplays.com
www.normanmaineplays.com
  Est. 2005. Plays for community,
  professional and university theatre.
  Response: 2-3 mos. Preferred Genre(s):
  Plays or Musicals. Preferred Length:
  Any length. Submission Materials: See
  website.

**Original Works Publishing**
4611 1/2 Ambrose Ave., Los Angeles, CA
  90027
Jason Aaron Goldberg, President
info@originalworksonline.com
www.originalworksonline.com
  Est. 2000. Submitted material must
  have been produced. Response: 1-2
  months. Preferred Genre(s): Plays.
  Preferred Length: Any length.
  Submission Materials: See website.

**PAJ: A Journal of Performance and
Art**
Box 532, Village Sta., New York, NY
  10014
Bonnie Marranca, Editor
Tel: (212) 243-3885
Fax:(212) 243-2885
pajpub@mac.com
www.mitpressjournals.org/paj
  Est. 1976. Response: 2 mos query, 2
  mos script. Preferred Genre(s): Plays.
  Preferred Length: One-Act. Submission
  Materials: Query and synopsis only.

**Players Press Inc.**
Box 1132, Studio City, CA 91614
Robert W. Gordon, VP Editor
Tel: (818) 789-4980
playerspress@worldnet.att.net

Est. 1960. Response: 2 wks query, 6
mos script. Preferred Genre(s): All
genres. Preferred Length: Any length.
Submission Materials: Query letter &
SASE.

**Playscripts, Inc.**
450 Seventh Ave., Suite 809, New York,
  NY 10123
Mark Armstrong, Literary Director
Tel: (866) 639-7529
Fax:(888) 203-4519
submissions@playscripts.com
www.playscripts.com
  Est. 1998. Acting editions sold and
  performances licensed to
  amateur/professional venues
  worldwide. Musicals by agent
  submission only. Preferred Genre(s):
  Plays. Preferred Length: Any length.
  Submission Materials: See website.
  Deadline(s): Rolling

**Poems & Plays**
MTSU English Dept., Murfreesboro, TN
  37132
Gaylord Brewer, Editor
Tel: (615) 898-2712
Fax:(615) 898-5098
gbrewer@mtsu.edu
www.mtsu.edu/english/poemsandplays/
  Est. 1993. Work must be unpublished.
  Response: 3 mos. Preferred Genre(s):
  Plays. Preferred Length:
  10-min./10pgs.. Submission Materials:
  Complete script, SASE. Deadline(s):
  Nov 30, 2011

**Rodgers & Hammerstein Organization
Theatricals**
229 W. 28th St., Fl. 11, New York, NY
  10001
Lissi Borshman, Amateur Licensing
  Representative
Tel: (212) 564-4000
Fax:(212) 268-1245
theatre@rnh.com
www.rnhtheatricals.com
  Titles must be returned within 2 weeks
  after closing in perfect condition.
  Quotes expire 3 months after created.
  Submission Materials: Application.

**Samuel French Inc.**
45 W. 25th St., New York, NY 10010
Roxane Heinze-Bradshaw, Managing
  Editor
Tel: (212) 206-8990
Fax:(212) 206-1429
publications@samuelfrench.com
www.samuelfrench.com
  Est. 1830. Performances licensed for
  amateur, stock, professional and
  foreign venues in all media. Respons: 2
  mos. Preferred Genre(s): All genres.
  Preferred Length: Any length.
  Submission Materials: Query, sample,
  SASE.

**Smith and Kraus**
Box 127, Lyme, NH 03768
Marisa Smith, Publisher
Tel: (603) 643-6431
Fax:(603) 643-1831
editor@smithkraus.com
www.smithkraus.com
  Response: 3 wks query; 4 mos script.
  Preferred Genre(s): Plays. Preferred
  Length: One-act or Full-length.
  Submission Materials: Query and
  synopsis only.

**Speert Publishing**
New York, NY
Eleanore Speert, President
Tel: (212) 979-7656
espeert@speertpublishing.com
www.speertpublishing.com
  Self-publishing services for acting
  editions of original plays. Response: 1
  wk. Preferred Genre(s): Plays.
  Preferred Length: Any length.
  Submission Materials: Query letter
  only.

**Tams-Witmark Music Library Inc.**
560 Lexington Ave., New York, NY
  10022
Sargent L. Aborn, President
Tel: (212) 688-2525
Fax:(212) 688-3232
info@tamswitmark.com
www.tams-witmark.com

Classic broadway musicals for stage
performance around the world.
Preferred Genre(s): Musical theatre.
Preferred Length: Any length.
Submission Materials: See website.

**Theatrefolk**
P.O. Box 1064, Crystal Beach, ON
  L0S-1B0 Canada
Craig Mason, Publisher
Tel: (866) 245-9138
Fax:(877) 245-9138
tfolk@theatrefolk.com
www.theatrefolk.com
  We publish plays specifically for
  student performers. Production: simple.
  Response: 6-8 wks. Preferred Genre(s):
  All genres. Preferred Length: One-act
  or Full-length. Submission Materials:
  Complete script. Deadline(s): Year
  round

**TheatreForum**
9500 Gilman Dr., MCO344, La Jolla, CA
  92093
Adele Edling Shank, Editor
Fax:(858) 534-1080
ashank@ucsd.edu
www.theatreforum.org
  Plays must have been professionally
  produced. Submit via email. Preferred
  Genre(s): Plays. Preferred Length:
  Full-length. Submission Materials:
  Query letter only.

**Theatrical Rights Worldwide**
1359 Broadway, #914, New York, NY
  10018
Steve Spiegel, President & CEO
Tel: (646) 736-3232
Fax:(866) 378-9758
licensing@theatricalrights.com
www.theatricalrights.com
  Est. 2006. Work must be unpublished.
  Response: 3-6 mos. Preferred Genre(s):
  Musical theatre. Preferred Length:
  One-act or Full-length. Submission
  Materials: query, full script, audio,
  SASE.

# Career Development Opportunities

## Colonies & Residencies

**Altos de Chavon**
66 5th Ave., #819D, New York, NY
10011
Carmen Lorente, Program Coordinator
Tel: (212) 229-5370
Fax:(212) 229-8988
altos@earthlink.net
www.altosdechavon.com
Est. 1981. 3 1/2 mo. residencies in La
Romana, Dominican Rep, for visual
artists, writers, musicians, and
architects. Summary of work, critiques
of previous work required. Submission
Materials: Query and synopsis only.
Fee: Yes. Deadline(s): 8/15/2011

**Atlantic Center for the Arts**
1414 Art Center Ave., New Smyrna
Beach, FL 32168
James Frost, Program Manager
Tel: (386) 427-6975
Fax:(386) 427-5669
program@atlanticcenterforthearts.org
www.atlanticcenterforthearts.org
Est. 1982. Residencies of 3 wks w/
master artists. Workspace incl black
box theater, music/recording studio,
dance studio, art & sculpture studios,
digital lab and resource library.
Submission Materials: See website.
Fee: Yes.

**Bellagio Center Creative Arts
Residencies**
Villa Serbelloni, Via Roma 1, Bellagio,
Lake Como 22021 Italy
Tel: 39-031-9551
Fax:(390) 319-5525 Ext 9
bellagio_res@rockfound.org
www.rockfound.org/bellagio
Preferred Genre(s): All genres.
Submission Materials: See website.
Fee: Yes.

**Byrdcliffe Arts Colony Artist-in-
Residence (AIR)**
34 Tinker St., Woodstock, NY 12498
Katherine Burger, Director, Artist in
Residence
Tel: (845) 679-2079
Fax:(845) 679-4529
wguild@ulster.net
www.woodstockguild.org
Est. 1980 Catskill Mountains,
Woodstock, NY. Four, 4-week sessions
per season. Application on website.
Additional ph # May - September
ONLY 845 679 8540 Preferred
Genre(s): Plays or Musicals. Preferred
Length: Any length. Submission
Materials: Application, SASE. Fee:
Yes. Deadline(s): 3/1/2011

**Camargo Foundation**
1 Ave Jermini, Cassis, 13260 France
Leon Selig, Director
Tel: 0 (113) 344-2011 Ext 157
Fax:0 (113) 344-2013 Ext 657
apply@camargofoundation.org
www.camargofoundation.org
Interdisciplinary residency program
includes thirteen furnished apartments,
a reference library and three art/music
studios. Residencies are one semester.
See website for complete online
application requirements. Preferred
Genre(s): All genres. Preferred Length:
Any length. Submission Materials: See
website. Fee: Yes. Deadline(s):
1/12/2011

**Centrum Artistic Residencies Program**
Box 1158, Port Townsend, WA 98368
Lisa Werner, Director of Operations
Tel: (360) 385-3102
lisa@centrum.org
www.centrum.org/residencies

Est. 1980. Awarded in one week blocks, residencies may be of any duration, time and space permitting. Submit proposal of work focused on w/resume and work sample. Preferred Genre(s): All genres. Submission Materials: See website. Fee: Yes. Deadline(s): Rolling

**Dorland Mountain Arts Colony**
Box 6, Temecula, CA 92593
Karen Parrott, Executive Director
Tel: (909) 302-3837
Fax:(908) 696-2855
info@dorlandartscolony.org
www.dorlandartscolony.org
Est. 1979. 1 -2 month residencies in southern CA. Submission Materials: Application. Fee: Yes. Deadline(s): Mar 1 2011 , 9/1/2011

**Edward Albee Foundation**
Edward Albee Foundation, 14 Harrison St., New York, NY 10013
Jakob Holder, Secretary
Tel: (212) 226-2020
Fax:(212) 226-5551
info@albeefoundation.org
www.albeefoundation.org
Est. 1966. Residencies of 4 -6 weeks (Jun-Sep) in Montauk, NY, for writers, composers and visual artists. Submission Materials: Full script, SASE, application form. Deadline(s): 3/1/2011

**Gell Center of the Finger Lakes**
740 University Ave., Rochester, NY 14607
Kathy Pottetti, Director Operations/Programming
Tel: (585) 473-2590
Fax:(585) 442-9333
Kathyp@wab.org
www.wab.org
Submission Materials: Sample. Fee: Yes.

**Hawthornden Retreat for Writers**
Hawthornden Castle, Lasswade, EH18 1EG Scotland
S.M. Gaskell, Director
Tel: 0 (131) 440-2180
Fax:0 (131) 440-1989
office@hawthornden.com

Est. 1982. Residencies of 4 wks (Feb-Jul, Sep-Dec) in 17th-century castle, 40-min bus to Edinburgh. Residents housed in study bedrooms. Phone:44-131-440 -2180; fax: 44-131-440-1989. Author must be produced or published. Submission Materials: Application, 10 - 15 pg sample. Deadline(s): 6/30/2011

**Headlands Center for the Arts**
944 Fort Barry, Sausalito, CA 94965
Holly Blake, Residency Manager
Tel: (415) 331-2787
Fax:(415) 331-3857
info@headlands.org
www.headlands.org
Est. 1987. Hosts 30 subsidized studio rentals/residencies for artists of all disciplines per year from 1 to 3 mos. Response: 4-5 mos. Submission Materials: See website.

**Hedgebrook**
2197 Millman Rd., Langley, WA 98260
Amy Wheeler, Executive Director
Tel: (360) 579-2140
Fax:(360) 321-2171
connect@hedgebrook.org
www.hedgebrook.org
Est. 1988. No cost writing retreat residencies of 2 - 6 wks in 48-acre retreat on Whidbey Island. Author must be female. Submission Materials: Application. Fee: Yes. Deadline(s): 9/24/2011

**Helene Wurlitzer Foundation of New Mexico**
P.O. Box 1891, Taos, NM 87571
Michael Knight, Executive Director
Tel: (575) 758-2413
Fax:(575) 758-2559
HWF@taosnet.com
www.wurlitzerfoundation.org
Est. 1956. Rent and utility fee free residences of 3 mos (Jan-Nov) for visual artists, writers and composers. Deadline: Jan 2011 for residency in 2012. Submission Materials: Application. Deadline(s): 1/18/2011

**International Writing Program (IWP)**
430 N. Clinton St., Iowa City, IA 52242
Christopher Merrill
Tel: (319) 335-0128
Fax:(319) 335-3843
iwp@uiowa.edu
iwp.uiowa.edu
   Est. 1967. For published writers of
   fiction, poetry, drama, or screenplays
   who are not US residents but are
   proficient in English. Aug.-Nov. 3 mo.
   residency.

**La MaMa Playwright Retreat**
74-A E. 4th St., New York, NY 10003
Est. 2007. Fee: Yes.

**Lanesboro Residency Program
Fellowships**
103 Parkway Ave. N., Box 152,
   Lanesboro, MN 55949
Sara Decker, Program/Marketing Director
Tel: (507) 467-2446
Fax:(507) 467-4446
Info@lanesboroarts.org
www.lanesboroarts.org
   Retreat space also available for rent.
   Submission Materials: Application.
   Fee: Yes. Deadline(s): 6/30/2011

**Ledig House Writers Residency
Program**
Art Omni Ledig House, 55 5th Ave., Fl.
   15, New York, NY 10003
DW Gibson, Executive Director
Tel: (212) 206-6060
Fax:(212) 206-6114
writers@artomi.org
www.artomi.org
   Est. 1992. Residencies (Mar-Jun, Sep-
   Nov) in Catskill Mts. Residents
   provided with separate or combined
   work/bedroom areas. All meals
   included. Submission Materials: Query,
   10pg sample, bio, SASE. Fee: Yes.
   Deadline(s): 10/20/2011

**MacDowell Colony**
100 High St., Peterborough, NH 03458
Courtney Bethel, Admissions Director
Tel: (603) 924-3886
Fax:(603) 924-9142
admissions@macdowellcolony.org
www.macdowellcolony.org

Est. 1907. Residencies/studios for up to
8 wks (Jun-Sep, Oct-Jan, Feb-May).
Multiple deadlines. Financial assistance
available. Response: 10 weeks
Submission Materials: Application.
Fee: Yes. Deadline(s): Multiple

**Millay Colony for the Arts**
454 East Hill Rd, Box 3, Austerlitz, NY
   12017
Calliope Nicholas, Residency Director
Tel: (518) 392-3103
Fax:(518) 392-4944
apply@millaycolony.org
www.millaycolony.org
   Est. 1973. Month-long residencies
   (Apr-Nov) on former estate of Edna St.
   Vincent Millay for writers, visual
   artists, composers. No cost for
   residency. Response: by Feb. 2012.
   Submission Materials: See website.
   Fee: Yes. Deadline(s): 10/1/2011

**Montana Artists Residency**
Box 8, Basin, MT 59631
Debbie Sheehan, Residency Coord.
Tel: (406) 225-3500
mar@mt.net
www.montanarefuge.org
   Est. 1993. Writer residencies of varying
   lengths/configurations. See website for
   full information/fees. Submission
   Materials: See website. Fee: Yes.
   Deadline(s): 4/15/2011, 5/15/2011

**Shenandoah International Playwrights**
Box 1, Verona, VA 24482
Tel: (540) 248-1868
Fax:(540) 248-7728
theatre@shenarts.org
www.shenanarts.org
   Est. 1977. Up to 12 playwrights (from
   around the US and the world) work
   with dramaturgs, directors and actors in
   Jul-Aug, culminating in invited
   readings. Preferred Genre(s): All
   genres. Preferred Length: Full-length.
   Submission Materials: See website.
   Fee: Yes. Deadline(s): See website

**Sundance Institute Playwrights Retreat at Ucross**
180 Varick St., Suite 1330, New York, NY 10014
Christopher Hibma, Associate Director
Tel: (646) 822-9563
Fax:(310) 360-1969
theatre@sundance.org
www.sundance.org
  Est. 2001. 18-day retreat for 5 playwrights and 1 theater composer at Ucross Foundation, Clearmont, WY. Submission Materials: See website.

**The Field Artward Bound Residency Program**
161 6th Ave., Fl. 14, New York, NY 10013
Patricia Burgess
Tel: (212) 691-6969
Fax:(212) 255-2053
patricia@thefield.org
www.thefield.org
  Residencies of 10-14 days (Jun-Sep) at rural facilities outside NYC. Fees: free ($100 refundable deposit). Response: 1 mo. Preferred Genre(s): Plays. Preferred Length: 10 min . Submission Materials: Application. Deadline(s): See website

**Tyrone Guthrie Centre**
Annaghmakerrig, Newbliss, Ireland
Dr. Pat Donlon, Resident Director
Tel: (353) 475-4003
Fax:(353) 475-4380
info@tyroneguthrie.ie
www.tyroneguthrie.ie
  Est. 1981. Year-round residencies of varying duration in private rooms, studios, self-catering farmyard cottages. Response: 1 mo. Submission Materials: Application. Fee: Yes.

**U.S./Japan Creative Artists' Program**
1201 15th St. NW, #330, Washington, DC 20005
Margaret P. Mihori, Executive Director
Tel: (202) 653-9800
Fax:(202) 418-9802
jusfc@jusfc.gov
www.jusfc.gov
  Est. 1979. 5-mo residency in Japan for produced professional US artists with financial assistance. Submission Materials: Application. Fee: Yes. Deadline(s): 2/1/2011

**Ucross Foundation Residency Program**
30 Big Red Ln., Clearmont, WY 82835
Ruth Salvatore, Residency Manager
Tel: (307) 737-2291
Fax:(307) 737-2322
www.ucrossfoundation.org
  Est. 1981. Residencies of 2 weeks to 6 weels (Feb-Jun, Jul-Nov) near Big Horn Mts. Residents are provided living & studio space plus meals. Submission Materials: See website. Fee: Yes. Deadline(s): 3/1/2011, 10/1/2011

**Virginia Center for the Creative Arts (VCCA)**
154 San Angelo Dr., Amherst, VA 24521
Sheila Pleasants, Director of Artists' Services
Tel: (434) 946-7236
Fax:(434) 946-7239
vcca@vcca.com
www.vcca.com
  Est. 1971. Residencies of 2 wks-2 mos on 12-acre hilltop in foothills of Blue Ridge Mts near Sweet Briar College. Does not accept scholarly projects. Response: 2 mos. Submission Materials: Application, full script. Fee: Yes. Deadline(s): 1/15/2011, 5/15/2011 & 9/15/2011

**William Inge Center for the Arts**
Box 708, 1057 W. College Ave., Independence, KS 67301
Peter Ellenstein, Artistic Director
Tel: (620) 332-5490
info@ingecenter.org
www.ingecenter.org
  Est. 2002. 2 playwrights in 9-wk residency at Inge home (Sep-Nov or Mar-May), with 1-wk Actors' Equity Reading workshop of new play and some teaching. Response: 6 mos. Preferred Genre(s): Plays. Preferred Length: Full-length. Submission Materials: See website. Deadline(s): rolling

**Yaddo**
Box 395, Saratoga Springs, NY 12866
Candace Wait, Program Director
Tel: (518) 584-0746
Fax:(518) 584-1312
chwait@yaddo.org
www.yaddo.org
    Est. 1900. Residencies of 2 wks-2 mos
    on 400-acre turn-of-century estate in

Saratoga Springs, NY. Free
room/board/private studio space. See
website for submission materials.
Preferred Genre(s): All genres.
Submission Materials: See website.
Fee: Yes. Deadline(s): 8/1/2011

# Conferences & Festivals

**Actors Theatre of Louisville, Humana
Festival [KY]**
316 W. Main St., Louisville, KY 40202
Amy Wegener
Tel: (502) 584-1265
Fax:(502) 561-3300
awegener@actorstheatre.org
www.actorstheatre.org/
    humana_submission.htm
    Est. 1976. Festival of 10-15 produced
    plays in Mar-Apr, incl. premieres and
    second productions. No electronic
    submissions. Preferred Genre(s): All
    genres. Preferred Length: Any length.
    Submission Materials: Agent only
    submissions.

**Alabama Shakespeare Festival**
1 Festival Dr., Montgomery, AL 36117
Nancy Rominger, Artistic Assoc.
Tel: (334) 271-5300
Fax:(334) 271-5348
www.asf.net
    Est. 1972. Southern Writers Project
    develops new plays with Southern or
    African-American themes by Southern
    or African-American writers. Preferred
    Genre(s): All genres. Preferred Length:
    Full-length. Submission Materials: See
    website.

**American College Theater Festival
(ACTF)**
Kennedy Center, Washington, DC 20566
Susan Shaffer, Co-Manager Administrator
Tel: (202) 416-8857
Fax:(202) 416-8802
kcactf@kennedy-center.org
www.KCACTF.org

Est. 1969. National fest of student
productions, selected from regional
college fests. Preferred Genre(s): All
genres. Preferred Length: Any length.
Submission Materials: Query, synopsis,
full script, SASE. Deadline(s): Dec 1
2011

**Appalachian Festival of Plays and
Playwrights**
PO Box 867, Abingdon, VA 24212
Nicholas Piper, Director
Tel: (276) 619-3316
Fax:(276) 619-3335
apfestival@bartertheatre.com
www.bartertheatre.com/festival
    Est. 2001. Appalacian playwrights or
    work with Appalacian settings &
    themes. Stagings of 2 plays from
    previous AFPP, and readings w/cash
    award of 6 new scripts in 2-wk fest,
    judged by panel. Must be
    unproduced/unpublished. Preferred
    Genre(s): Plays. Preferred Length:
    Full-length. Submission Materials:
    Complete script & SASE. Deadline(s):
    3/31/2011

**Arkansas Writers Conference**
1115 Gillette Drive, Little Rock, AR
72227
Clovita Rice
Tel: (501) 915-0708
jdaviscpa@aol.com
www.geocities.com/penwomen
    Seeking work featuring older characters
    and concerns of seniors. Preferred
    Genre(s): All genres. Preferred Length:
    One-act or Full-length. Submission

Materials: Complete script.
Deadline(s): Apr 30 2011

**Ashland New Plays Festival**
Box 3314, Ashland, OR 97520-0453
Frederick F. Wright, President
Tel: (541) 488-7995
Fax:(541) 472-0512
info@ashlandnewplays.org
www.ashlandnewplays.org
Est. 1992. Annual Oct. fest with 12 hrs
rehearsal for 2 unstaged readings w/
prof director and actors. Must speak to
U.S. audience. Production: cast limit 8.
Response time: by 8/2011 Preferred
Genre(s): Plays. Preferred Length:
Full-length. Submission Materials: See
website. Deadline(s): Jan 15 2011

**Attic Theatre One-Act Marathon**
5429 W. Washington Blvd., Los Angeles,
CA 90016
Jaime Gray, Literary Manager
Tel: (323) 525-0600
Fax:(323) 525-0661
litmanager@attictheatre.org
www.attictheatre.org
3-10 entries selected for
production/reading in marathon. Panel
from L.A. theater community chooses
2 winners. Production: cast limit 8,no
orchestra, unit set. Response time: 4
mos. Preferred Genre(s): Plays.
Preferred Length: One-Act. Submission
Materials: See website. Deadline(s):
2/28/2011

**Bay Area Playwrights Festival (BAPF)**
1616 16th Street, Suite 350, San
Francisco, CA 94103
Jonathan Spector, Literary Manager
Tel: (415) 626-2176
literary@playwrightsfoundation.org
www.playwrightsfoundation.org
Est. 1976. 2-wk July fest of 5-6 full-
length plays by US writers.
Submissions not returned. Response
time: 4 mos. Preferred Genre(s):
Comedy. Preferred Length: One-act or
Full-length. Submission Materials:
Query and full script. Deadline(s):
11/30/2011

**Boomerang Theatre Company**
P.O. Box 237166, Ansonia Station, New
York, NY 10023
Tim Errickson, Literary Manager
Tel: (212) 501-4069
info@boomerangtheatre.org
www.boomerangtheatre.org
Est. 1999. Annual reading series of
new plays. Preferred Genre(s): Plays.
Preferred Length: Full-length.
Submission Materials: Query, synopsis,
10-pg sample, resume,SASE.
Deadline(s): 9/30/2011

**Boston Theater Marathon**
www.bu.edu/btm
Est. 1999. 50 10-min plays by New
England playwrights by 50 New
England theaters over 10 hrs in 1 day.
Production: small orchestra, minimal
set. Response time: 4 mos. Alternate
website: www.bostonplaywright.org
Preferred Genre(s): Comedy. Preferred
Length: 10-min./10pgs.. Submission
Materials: Complete script, SASE.
Deadline(s): Nov 15 2011

**Centre Stage New Play Festival**
Box 8451, Greenville, SC 29604
Brian Haimbach, New Play Fesitval
Director
Tel: (864) 233-6733
Fax:(864) 233-6733
haimbach@hotmail.com
www.centrestage.org
Est. 2002. Winner of festival gets
production & development assist.
Scripts must be
unpublished/unproduced and sent via
US Mail. Scripts not returned. Cast
limit 5 actors. Preferred Genre(s):
Plays. Preferred Length: Full-length.
Submission Materials: See website.
Deadline(s): 2/1/2011

**Cleveland Public Theatre New Plays
Festival**
6415 Detroit Ave., Cleveland, OH 44102
Tel: (216) 631-2727
Fax:(216) 631-2575
cpt@en.com
www.cptonline.org

Biennial four-week festival of staged readings. Assistance: room/board, travel, per diem Frequency: biennial Production: cast of up to 10,simple set Preferred Genre(s): All genres. Preferred Length: Full-length. Submission Materials: Synopsis, sample, SASE.

## Collaboraction: Sketchbook Festival

437 N. Wolcott, #201, Attn: SKBK06, Chicago, IL 60622
Anthony Moseley, Executive Artistic Director
Tel: (312) 226-9633
Fax:(312) 226-6107
becky@collaboraction.org
www.collaboraction.org/
Annual festival of short plays. Email submissions. Check website for details. Preferred Genre(s): Audience Participation. Preferred Length: One-act or Full-length. Submission Materials: Application, full script. Deadline(s): Dec 15 2011

## Cultural Conversations

116 Arts Bldg., Penn State University School of Theatre, University Park, PA 16802
Susan Russell, Artistic Director
Tel: (814) 863-1451
sbr13@psu.edu
www.culturalconversations.psu.edu
Est. 2007. Readings of new plays by actors 15 - 35 addressing themes of local and global diversity. No SASE, scripts are recycled. Response: by 1/15 of each year. Preferred Genre(s): Plays. Preferred Length: Full-length. Submission Materials: Complete script. Deadline(s): Oct 31 2011

## Firehouse Theatre Project's Festival of New American Plays

1609 W. Broad St., Richmond, VA 23220
Carol Piersol, Artistic Director
Tel: (804) 355-2001
Fax:(804) 355-0999
info@firehousetheatre.org
www.firehousetheatre.org
Est. 2003. Submit script and prof recommendation by US mail

w/author's info on removable cover page. Submissions not returned. Response: 7 mos. Preferred Genre(s): All genres. Preferred Length: Any length. Submission Materials: Complete script. Deadline(s): Jun 30 2011

## Fresh Fruit Festival

145 E. 27th St., #1-A, New York, NY 10016
Carol Polcovar, Artistic Director
Tel: (212) 857-8701
artisticdirector@freshfruitfestival.com
www.freshfruitfestival.com
Est. 2003. Work submitted must be unproduced in NYC and unoptioned. Response: 2 mos. Preferred Genre(s): Plays or Musicals. Special Interest: LGBT. Preferred Length: One-act or Full-length. Submission Materials: Application posted on website. Deadline(s): Feb 15 2011

## FusionFest

8500 Euclid Ave., Cleveland, OH 44106
Seth Gordon, Associate Artistic Director
Tel: (216) 795-7000
Fax:(216) 795-7007
sgordon@clevelandplayhouse.com
www.clevelandplayhouse.com
Est. 1995. Reading series of unoptioned/unproduced new plays. Author must be resident of Ohio. Response: 6 mos. Submission Materials: Agent only submissions.

## FutureFest

1301 E. Siebenthaler Ave., Dayton, OH 45414
Fran Pesch, FutureFest Program Director
Tel: (937) 424-8477
dp_futurefest@yahoo.com
www.daytonplayhouse.org
Est. 1990. Adjudicated July festival of new work. Work must be longer than 75 minutes. Submissions not returned. Preferred Genre(s): Plays. Preferred Length: Full-length. Submission Materials: Synopsis and full script. Deadline(s): Oct 31 2011

**Genesis Festival**
P.O. Box 238, 7 Livingston Ave., New
    Brunswick, NJ 08901
Marshall Jones, Executive Director
Tel: (732) 545-8100
Fax:(732) 907-1864
www.crossroadstheatrecompany.org
    Submission Materials: Query, synopsis,
    30pg sample, bio. Deadline(s): Dec 31
    2011

**Indo-American Arts Council Inc.
(IACC)**
517 East 87th Street, Suite 1B, New
    York, NY 10128
Aroon Shivdasani, Executive Director
Tel: (212) 529-2347
Fax:(212) 477-4106
aroon@iaac.us
www.iaac.us
    Est. 1998. Annual film and playwrights
    festivals. Preferred Genre(s): Plays.
    Preferred Length: Any length.
    Submission Materials: Application,
    synopsis, full script, video, SASE.
    Deadline(s): Aug 1 2011

**Inspirato Festival**
124 Broadway Ave., Ste. 112, Toronto,
    ON M4P-1V8 Canada
Dominik Loncar
Tel: (416) 832-222
inspirato@ca.inter.net
www.inspiratofestival.ca
    Preferred Genre(s): Plays. Preferred
    Length: 10-min./10pgs.. Submission
    Materials: Complete script.
    Deadline(s): Dec. 31, 2011

**International Mystery Writers' Festival**
101 Daviess St., Owensboro, KY 42303
Donna Conkwright, Program Director
Tel: (270) 687-2770
Fax:(270) 687-2775
dconkwright@riverparkcenter.org
www.newmysteries.org
    Est. 2007. Accepts unproduced plays,
    teleplays or short screenplays in
    mystery/thriller genre. Submissions not
    returned. Response: 3 mos. Preferred
    Genre(s): Mystery. Preferred Length:
    Any length. Submission Materials:
    Complete script. Deadline(s):
    10/31/2011

**Jewish Ensemble Theater Festival of
New Plays**
Jewish Ensemble Theater, 6600 W. Maple
    Rd., West Bloomfield, MI 48322
Christopher Bremer, Managing Director
Tel: (248) 788-2900
Fax:(248) 788-5160
c.bremer@jettheatre.org
www.jettheatre.org
    Est. 1989. Submit by US mail only.
    Production: cast limited to 8. Preferred
    Genre(s): Plays or Musicals. Preferred
    Length: One-act or Full-length.
    Submission Materials: Complete script
    & SASE. Deadline(s): August 1st each
    year

**Kitchen Dog Theater (KDT) New
Works Festival**
3120 McKinney Ave., #100, Dallas, TX
    75204
Tina Parker, Co-Artistic Director
Tel: (214) 953-2258
Fax:(214) 953-1873
tina@kitchendogtheater.org
www.kitchendogtheater.org
    Est. 1990. Winner receives production,
    travel stipend, and royalty; 7 finalists
    receive reading. Submit by US mail
    only. Submissions recycled, not
    returned. Response: 8 mos. Preferred
    Genre(s): Plays. Preferred Length:
    Full-length. Submission Materials:
    Complete script. Deadline(s): January
    1st

**Lark Play Development Center:
Playwrights' Week**
939 8th Ave., #301, New York, NY
    10019
Andrea Hiebler, Literary Coodinator
Tel: (212) 246-2676
Fax:(212) 246-2609
andreah@larktheatre.org
www.larktheatre.org
    Submissions accepted Aug-Nov for a
    fest of public dev. readings the
    following fall. Response: 9 mos.
    Preferred Genre(s): Plays. Preferred
    Length: Full-length. Submission
    Materials: Application, full script.
    Deadline(s): Nov 15 2011

**Last Frontier Theatre Conference**
Box 97, Valdez, AK 99686
Dawson Moore, Coordinator
Tel: (907) 834-1614
Fax:(907) 834-1611
dmoore@pwscc.edu
www.pwscc.edu/conference
   Est. 1993. Application free. See
   website for conference fees. Work must
   not have been professionally produced.
   Preferred Genre(s): Plays. Preferred
   Length: Full-length. Submission
   Materials: Synopsis and full script.
   Deadline(s): 12/20/2011

**Lavender Footlights Festival**
P.O. Box 942107, Miami, FL 33194
Ryan Capiro, Aristic Director
Tel: (305) 433-8111
Fax:(305) 672-7818
Ryan@Lavenderfootlights.org
www.lavenderfootlights.org
   Est. 2000. Fest of readings with gay
   and lesbian themes. Preferred Genre(s):
   Plays. Special Interest: LGBT.
   Preferred Length: Full-length.
   Submission Materials: Synopsis, full
   script, SASE . Deadline(s): 12/1/2011

**Little Festival of the Unexpected**
Portland Stage, Box 1458, Portland, ME
   04104
Daniel Burson, Literary Manager
Tel: (207) 774-1043
Fax:(207) 774-0576
dburson@portlandstage.com
www.portlandstage.com
   Est. 1989. 1-wk fest of new plays
   (unproduced, unpublished, unoptioned)
   with writers developing work thru
   staged readings. Production: cast limit
   8. US mail submission only. Preferred
   Genre(s): Plays. Preferred Length:
   Full-length. Submission Materials:
   Query, synopsis and 10-pg sample.
   Deadline(s): Rolling

**National Black Theatre Festival**
610 Coliseum Dr., Winston-Salem, NC
   27106
Larry Leon Hamlin, Producer & Artistic
   Director
Tel: (336) 723-2266
nbtf@bellsouth.net
www.nbtf.org
   Est. 1989. Biennial (odd years) fest in
   Aug of productions about the Black
   experience. Preferred Genre(s): All
   genres. Special Interest:
   African-American. Preferred Length:
   Full-length. Submission Materials: See
   website. Deadline(s): See website

**New Jersey Playwrights Festival of
New Plays**
Box 1663, Bloomfield, NJ 07003
Lenny Bart, Artistic Director
Tel: (973) 259-9187
Fax:(973) 259-9188
info@12mileswest.org
www.12mileswest.org
   Annual fest of plays by NJ
   playwrights. Production: cast of 2-7,
   unit set. Response: 1 yr. Preferred
   Genre(s): All genres. Preferred Length:
   Any length. Submission Materials: See
   website.

**New Play Festival**
Denver Center, 1101 13th Street, Denver,
   CO 80204
Chad Henry, Literary Assoc.
Tel: (303) 572-4456
Fax:(303) 893-3206
chenry@dcpa.org
www.dcpa.org
   Est. 2005. Rehearsed reading of new
   work for industry and general
   audience. Response: up to 6 mos.
   Preferred Genre(s): Plays or Musicals.
   Preferred Length: Full-length.
   Submission Materials: Complete script
   & SASE. Deadline(s): Rolling

**New Professional Theatre Writers Festival**
229 W. 42nd St., #501, New York, NY 10036
Mark D. Wood, Literary Manager
Tel: (212) 398-2666
Fax:(212) 398-2924
newprof@aol.com
www.newprofessionaltheatre.org
 Est. 1991. Annual fest of work by African-Americans, Asians, and Latinos. Also business seminars, mentoring, and 2-wk residencies. Preferred Genre(s): All genres. Preferred Length: Full-length. Submission Materials: See website. Deadline(s): Jun 1 2011

**New York City 15-Minute Play Fest**
American Globe Turnip Fest, 145 W. 46th St., Fl. 3, New York, NY 10036
Elizabeth Keefe, Executive Director
Tel: (212) 869-9809
Fax:(212) 869-9807
liz@americanglobe.org
www.americanglobe.org
 Est. 1993. 2-wk fest in May of 4-5 new plays each night. Production: cast of 2-10, no set. Response: 2 mos. Preferred Genre(s): Plays. Preferred Length: 15 min.. Submission Materials: Complete script & SASE. Deadline(s): Dec 15 2011

**New York Musical Theatre Festival (NYMF)**
242 W. 38th St., #1102, New York, NY 10018
Jess McLeod, Assoc Programming Dir
Tel: (212) 664-0979
Fax:(212) 664-0978
www.nymf.org
 DROPPED.

**Penobscot Theatre**
131 Main Street, 4th Floor, Bangor, ME 04401
Scott RC Levy, Producing Artistic Director
Tel: (207) 947-6618
info@penobscottheatre.org
www.penobscottheatre.org

2 wk. New Play Fest. featuring readings & workshops. Response: by 5/1/11. Preferred Genre(s): All genres. Preferred Length: Any length. Submission Materials: Cover letter. Deadline(s): Feb 14 2011

**Playfest - Harriett Lake Festival of New Plays**
812 E. Rollins St., #100, Orlando, FL 32803
Patrick Flick, Dir., New Play Development & Casting
Tel: (407) 447-1700
Fax:(407) 447-1701
patrickf@orlandoshakes.org
www.orlandoshakes.org
 Est. 1989. 10 new plays receive readings, 2-3 developmental in Festival of new plays. Preferred Genre(s): Plays. Preferred Length: Full-length. Submission Materials: See website. Deadline(s): Aug 1 2011

**Premiere Stages Play Festival**
Hutchinson Hall, 1000 Morris Ave., Union, NJ 07083
John Wooten, Producing Artistic Dir.
Tel: (908) 737-5526
Fax:(908) 737-4636
premiere@kean.edu
www.kean.edu/premierestages
 Est. 2004. Annual fest for playwrights born or living in NJ, CT, NY, PA. Three public readings in Apr, full Equity production of winner in Jul. Frequency: annual Production: cast limit 8 See website for details Preferred Genre(s): Contemporary - comedy or drama. Preferred Length: Full-length. Deadline(s): Jan 15 2011

**Samuel French, Inc. Off-Off-Broadway Short-Play Festival**
45 W. 25 St., New York, NY 10010
Kenneth Dingledine, Festival Coordinator
Tel: (212) 206-8990
Fax:(202) 206-1429
oobfestival@samuelfrench.com
www.samuelfrench.com
 Est. 1976. Summer 1-wk fest in NYC. 40 shows. 6 finalists chosen for publication and representation by

Samuel French. Preferred Genre(s): Plays. Preferred Length: 10 min and one-acts. Submission Materials: Application, full script. Deadline(s): See website

**San Francisco Fringe Festival (SFFF)**
156 Eddy St., San Francisco, CA 94102
Christina Augello
Tel: (415) 931-1094
www.sffringe.org
  Preferred Genre(s): All genres. Preferred Length: Any length. Submission Materials: See website. Deadline(s): See website

**Seven Devils Playwrights Conference**
343 E. 30th St., #19-J, New York, NY 10016
Jeni Mahoney, Co-Artistic Director
Tel: (917) 881-9114
jeni@idtheater.org
www.idtheater.org
  Est. 2001. 2-wk play new play development conference in McCall, ID, ending w/fully staged readings. Preferred Genre(s): Plays. Preferred Length: One-act or Full-length. Submission Materials: See website. Deadline(s): Nov 15 2011

**Short Attention Span PlayFEST**
Atlantis Playmakers, 5261 Whitsett Avenue #20, Valley Village, CA 91607
Kimberly Davis Basso, Artistic Director
Tel: (978) 667-0550
kdb@atlantisplaymakers.com
www.atlantisplaymakers.com
  Est. 1998. Preferred Genre(s): Plays. Submission Materials: See website. Deadline(s): See website

**Southern Appalachian Playwrights' Conference**
Box 1720, Mars Hill, NC 28754
Rob Miller, Managing Director
Tel: (828) 689-1384
Fax:(828) 689-1272
sart@mhc.edu
www.sartplays.org
  Est. 1981. Readings & critique of 5/6 plays in 3-day conference at Mars Hill Coll. Submissions must abide the

specific guidelines. See website. Response: Aug/Sept. Preferred Genre(s): Plays or Musicals. Preferred Length: Full-length. Submission Materials: See website. Deadline(s): Oct 31 2011

**Summer Play Festival (SPF)**
Box 778, New York, NY 10108
Sarah Bagley, Literary Coordinator
Tel: (212) 279-4040
Fax:(212) 297-4041
info@spfnyc.com
www.spfnyc.com
  Est. 2003. Submit via email. Production: cast limit 10. Preferred Genre(s): Plays. Preferred Length: Any length. Submission Materials: Application, full script. Deadline(s): 11/1/2010

**Teatro del Pueblo**
209 West Page St., Ste 208, St. Paul, MN 55107
Alberto Justiniano
Tel: (651) 224-8806
Fax:(651) 298-5796
al@teatrodelpueblo.org
www.teatrodelpueblo.org
  Looking for 15 to 50 min one-act plays dealing with poltical issues pertaining to Latino Social Justice. Preferred Genre(s): Plays. Special Interest: Latino. Preferred Length: One-Act. Submission Materials: Synopsis, complete script. Deadline(s): Sept. 15, 2011

**Tennessee Williams/New Orleans Literary Festival**
938 Lafayette St., #514, New Orleans, LA 70113
Laura Miller, Contest Coordinator
Tel: (504) 581-1144
Fax:(504) 581-3270
info@tennesseewilliams.net
www.tennesseewilliams.net
  Production: small, minimal. Preferred Genre(s): Plays. Preferred Length: One-Act. Submission Materials: See website. Deadline(s): 11/1/2011

**The Many Voices Project**
1105 W. Chicago Ave., Chicago, IL
60622
Ilesa Duncan, Outreach Director
Tel: (312) 633-0630
Fax:(312) 633-0630
iduncan@chicagodramatists.org
www.chicagodramatists.org
Contest and developmental showcase
for US playwrights of color in 2-wk
Jul fest of staged readings. Work must
be previously unproduced. Response: 2
mos. Preferred Genre(s): Plays or
Musicals. Special Interest:
African-American. Preferred Length:
One-act or Full-length. Submission
Materials: Full Script, cast breakdown,
bio, SASE.

**Theatre Building Chicago**
1225 W. Belmont Ave., Chicago, IL
60657
Allan Chambers, Artistic Director
Tel: (773) 929-7367
Fax:(773) 327-1404
allan@theatrebuildingchicago.org
www.theatrebuildingchicago.org
Est. 1984. Production: cast limit 16,
piano only, no set. Response: 3 mos.
Preferred Genre(s): Musical theatre.
Preferred Length: Full-length.
Submission Materials: Application.
Deadline(s): 10/1/2011

**Theatre Three [NY] One-Act Play
Festival**
Box 512, 412 Main St., Port Jefferson,
NY 11777
Jeffrey Sanzel, Executive Artistic Director
Tel: (631) 928-9202
Fax:(631) 928-9120
www.theatrethree.com

Est. 1969. Festival of one-act plays in
March. Production: 2-8, minimal set.
Response: 8 mos. Preferred Genre(s):
Plays. Preferred Length: 10 min and
one-acts. Submission Materials: See
website. Deadline(s): 9/30/2011

**Year-End Series (YES) New Play
Festival**
Northern Kentucky University, One Nunn
Drive, Fine Arts 228, Highland
Heights, KY 41099
Sandra Forman, Project Director
Tel: (859) 572-6303
Fax:(859) 572-6057
forman@nku.edu
www.nku.edu/~theatre
Est. 1983. Biennial (odd yrs) fest in
April of 3 new works receive full
productions. Playwrights flown in for
final wk of rehearsals and opening
night. Preferred Genre(s): Plays or
Musicals. Preferred Length:
Full-length. Submission Materials: Full
script, synopsis, character breakdown,
SASE. Deadline(s): Not accepting
submissions until 2012.

## Conferences & Festivals (Fee Charged)

**Actors' Playhouse National Children's Theatre Festival**
280 Miracle Mile, Coral Gables, FL 33134
Earl Maulding, Dir, TYA
Tel: (305) 444-9293 Ext 615
Fax:(305) 444-4181
maulding@actorsplayhouse.org
www.actorsplayhouse.org
Est. 1994. Annual 4-day fest. Winning show wins $500 plus production. See website. Production: cast limit 8, touring set. Preferred Genre(s): Children's Musicals. Special Interest: Theatre for Young Audiences. Submission Materials: Full Script, Vocal Score, Vocal Recording. Deadline(s): 4/1/2011

**Baltimore Playwrights Festival**
Box 38537, Baltimore, MD 21231
Miriam Bazensky, Chair
chairman@baltimoreplaywrightsfestival.org
www.baltimoreplaywrightsfestival.com
Est. 1981. Plays chosen for 3-wk summer production and selected public readings. Preferred Genre(s): All genres. Preferred Length: Full-length. Submission Materials: Synopsis, full script (3 copies). Deadline(s): 4/1/2011, 9/30/2011

**Cincinnati Fringe Festival**
1120 Jackson Street, Cincinnati, OH 45202
Eric Vosmeier
Tel: (513) 300-5669
Fax:(513) 421-3435
fringesubmissions@knowtheatre.com
www.cincyfringe.com
Est. 2003. Annual Fringe Festival late May/early June. Submissions not returned. Response time: 3 mos. Preferred Genre(s): Plays or Musicals. Preferred Length: One-act or Full-length. Submission Materials: Application. Deadline(s): 12/30/2011

**Edinburgh Festival Fringe**
180 High St., Edinburgh, EH1 1QS
Paul Gudgin, Director
Tel: (441) 312-2600 Ext 26
admin@edfringe.com
www.edfringe.com
Est. 1947. To participate, you need to organize every aspect of bringing your production to Edinburgh. Preferred Genre(s): All genres. Preferred Length: Any length. Submission Materials: See website. Deadline(s): See website

**Juneteenth Legacy Theatre**
605 Water St. #21B, New York, NY 10002
Loma Littleway
Tel: (502) 636-4200
Fax:(502) 561-2149
juneteenthlegacy@aol.com
www.juneteenthlegacytheatre.com
Est. 1999. Staged readings on African-American experience in 19th-20th centuries. Preferred Genre(s): Plays or Musicals. Special Interest: African-American. Preferred Length: Any length. Submission Materials: Complete script (4 copies). Deadline(s): 3/15/2011

**Long Beach Playhouse New Works Festival**
5021 East Anaheim Street, Long Beach, CA 90804
Jo Black-Jacob, New Works Literary Manager
Tel: (562) 494-1014 Ext 526
joblack@dslextreme.com
newworks@lbplayhouse.org
www.lbph.com
Est. 1989. Spring fest of 4 new unproduced plays in staged readings. Production: cast limit 10, limited set. Response: 3 mos after festival. Preferred Genre(s): Plays. Preferred Length: Full-length. Submission Materials: See website. Deadline(s): September 30th , Year Round

**National Alliance for Musical Theatre (NAMT)**
520 8th Ave., #301, New York, NY 10018
Kathy Evans, Executive Director
Tel: (212) 714-6668
Fax:(212) 714-0469
info@namt.org
www.namt.org
Est. 1985. Equity Showcase of 8 musicals in 45-min presentations over 2 days. Participants receive stipend from NAMT. Invitation is industry only. Response: 6 mos. Preferred Genre(s): Musical theatre. Preferred Length: Full-length. Submission Materials: Application, full script, cd. Deadline(s): See website

**Old Opera House Theatre Company New Voice Play Festival**
204 N. George St., Charles Town, WV 25414
Steven Brewer, Managing and Artistic Director
Tel: (304) 752-4420
ooh@oldoperahouse.org
www.oldoperahouse.org
Est. 2001. Call or email for application and deadlines. One act play festival-plays 10 to 40 minutes in length. Preferred Genre(s): Plays. Preferred Length: 10 min and one-acts. Submission Materials: See website. Deadline(s): 3/1/2011

**Raymond J. Flores Short Play Festival (Around the Block)**
5 E. 22nd St., #9-K, New York, NY 10010
Carlos Jerome, President
Tel: (212) 673-9187
info@aroundtheblock.org
www.aroundtheblock.org
Est. 2004. Theme: Urban life and dreams. Must include a one paragraph synopsis in English. Email submissions only. Preferred Genre(s): Plays. Preferred Length: 10 min and one-acts. Submission Materials: Application, full script, bio (1pg). Deadline(s): 11/30/2011

**ShowOff! Ten-Minute Playwriting Festival**
Camino Real Playhouse, 31776 El Camino Real, San Juan Capistrano, CA 92675
Tom Scott, President
Tel: (949) 248-0808
Fax:(949) 248-0808
box_office@sbcglobal.net
www.caminorealplayhouse.org
Est. 1993. Material must be unpublished. Response: 3 mos. Preferred Genre(s): Plays. Preferred Length: 10-min./10pgs.. Submission Materials: Complete script. Deadline(s): 10/15/2011

**Theater Resources Unlimited (TRU)/TRU Voices**
Players Theater, 115 MacDougal St., New York, NY 10012
Bob Ost, Executive Director
Tel: (212) 714-7628
Fax:(212) 864-6301
trunltd@aol.com
www.truonline.org
New plays & musicals readings series. Prefer submissions from producers, but writers welcome to submit. Production: cast limit 12 (with doubling). Response: 3 to 6 mos. Preferred Genre(s): Plays or Musicals. Preferred Length: Full-length. Submission Materials: See website. Deadline(s): 1/7/2011 , 8/22/2011

**Utah Shakespearean Festival: New American Playwrights Projec**
351 W. Center St., Cedar City, UT 84720
Charles Metten, Director, NAPP
Tel: (435) 586-7880
Fax:(435) 865-8003
metten@bard.org
www.bard.org
Aug fest of 4 play readings, with writers in residence. Production: cast of 8-10, set limit 2, flexible stage. Unproduced, w/single author. Preferred Genre(s): Plays. Preferred Length: Full-length. Submission Materials: Complete script. Deadline(s): 12/1/2011

**Weathervane Playhouse**
1301 Weathervane Lane, Akron, OH
  44313
Tel: (330) 678-3893
Fax:(330) 873-2150
10minuteplay@weathervaneplayhouse.com
www.weathervaneplayhouse.com

Material must be unproduced. See
website for details. Preferred Genre(s):
All genres. Preferred Length: 10-30
min.. Submission Materials:
Application, full script, bio (1pg).
Deadline(s): 5/11/2010

## Contests

**American Scandinavian Foundation
Translation Prize**
58 Park Ave., New York, NY 10016
Tel: (212) 879-9779
Fax:(212) 686-2115
grants@amscan.org
www.amscan.org
  Est. 1979. Prize for best translation of
  drama written after 1800 by a
  Scandinavian author (Danish, Finnish,
  Icelandic, Norwegian, Swedish).
  Preferred Genre(s): Translation.
  Preferred Length: One-act or Full-
  length. Submission Materials: See
  website. Deadline(s): 6/1/2011

**Anna Zornio Memorial Children's
Theatre Playwriting Award**
UNH Theatre/Dance Dept., PCAC, 30
  Academic Way, Durham, NH 03824
Michael Wood, Administrative Manager
Tel: (603) 862-3038
Fax:(603) 862-0298
mike.wood@unh.edu
www.unh.edu/theatre-dance/zornio
  Est. 1979. Quadrennial cash/production
  award for unproduced, unpublished
  children's work for residents of U.S.
  and Canada. Preferred Genre(s): All
  genres. Special Interest: Theatre for
  Young Audiences. Preferred Length:
  Full-length. Submission Materials: See
  website. Deadline(s): 3/2/2012

**Arena Stage Student Ten-Minute Play
Competition**
1101 6th St., SW, Washington, DC 20024
Tel: (202) 234-5782
Fax:(202) 488-4056
education@arenastage.org
www.arenastage.org
  Preferred Length: 10-min./10pgs..

**Arthur W. Stone New Play Award**
Louisiana Tech University, Box 8608,
  Ruston, LA 71272
Louisiana Tech University
Tel: (318) 257-2711
Fax:(318) 257-4571
stoneplaywritingaward@yahoo.com
performingarts.latech.edu
  Est. 2006. Email (DOC, FDR, RTF
  formats) 9/11 themed work only.
  Submit author bio and production
  history. Preferred Genre(s): Plays or
  Musicals. Preferred Length:
  Full-length. Submission Materials:
  Synopsis and full script.

**Babes With Blades - Joining Sword
and Pen**
Babes With Blades, 1205 W. Farwell #2,
  Chicago, IL 60626
Morgan Manasa
swordandpen@babeswithblades.org
www.babeswithblades.org
  Est. 1997. New play development
  program and contest. Work must
  include fighting roles for women!
  Preferred Genre(s): All genres.
  Submission Materials: See website.

**Baker's Plays High School Playwriting
Contest**
45 W. 25th Street #9, New York, NY
  10010
Roxane Heinze-Bradshaw, Managing
  Editor
Tel: (212) 255-8085
Fax:(212) 627-7753
publications@bakersplays.com
www.bakersplays.com
  Est. 1989. For student plays, preferably
  about HS experience. Plays must be
  accompanied by complete application

form. Preferred Genre(s): All genres.
Preferred Length: One-act or Full-
length. Submission Materials: Full
script, SASE, application form.
Deadline(s): 1/30/2011

**Beverly Hills Theatre Guild Julie
Harris Playwright Awards**
Beverly Hills Theatre Guild, Box 148,
  Beverly Hills, CA 90213
Candace Coster, Coordinator
Tel: (310) 273-3390
www.beverlyhillstheatreguild.org
  Preferred Genre(s): Comedy. Preferred
  Length: Full-length. Submission
  Materials: query, application, full
  script. Deadline(s): 8/1–11/1/2011

**Brevard Little Theatre New-Play
Competition**
P.O. Box 426, Brevard, NC 28712
June Stacy, Coordinator
Tel: (828) 883-2751
jstacy@comporium.net
www.brevardlittletheatre.com
  Multiple submissions OK. Production:
  cast limit: 10, simple set. Preferred
  Genre(s): Plays. Preferred Length:
  One-act or Full-length. Submission
  Materials: Query, full script, SASE.
  Deadline(s): 7/31/2010

**Christopher Brian Wolk Award**
Abingdon Theatre, 312 W. 36th St., 6th
  floor, New York, NY 10018
Kim T. Sharp, Literary Manager
Tel: (212) 868-2055
Fax:(212) 868-2056
ksharp@abingdontheatre.org
www.abingdontheatre.org
  Est. 2001. Mail entire
  unproduced/unoptioned script
  w/character breakdown, prod hist, bio.
  See website for full guidelines.
  Production: cast limit 8. Response
  time: 3 - 6 mos. Preferred Genre(s):
  Plays. Preferred Length: Full-length.
  Submission Materials: See website.
  Deadline(s): 6/1/2011

**Clauder Competition for New England
Playwrights**
Portland Stage, Box 1458, Portland, ME
  04104
Daniel Burson, Literary Manager
Tel: (207) 774-1043
Fax:(207) 774-0576
dburson@portlandstage.org
www.portlandstage.org
  Est. 1981. Competition for
  unpublished/unproduced work from
  New England writers (current or
  former resident; student). Frequency:
  every 3 years. Production: cast limit 8.
  Preferred Genre(s): All genres.
  Preferred Length: Full-length.
  Submission Materials: Complete script.
  Deadline(s): 3/1/2012

**David C. Horn Prize**
Yale Univ. Press, Box 209040, New
  Haven, CT 06520
Alison MacKeen, Editor
Tel: (203) 432-0975
Fax:(203) 436-1064
www.dchornfoundation.org
  Est. 2006. Submissions not returned.
  Preferred Genre(s): Plays. Preferred
  Length: Full-length. Submission
  Materials: See website. Deadline(s):
  6/1–8/15/2011

**Dorothy Silver Playwriting
Competition**
Mandel Jewish Community Center, 26001
  S. Woodland Ave., Beachwood, OH
  44122
Deborah Bobrow, Coordinator
Tel: (216) 593-6278
Fax:(216) 831-7796
dbobrow@mandeljcc.org
www.mandeljcc.org
  Award for original works of significant,
  fresh perspective on Jewish experience.
  US mail only. Response: 4 mos
  Preferred Genre(s): Plays or Musicals.
  Preferred Length: Full-length.
  Submission Materials: Full Script,
  audio, SASE. Deadline(s): 12/31/2011

**Edgar Allan Poe Award for Best Play**
1140 Broadway, St. 1507, New York, NY
    10001
Margery Flax, Admin Director
Tel: (212) 888-8171
Fax:(212) 888-8107
mwa@mysterywriters.org
www.mysterywriters.org
    Est. 1945. Material submitted must
    have already been produced. Preferred
    Genre(s): Plays or Musicals. Preferred
    Length: One-act or Full-length.
    Submission Materials: See website.
    Deadline(s): 11/30/2011

**Essential Theatre Playwriting Award**
1414 Foxhall Lane #10, Atlanta, GA
    30316
Peter Hardy, Producing Artistic Director
Tel: (404) 212-0815
pmhardy@aol.com
www.essentialtheatre.com
    Material must be unproduced of at
    least an hour's length. Writer must be
    resident of GA. Preferred Genre(s):
    Plays or Musicals. Preferred Length:
    One-act or Full-length. Submission
    Materials: Complete script.
    Deadline(s): 4/23/2011

**Garrard Best Play Competition**
1101 Honor Heights Dr., Muskogee, OK
    74401
Marie L. Wadley, President
Tel: (918) 683-1701
Fax:(918) 683-3070
5civilizedtribes@sbcglobal.net
www.fivetribes.org
    Biennial (even yrs) competition for
    playwrights of Cherokee, Chickasaw,
    Choctaw, Creek or Seminole lineage
    that reflect the history, culture, or
    traditions of the Five Civilized Tribes.
    Preferred Genre(s): All genres. Special
    Interest: Native American. Submission
    Materials: Full Script (4 copies), proof
    of heritage, bio. Deadline(s): 7/7/2011

**George R. Kernodle Playwriting
Contest**
619 Kimpel Hall, Fayetteville, AR 72701
Roger Gross, Director
Tel: (479) 575-2953
Fax:(479) 575-7602
rdgross@uark.edu
www.uark.edu
    Preferred Genre(s): All genres.
    Submission Materials: See website.

**Goshen College Peace Playwriting
Contest**
1700 S. Main St., Goshen, IN 46526
Douglas Caskey, Director of Theatre
Tel: (574) 535-7393
Fax:(574) 535-7660
douglc@goshen.edu
www.goshen.edu
    Preferred Genre(s): Plays. Preferred
    Length: 10 min and one-acts.
    Submission Materials: Synopsis, full
    script, resume . Deadline(s):
    12/31/2011

**Jane Chambers Playwriting Award**
Dept. of Perf. Arts, Georgetown U., 108
    Davis Center, Box 571063,
    Washington, DC 20057
Maya Roth
Tel: (202) 687-1327
mer46@georgetown.edu
www.athe.org/wtp/html/chambers.html
    Award for plays and performance texts
    by females that reflect a feminist
    perspective and contain a majority of
    opportunities for women performers.
    Submissions not returned. Preferred
    Genre(s): All genres. Special Interest:
    Feminist. Preferred Length: Any
    length. Submission Materials:
    Application, synopsis, full script (3)
    resume. Deadline(s): 2/15/2011

**Jane Chambers Student Playwriting
Award**
230 W. 56th St., #65-A, New York, NY
    10019
Jen-Scott Mobley
jen-scottm@nyc.rr.com
www.athe.org/wtp/html/chambers.html
    Award for plays and texts by female
    students that reflect a feminist

perspective and contain a majority of opportunities for women performers. Submissions not returned. Preferred Genre(s): All genres. Special Interest: Feminist. Preferred Length: Full-length. Submission Materials: Application, synopsis, full script (2), resume. Deadline(s): 2/15/2011

**Laity Theatre Company**
3053 Rancho Vista Blvd. Ste. H336, Palmdale, CA 93551
James Goins
Tel: (888) 732-6092
Fax:(661) 430-5423
contact@laityarts.org
www.laityarts.org
Seeking unproduced/unpublished material for readings/workshops thematically linked to women, theatre for young audiences, writers of color and people w/disabilities. Preferred Genre(s): Plays. Preferred Length: Any length. Submission Materials: Query, synopsis, 15pg sample. Deadline(s): 3/15/2011

**LiveWire Chicago Theatre**
P.O. Box 11226, Chicago, IL 60611
Josh Weinstein
Tel: (312) 533-4666
livewirechicago@gmail.com
www.livewirechicago.com/vision
Annual short play festival surrounding a central theme. Work must be previously unproduced. See website for theme guidelines, submission criteria, deadlines and more info. Preferred Genre(s): Plays. Preferred Length: 10 min and one-acts. Submission Materials: Complete script. Deadline(s): See website

**MetLife Foundation's Nuestras Voces National Playwriting Com**
Repertorio Espanol, 138 E. 27th St., New York, NY 10016
Allison Astor-Vargas, Special Projects Manager
Tel: (212) 225-9950
Fax:(212) 225-9085
aav@repertorio.org
www.repertorio.org/opportunities

Author must be related to Hispanics in the US. Preferred Genre(s): Plays or Musicals. Special Interest: Latino. Preferred Length: Full-length. Submission Materials: Application, full script (2 copies, anonymous). Deadline(s): 6/1/2011

**Mississippi Theatre Association**
1297 Bardwell Road, Starkville, MS 39759
Kris Lee
Tel: (812) 320-3534
tklee1976@gmail.com
www.mta-online.org
This competition is open to all Mississippi writers either in state or abroad. Submit via email. Preferred Genre(s): Comedy or Variety. Preferred Length: Full-length. Submission Materials: Application, synopsis, full script. Deadline(s): 9/1/2011

**Naples Players ETC**
701 5th Ave. S., Naples, FL 34102-6662
Joe Moran
Tel: (239) 434-7340
venus46@naples.net
www.naplesplayers.com
Writer must reside in Collier, Lee, Charlotte, Glades or Hendry counties in Florida and may not be a member of the anonymous judging panel. Preferred Genre(s): Comedy or Variety. Preferred Length: 10-30 min.. Submission Materials: See website. Deadline(s): 5/31/2011

**National Latino Playwriting Award**
Arizona Theatre Company, 343 S. Scott Avenue, Tucson, AZ 85701
Elaine Romero, Playwright in Residence
Tel: (520) 884-8210
Fax:(520) 628-9129
eromero@arizonatheatre.org
www.aztheatreco.org
Must be resident of US, or Mexico; Latino. Preferred Genre(s): All genres. Special Interest: Latino. Preferred Length: Full-length. Submission Materials: See website. Deadline(s): 12/31/2010

**National Ten-Minute Play Contest**
Actors Theatre of Louisville, 316 W.
  Main St., Louisville, KY 40202
Sarah Lunnie, Literary Associate
Tel: (502) 584-1265
Fax:(502) 561-3300
slunnie@actorstheatre.org
www.actorstheatre.org/humana_contest.htm
  Est. 1989. Preferred Genre(s): Plays.
  Preferred Length: 10 min. Submission
  Materials: Complete script.
  Deadline(s): 11/1/2011

**North Carolina New Play Project
(NCNPP)**
Greensboro Playwrights Forum,
  Greensboro Cultural Center, 200 N.
  Davie St., Box 2, Greensboro, NC
  27401
Stephen Hyers, Director
Tel: (336) 335-6426
Fax:(336) 373-2659
drama@greensboro-nc.gov
www.playwrightsforum.org
  Work must be unpublished/unproduced.
  Email submission. Author must be a
  resident of NC. Production: small cast,
  simple set. Response: 6 mos. Preferred
  Genre(s): Plays. Preferred Length:
  Full-length. Submission Materials: 10-
  pg sample. Deadline(s): 8/15/2011

**Ohioana Career Award**
274 E. 1st Ave., #300, Columbus, OH
  43201
Linda Hengst, Executive Director
Tel: (614) 466-3831
Fax:(614) 728-6974
ohioana@ohioana.org
www.ohioana.org
  Est. 1943. Award to native Ohioan for
  outstanding professional
  accomplishments in arts and
  humanities. Submission Materials: See
  website. Deadline(s): 12/31/2011

**Ohioana Citations**
274 E. 1st Ave., #300, Columbus, OH
  43201
Linda Hengst, Executive Director
Tel: (614) 466-3831
Fax:(614) 728-6974
ohioana@ohioana.org
www.ohioana.org

Est. 1945. Award for outstanding
contributions and accomplishments in
specific area of arts and humanities.
Must be native or at least five year
resident of OH. Submission Materials:
See website. Deadline(s): 12/31/2011

**Ohioana Pegasus Award**
274 E. 1st Ave., #300, Columbus, OH
  43201
Linda Hengst, Executive Director
Tel: (614) 466-3831
Fax:(614) 728-6974
ohioana@ohioana.org
www.ohioana.org
  Est. 1964. Award for unique or
  outstanding contributions or
  achievements in arts and humanities,
  given at discretion of trustees. Must be
  OH native or at least five year resident.
  Submission Materials: See website.
  Deadline(s): 12/31/2011

**One-Act Playwriting Competition**
900 N. Benton Ave., Springfield, MO
  65802
Dr. Mick Sokol, Asst Professor, Theatre
Tel: (417) 873-6821
Fax:(417) 873-7572
msokol@drury.edu
www.drury.edu
  Est. 1984. Preferred Genre(s): Plays.
  Preferred Length: One-Act. Submission
  Materials: Complete script & SASE.
  Deadline(s): 12/1/2011

**PEN/Laura Pels Foundation Awards
for Drama**
588 Broadway, #303, New York, NY
  10012
Nick Burd, Coordinator
Tel: (212) 334-1660
Fax:(212) 334-2181
awards@pen.org
www.pen.org
  Est. 1998. Award to US playwright in
  mid-career writing in English. See
  website for details. Submission
  Materials: See website. Deadline(s):
  1/16/2011

**Playwrights First Award**
15 Gramercy Park S., New York, NY
10003
Emily Andrew
Tel: (212) 744-1312
   (212) 677-1966
emilyandren@earthlink.net
   Est. 1993. Annual. Response Time: by
   5/01/12. Award: $1,000 and
   professional reading. Preferred
   Genre(s): All genres. Preferred Length:
   Full-length. Submission Materials:
   Query, full script, resume. Deadline(s):
   9/15/2011

**Richard Rodgers Awards for Musical Theater**
633 W. 155th St., New York, NY 10032
Jane E. Bolster, Richard Rodgers Awards
   Coord.
Tel: (212) 368-5900
Fax:(212) 491-4615
academy@artsandletters.org
www.artsandletters.org
   Est. 1978. Awards for musicals by
   writers and composers not already
   established in field. Preferred Genre(s):
   Musical theatre. Submission Materials:
   Application, synopsis, full script, audio,
   SASE. Deadline(s): 11/2/2011

**Robert Chesley Award**
828 N. Laurel Ave., Los Angeles, CA
90046
Victor Bumbalo, President
Tel: (323) 658-5981
VictorTom@aol.com
   Est. 1991. In honor of Robert Chesley
   (1943-90) to recognize gay and lesbian
   themed work. Nominations open in
   early fall. Preferred Genre(s): Plays.
   Special Interest: LGBT. Preferred
   Length: Full-length. Submission
   Materials: Complete script & SASE.
   Deadline(s): Early fall

**Robert J. Pickering Award for Playwriting Excellence**
89 Division St., Coldwater, MI 49036
J. Richard Colbeck, Award Chair
Tel: (517) 279-7963
Fax:(517) 279-8095

Est. 1984. Award for unproduced plays
and musicals. Preferred Genre(s): Plays
or Musicals. Preferred Length:
Full-length. Submission Materials:
Complete script & SASE. Deadline(s):
12/31/2011

**Ruby Lloyd Apsey Award**
Alabama Univ., Birmingham, ASC 255,
   1530 3rd Ave. S., Birmingham, AL
   35294
Lee Shackleford, Resident Playwright
Tel: (205) 975-8755
Fax:(205) 934-8076
leeshack@uab.edu
theatre.hum.uab.edu
   Biennially (even years) UAB seeks
   new/full-length work on racial or
   ethnic issues, w/ ethnically diverse
   casting. Prefer recyclable hard copy
   sent by US mail. Preferred Genre(s):
   Plays. Preferred Length: Full-length.
   Submission Materials: Complete script.
   Deadline(s): 12/1/2012

**Santa Cruz Actors' Theatre Play Contests**
1001 Center St., #12, Santa Cruz, CA
95060
Gary Gerringer, Office Manager
Tel: (831) 425-1003
Fax:(831) 425-7560
admin@santacruzactorstheatre.org
www.santacruzactorstheatre.org
   Est. 1985. Contests for full and ten
   minute long plays as well as for young
   playwrights. Preferred Genre(s): Plays.
   Preferred Length: Any length.
   Submission Materials: See website.
   Deadline(s): See website

**Scholastic Art & Writing Awards**
557 Broadway, New York, NY 10012
Alex Tapino, Sr Mgr, National Programs
Tel: (212) 343-7729
Fax:(212) 389-3939
info@artandwriting.org
www.artandwriting.org
   Est. 1923. National awards in 2
   categories (grades 7-8; grades 9-12),
   selected from regional contests.
   Regional deadlines vary. Regional Gold
   Key works are considered for national

awards. Preferred Genre(s): Plays.
Preferred Length: 10 min and one-acts.
Submission Materials: Application, full
script. Deadline(s): See website

**STAGE International Script
Competition**
Professional Artists Lab, CNSI-MC 6105,
 3241 Elings Hall Building 266, Santa
 Barbara, CA 93106-6105
Tel: (805) 893-7244
kawalek@filmandmedia.ucsb.edu
stage@cnsi.ucsb.edu
www.stage.cnis.ucsb.edu Preferred
 Length: Full-length. Submission
 Materials: See website.

**Summerfield G. Roberts Award**
1717 8th St., Bay City, TX 77414
Janet Hickl, Administrative Assistant
Tel: (979) 245-6644
Fax:(979) 244-3819
srttexas@srttexas.org
www.srttexas.org/sumfield.html
 Award for creative writing about the
 Republic of Texas, to encourage
 literature & research about the events
 and personalities of 1836-46.
 Submission Materials: Complete script,
 SASE. Deadline(s): 1/15/2011

**Susan Smith Blackburn Prize**
3239 Avalon Pl., Houston, TX 77019
Emilie Kilgore, Founder/President
Tel: (713) 308-2842
Fax:(713) 654-8184
www.blackburnprize.org
 Est. 1978. Plays accepted only from
 specified source theaters in US, UK
 and Ireland. Writers should bring their
 work to the attention of the theatre
 companies listed on website. Preferred
 Genre(s): Comedy. Preferred Length:
 Any length. Submission Materials:
 Complete script, SASE. Deadline(s):
 9/15/2011

**TeCo Theatrical Productions New Play
Competition**
215 South Tyler Street, Dallas, TX 75208
Teresa Coleman Walsh, Executive Artistic
 Director
Tel: (214) 948-0716
Fax:(214) 948-3706
teresa@tecotheater.org
www.tecotheater.org
 Est. 1993. Author must be resident of
 Dallas. Submit: unoptioned/
 unpublished/unproduced by US mail.
 Production: cast limit 4, minimal set
 and costume changes. Response: 2
 mos. Preferred Genre(s): Plays.
 Preferred Length: One-Act. Submission
 Materials: Complete script.
 Deadline(s): 12/6/2011

**The Ten Minute Musicals Project**
Box 461194, West Hollywood, CA 90046
Michael Koppy, Producer
info@TenMinuteMusicals.org
www.TenMinuteMusicals.org
 Est. 1989. Production: cast limit 10.
 Preferred Genre(s): Musical theatre.
 Preferred Length: 10 min and one-acts.
 Submission Materials: full
 script,audio,lead sheets/score,SASE.
 Deadline(s): 8/31/2011

**University of Wyoming Amy & Eric
Burger Essays on Theatre Contest**
Univ. of Wyoming c/o Dr. Jim Volz,
 Theatre & Dance, PO Box 6850,
 Fullerton, CA 92834
Jim Volz, President, Consultant for the
 Arts
jvolz@fullerton.edu
 Seek unpublished essays (bet. 1800 &
 7500 words) on Theatre/Drama for
 award. Email Dr. Volz
 (jvolz@fullerton.edu) for submission
 requirements. Winner notified by June
 2011. Preferred Genre(s): All genres.
 Submission Materials: 2 copies of
 essay. Deadline(s): 3/11/2011

**Valencia Character Company**
Box 3028, Orlando, FL 32802
Julia Gagne, Artistic Director
Tel: (407) 582-2296
Fax:(407) 249-3943
jgagne@valenciacc.edu
valenciacharacterco.com
    Est. 1991. Winning script receives
    development and full production.
    Author must be FL resident.
    Production: some college age.
    Response: 2 mos. Preferred Genre(s):
    Plays. Preferred Length: Full-length.
    Submission Materials: Complete script.
    Deadline(s): 6/1/2011 , 10/15/2011

**Vermont Playwrights Award**
Valley Players, P.O. Box 441, Waitsfield,
    VT 05673
Sharon Kellermann, Coordinator
Tel: (802) 583-6767
valleyplayers@madriver.com
www.valleyplayers.com
    Est. 1982. Must be resident of ME,
    NH, VT. Work must be unoptioned,
    unpublished, unproduced. Preferred
    Genre(s): Plays. Preferred Length:
    Full-length. Submission Materials:
    Application, full script, SASE.
    Deadline(s): 2/1/2011

**WordBRIDGE Playwrights Laboratory**
221 Brooks Center, Dept. of Performing
    Arts, Clemson, SC 29634
Mark Charney David White
Tel: (864) 656-5415
Fax:(864) 656-1013
cmark@clemson.edu
dave@wordbridge.org
www.wordbridge.org
    Email submissions by student/grad
    student or pre-professional starting in
    late fall only, deadline January 1st; see
    website for full details. Preferred
    Genre(s): Plays. Special Interest:
    Theatre for Young Audiences. Preferred
    Length: One-act or Full-length.
    Submission Materials: Application, full
    script. Deadline(s): 1/1/2011

**Write a Play! NYC Contest**
Young Playwrights Inc, Post Office Box
    5134, New York, NY 10185
Amanda Junco, Artistic Director
Tel: (212) 594-5440
Fax:(212) 684-4902
admin@youngplaywrights.org
www.youngplaywrights.org
    Contest open to all NYC students in 3
    categories: elementary, middle and high
    school. All receive certificate of merit,
    written evaluation, and invitation to
    awards ceremony. Preferred Genre(s):
    Plays. Special Interest: Theatre for
    Young Audiences. Preferred Length:
    Full-length. Submission Materials:
    Complete script. Deadline(s): 3/1/2011

**Young Connecticut Playwrights Festival**
Box 131, Newton, CT 06480
Bruce Post, Executive Director
Tel: (203) 270-2951
Fax:(203) 270-2951
brucepost@yahoo.com
    Est. 1996. 4 plays in professional
    staged readings at Waterbury Arts
    Magnet School. Author must be 12 -
    18 and resident of CT. Response: 1
    mo. Preferred Genre(s): Plays or
    Musicals. Preferred Length: One-Act.
    Submission Materials: Complete script
    & SASE. Deadline(s): 4/7/2011

**Young Playwrights Inc. National Playwriting Competition**
Young Playwrights, Inc., Post Office Box
    5134, New York, NY 10185
Amanda Junco, Exec Associate
Tel: (212) 594-5440
Fax:(212) 684-4892
admin@youngplaywrights.org
www.youngplaywrights.org
    Est. 1981. Young Playwrights Inc.
    identifies and develops young (18 and
    younger) US playwrights by involving
    them as active participants in the
    highest quality professional productions
    of their plays. Preferred Genre(s): No
    musicals or Adaptations. Preferred
    Length: Any length. Submission
    Materials: Complete script & SASE.
    Deadline(s): 1/3/2011

## Contests (Fee Charged)

**Arlene R. & William P. Lewis**
**Playwriting Contest for Women**
Theater & Media Arts Dept., Box 264,
  Provo, UT 84602
Elizabeth Funk, Administrative Assistant
Tel: (801) 422-7768
Fax:(801) 422-0564
tma_department@byu.edu
  Author must be female and submit 2
  copies of script. Preferred Genre(s): All
  genres. Preferred Length: Full-length.
  Submission Materials: Complete script
  & SASE.

**Aurora Theatre Company: Global Age**
**Project**
2081 Addison St., Berkeley, CA 94704
Matthew Graham Smith, GAP Producer
Tel: (510) 843-4042
Fax:(510) 843-4826
literary@auroratheatre.org
www.auroratheatre.org
  Celebrating fresh forward-looking
  visions of global significance.
  Response time: 5 months. Preferred
  Genre(s): Plays or Musicals. Preferred
  Length: One-act or Full-length.
  Submission Materials: Complete script.
  Deadline(s): 8/1/2011

**Charles M. Getchell Award, SETC**
P.O.Box 9868, Greensboro, NC 27429
Chris Hardin
Tel: (864) 656-5415
Fax:(864) 656-1013
hardin@apsu.edu
www.setc.org
  Submit full script via online application
  only. See website for eligibility
  guidelines. Preferred Genre(s): All
  genres. Preferred Length: Any length.
  Submission Materials: Application, full
  script. Deadline(s): 6/1/2011

**Community Theatre Association of**
**Michigan**
4026 Lester, Oscoda, MI 48750
Vincent Weiler, Playwriting Contest Chair
vweiler@ioscoresa.net
www.communitytheatre.org

Author must be a resident of Michigan.
Submit script by US Mail only.
Preferred Genre(s): Plays. Preferred
Length: One-act or Full-length.
Submission Materials: Complete script
& SASE. Deadline(s): 5/15/2011

**David Mark Cohen Playwriting Award**
Kennedy Center, Education Div.,
  Washington, DC 20566
Susan Shaffer, Co-Manager for Admin.
Tel: (202) 416-8857
Fax:(202) 416-8802
skshaffer@kennedy-center.org
www.kennedy-center.org/educatioctf
  Plays accepted only from college/univ.
  participating in KC/ACTF program.
  Preferred Genre(s): Plays. Preferred
  Length: Full-length, 10 min.
  Submission Materials: Application,
  synopsis, full script. Deadline(s):
  12/1/2011

**Dubuque Fine Arts Players One Act**
**Play Contest**
1686 Lawndale St., Dubuque, IA 52001
Gary Arms, Contest Coordinator
Tel: (583) 582-5502
gary.arms@clarke.edu
www.dbqoneacts.org
  Est. 1977. Unproduced/unpublished
  material must be sent via US Mail.
  Production: cast of 2-5, unit set.
  Response: 6 mos. Preferred Genre(s):
  Plays. Preferred Length: One-Act.
  Submission Materials: Application, full
  script (2 copies), SASE. Deadline(s):
  1/31/2011

**FirstStage One-Act Play Contest**
Box 38280, Los Angeles, CA 90038
Dennis Safren, Literary Manager
Tel: (323) 350-6271
firststagela@aol.com
www.firststagela.org
  Est. 1983. Staged readings of
  new/unproduced work. Submissions not
  returned. Response : 3 wks. Preferred
  Genre(s): Plays. Preferred Length:

One-Act. Submission Materials:
Complete script. Deadline(s):
11/25/2011

**FUSION Theatre Co.**
700 1st Street NW, Albuquerque, NM
  87102
Dennis Gromelski
Tel: (505) 766-9412
info@fusionabc.org
www.fusionabq.org
  Annual short works fest entitled "The
  Seven". Works must be
  unproduced/unpublished. Winner flown
  to NM for production. See website for
  details. Preferred Genre(s): Plays or
  Musicals. Preferred Length:
  10-min./10pgs.. Submission Materials:
  See website. Deadline(s): 4/15/2011

**Georgia College and State University**
Porter Hall CBX 066, Milledgeville, GA
  31061
Karen Berman, Pillars Playwriting Prize
Tel: (478) 445-1980
Fax:(478) 445-1633
kbermanth@aol.com
www.gcsu.edu/theatre
  Work must be unoptioned, unproduced,
  unpublished and author must be
  avail.for a short residency. Preferred
  Genre(s): Plays. Preferred Length:
  Full-length. Submission Materials: See
  website. Deadline(s): 12/1/2011

**Grawemeyer Award for Music
Composition**
Univ. of Louisville School of Music,
  Louisville, KY 40292
Marc Satterwhite, Director
Tel: (502) 852-1787
Fax:(502) 852-0520
GrawemeyerMusic@louisville.edu
www.grawemeyer.org
  Est. 1984. Preferred Length: Any
  length. Submission Materials: See
  website.

**Jackie White Memorial National
Children's Play Writing Contest**
309 Parkade Blvd., Columbia, MO 65202
Betsy Phillips, Director
Tel: (573) 874-5628
bybetsy@yahoo.com
www.cectheatre.org

Est. 1988. In memory of Jackie Pettit
White (1947-91). All scripts read and
recieve evaluation. Production: at least
7 speaking roles, sets appropriate for
community theaters. Preferred
Genre(s): Plays or Musicals. Preferred
Length: Full-length. Submission
Materials: Application, full script,
SASE. Deadline(s): 6/1/2011

**Jean Kennedy Smith Playwriting
Award**
Kennedy Center, Education Div.,
  Washington, DC 20566
Susan Shaffer, Co-Manager for
  Administration
Tel: (202) 416-8857
Fax:(202) 416-8802
skshaffer@kennedy-center.org
www.kennedy-center.org/educatioctf
  Award for a student-written play on
  disability. Plays accepted only from
  college/univ. participating in KC/ACTF
  program. Preferred Genre(s): Plays.
  Preferred Length: Full-length, 10 min.
  Submission Materials: See website.
  Deadline(s): 12/1/2011

**John Cauble Short Play Awards
Program**
Kennedy Center, Education Div.,
  Washington, DC 20566
Susan Shaffer, Co-Manager for Admin.
Tel: (202) 416-8857
Fax:(202) 416-8802
skshaffer@kennedy-center.org
www.kennedy-center.org/educatioctf
  Plays accepted only from college/univ.
  participating in KC/ACTF program.
  Preferred Genre(s): Plays. Preferred
  Length: One-Act. Submission
  Materials: Application, synopsis, full
  script. Deadline(s): 12/1/2011

**John Gassner Memorial Playwriting
Award**
NETC, 215 Knob Hill Dr., Hamden, CT
  06518
Joseph Juliano, Manager, Operations
Tel: (617) 851-8535
Fax:(203) 288-5938
mail@NETConline.org
www.NETConline.org

Est. 1967. Honors theater historian John Gassner for his lifetime dedication to all aspects of professional and academic theater. Seeking unproduced/unpublished plays. Response by 11/11. Preferred Genre(s): Plays. Preferred Length: Full-length. Submission Materials: Application, full script. Deadline(s): 4/15/2011

**Latino Playwriting Award**
Kennedy Center, Education Div.,
    Washington, DC 20566
Susan Shaffer, Co-Manager for Admin.
Tel: (202) 416-8857
Fax:(202) 416-8802
skshaffer@kennedy-center.org
www.kcactf.org
    The award will be presented to the author of the best student-written play by a Latino student playwright attending a college/university participating in KCACTF. Preferred Genre(s): Plays. Special Interest: Latino. Preferred Length: Full-length. Submission Materials: Application. Deadline(s): 10/1/2011

**Lionheart Theatre's Make the House Roar Prize**
Daphne Mintz, Prize Coordinator,
    Lionheart Theatre's Make the House Roar Prize, PO Box 1224, Norcross, GA 30091
Daphne Mintz, Prize Coordinator
Tel: (404) 514-6339
www.afterdinnertheatre.org
    Material must be unproduced. Preferred Genre(s): Comedy. Preferred Length: Full-length. Submission Materials: Complete script, Synopsis, character breakdowns. Deadline(s): 1/31/2011

**Lorraine Hansberry Playwriting Award**
Kennedy Center, Education Div.,
    Washington, DC 20566
Susan Shaffer, Co-Manager. for Admin.
Tel: (202) 416-8857
Fax:(202) 416-8802
skshaffer@kennedy-center.org
www.kennedy-center.org/educatioctf
    Award for a student-written play on the African-American experience. Plays accepted only from college/univ. participating in KC/ACTF program. Preferred Genre(s): Plays. Special Interest: African-American. Submission Materials: See website. Deadline(s): 10/1/2010

**Mark Twain Playwriting Award**
American Coll. Theater Festival,
    Education Ofc., Kennedy Center,
    Arlington, VA 22210
Susan Shaffer, Program Manager
Tel: (202) 416-8857
Fax:(202) 416-8802
skshaffer@kennedy-center.org
www.kennedy-center.org/educatioctf
    Plays accepted only from college/univ. participating in KC/ACTF program. Preferred Genre(s): Comedy. Preferred Length: Full-length. Submission Materials: Application.

**McLaren Memorial Comedy Playwriting Competition**
Midland MCT, 2000 W. Wadley Ave.,
    Midland, TX 79705
Andy Salcedo, McLaren Chair
Tel: (432) 682-2544
Fax:(432) 682-6136
tracy@mctmidland.org
mclaren1@mctmidland.org
www.mctmidland.org
    Est. 1989. Work must be unoptioned/unpublished/unproduced. Preferred Genre(s): Comedy. Preferred Length: One-act or Full-length. Submission Materials: Complete script & SASE. Deadline(s): End of February

**Musical Theater Award**
Kennedy Center, Education Div.,
    Washington, DC 20566
Susan Shaffer, Co-Manager for Admin.
Tel: (202) 416-8857
Fax:(202) 416-8802
skshaffer@kennedy-center.org
www.kennedy-center.org/educatioctf
    Plays accepted only from college/univ. participating in KC/ACTF program. Preferred Genre(s): Musical theatre. Preferred Length: Full-length, 10 min. Submission Materials: Application. Deadline(s): 10/1/2010

**National New Play Network**
c/o Woolly Mammoth Theatre Company,
  641 D Street NW, Washington, DC
  20004
Jason Loewith, Executive Director
Tel: (202) 312-5270
Fax:(202) 289-2446
jason@nnpn.org
www.nnpn.org
  Seeking political material unproduced
  in NYC. See website for
  fees/deadlines. Preferred Genre(s):
  Political. Preferred Length: Full-length.
  Submission Materials: See website.
  Deadline(s): check website for 2011
  deadlines

**National Student Playwriting Award**
John F. Kennedy Center for the Perf.
  Arts, Washington, DC 20566
Susan Shaffer, Co-Manager for Admin.
Tel: (202) 416-8857
Fax:(202) 416-8802
skshaffer@kennedy-center.org
www.kennedy-center.org/educatioctf
  Plays accepted only from college/univ.
  participating in KC/ACTF program.
  Preferred Genre(s): Plays. Preferred
  Length: Any length. Submission
  Materials: Application. Deadline(s):
  10/1/2010

**Paula Vogel Award for Playwriting**
John F. Kennedy Center for the
  Performing Arts, Washington, DC
  20566
Susan Shaffer, Co-Manager for Admin.
Tel: (202) 416-8857
Fax:(202) 416-8802
skshaffer@kennedy-center.org
www.kennedy-center.org/educatioctf
  Est. 2003. Award for a student-written
  play that celebrates diversity and
  encourages tolerance. Plays accepted
  only from college/univ. participating in
  KC/ACTF program. Preferred
  Genre(s): All genres. Preferred Length:
  Any length. Submission Materials:
  Application. Deadline(s): 10/1/2010

**Reverie Productions**
c/o Brooklyn Creative League, 540
  President Street, 3rd Floor, Brooklyn,
  NY 11215
Kimberly Wadsworth, Artistic Director
Tel: (212) 244-7803
Fax:(212) 244-7813
kimberly@reverieproductions.org
www.reverieproductions.org
  Est. 2002. Response: April. Preferred
  Genre(s): Plays. Preferred Length:
  One-act or Full-length. Submission
  Materials: Application, full script,
  SASE. Deadline(s): 12/15/2011

**SETC High School New Play Award**
700 Cobb Pkwy. N., Marietta, GA 30062
Nancy Gall-Clayton, Chair, Playwriting
  Contest
nancygallclayton@earthlink.net
www.setc.org/scholarship
  Author must be a student & resident of
  AL, FL, GA, KY, MS, NC, SC, TN,
  VA or WV and work must be
  unpublished/unproduced. Preferred
  Genre(s): Plays. Preferred Length:
  One-Act. Submission Materials:
  Complete script & SASE. Deadline(s):
  12/1/2011

**Stanley Drama Award**
Wagner College, One Campus Road,
  Staten Island, NY 10301
Todd Alan Price, Administrator
Tel: (718) 420-4338
Fax:(718) 390-3323
todd.price@wagner.edu
wagner.edu/stanleydrama/
  Est. 1957. Work must be unoptioned,
  unproduced, unpublished. Response: 6
  mos. Preferred Genre(s): Plays.
  Preferred Length: Full-length.
  Submission Materials: Full Script,
  audio, SASE. Deadline(s): 10/1/2011

**Ten-Minute Play Festival**
John F. Kennedy Center for the
  Performing Arts, Washington, DC
  20566
Susan Shaffer, Co-Manager for Admin.
Tel: (202) 416-8857
Fax:(202) 416-8802
skshaffer@kennedy-center.org
www.kennedy-center.org/educatioctf

Plays accepted only from college/univ. participating in KC/ACTF program. Preferred Genre(s): Plays. Preferred Length: 10-min./10pgs.. Submission Materials: Application, synopsis, full script. Deadline(s): 12/1/2011

**Theater for Youth Playwriting Award**
John F. Kennedy Center for the Performing Arts, Washington, DC 20566
Susan Shaffer, Co-Manager for Admin.
Tel: (202) 416-8857
Fax:(202) 416-8802
skshaffer@kennedy-center.org
www.kennedy-center.org/educatioctf
Award for student-written play appealing to young people in grades K-12. Plays accepted only from college/univ. participating in KC/ACTF program. Preferred Genre(s): Plays. Special Interest: Theatre for Young Audiences. Preferred Length: Any length. Submission Materials: Application.

**Theatre in the Raw Play Writing Contest**
3521 Marshall St., Vancouver, BC V5N 4S2 Canada
Jay Hamburger, Artistic Director
Tel: (604) 708-5448
Fax:(604) 708-1454
theatreintheraw@telus.net
www.theatreintheraw.ca
Est. 1994. Send unoptioned/unpublished/unproduced scripts via ground mail. Production: cast limit 6, set limit 2 (scene limit 3). Preferred Genre(s): Plays or Musicals. Preferred Length: 10 min . Submission Materials: Complete script & SASE. Deadline(s): 12/31/2011

**Theatre Oxford 10-Minute Play Contest**
PO Box 1321, Oxford, MS 38655
Alice Walker, Contest Director
Tel: (662) 236-5052
Fax:(662) 234-9266
theatreoxford@yahoo.com
www.10minuteplays.com

Est. 1998. Production: casts 2-4, minimal set, props. Only winners & finalists will be contacted. Work must be unoptioned, unproduced, unpublished. Submissions not returned. Preferred Genre(s): Plays. Preferred Length: 10 min . Submission Materials: Complete script. Deadline(s): 2/15/2011

**University of Central Missouri Competition**
Theater Dept., Martin 113, Warrensburg, MO 64093
Richard Herman, Chair
Tel: (660) 543-4020
Fax:(660) 543-8006
wilson@ucmo.edu
www.ucmo.edu/theatre
Est. 2001. Has produced children's plays for over 25 years. Now focused on world-premiere originals, through national competition. Special Interest: Theatre for Young Audiences. Submission Materials: See website. Deadline(s): See website

**Urban Stages Emerging Playwright Award**
555 8th Ave., Suite #1800, New York, NY 10018
Frances Hill, Artistic Director
Tel: (212) 421-1380
Fax:(212) 421-1387
urbanstage@aol.com
www.urbanstages.org
Est. 1986. Material must be unoptioned/unproduced/unpublished. Production: cast limit 7. Response: 3 mos. Preferred Genre(s): Plays. Preferred Length: Full-length. Submission Materials: Complete script.

## Grants & Fellowships

**Alabama State Council on the Arts**
201 Monroe St., Montgomery, AL 36130
Randy Shoults, Community Arts, Lit &
  Design Mgr.
Tel: (334) 242-4076
Fax:(334) 240-3269
randy.shoults@arts.alabama.gov
www.arts.alabama.gov
  Artist Fellowships and Artist in
  Education Residency in performing
  artists, literature, and visual artists.
  Must be 2 year resident of AL.
  Deadline(s): 3/1/2011

**Alaska State Council on the Arts
(ASCA)**
411 W. 4th Ave., #1-E, Anchorage, AK
  99501
Tel: (888) 278-7424
Fax:(907) 269-6601
aksca_info@eed.state.ak.us
www.eed.state.ak.us/aksca
  Est. 1966. Opportunities incl. quarterly
  career opportunity grants and biennial
  Connie Boochever Artist Fellowships
  (Aug 31 deadline, odd yrs). Preferred
  Genre(s): All genres. Preferred Length:
  Full-length. Submission Materials: 10-
  pg sample, audio. Deadline(s): See
  website for various deadlines

**American-Scandinavian Foundation
(ASF)**
58 Park Ave., New York, NY 10016
Tel: (212) 879-9779
Fax:(212) 249-3444
grants@amscan.org
www.amscan.org
  Grants for short visits and fellowships
  for full year of study or research in
  Denmark, Finland, Iceland, Norway or
  Sweden by U.S. citizens/residents.
  Proficient in host language preferred.
  Submission Materials: See website.
  Fee: Yes. Deadline(s): 11/1/2011

**Artist Trust**
1835 12th Ave., Seattle, WA 98122
Miguel Guillien, Program Manager
Tel: (206) 467-8734
Fax:(206) 467-9633
info@artisttrust.org
www.artisttrust.org
  Grants for Artist Projects (GAP)
  program. Assistance: $1,500 stipend.
  Response time: 4 mos. Must be
  resident of WA. Preferred Genre(s): All
  genres. Submission Materials:
  Application, 12 page sample, audio.
  Deadline(s): 6/11/2010

**Aurand Harris Fellowship**
c/o 8950 Koch Field Road at Silver
  Saddle, Flagstaff, AZ 86004
Mina H. Casmir, CTFA VP - Grants
info@childrenstheatrefoundation.org
www.childrenstheatrefoundation.org
  Est. 1958. For individuals with specific
  projects or with specific plans for
  developing excellence in children's
  theater. Preferred Genre(s): All genres.
  Special Interest: Theatre for Young
  Audiences. Submission Materials: See
  website.

**Connecticut Commission on Culture &
Tourism (CCT)**
One Constitution Plaza, 2nd Fl., Hartford,
  CT 06103
Tamara Dimitri, Arts Division
Tel: (860) 256-2720
Fax:(860) 256-2811
tamara.dimitri@ct.gov
www.cultureandtourism.org
  Artistic fellowship for resident of CT.
  Preferred Genre(s): All genres.
  Preferred Length: Any length.
  Submission Materials: See website.
  Deadline(s): Winter 2011 , Fall 2011

**Delaware Division of the Arts**
820 N. French St., Wilmington, DE
    19801
Kristin Pleasanton, Art & Artist Services
    Coordinator
Tel: (302) 577-8278
Fax:(302) 577-6561
kristin.pleasanton@state.de.us
www.artsdel.org
    Individual artists fellowships. Must be
    18+ and resident of DE. Submission
    Materials: Application, sample, SASE.
    Deadline(s): 8/2/2011

**Don and Gee Nicholl Fellowships**
1313 Vine St., Hollywood, CA 90028
Joan Wai, Program Manager
Tel: (310) 247-3010
Fax:(310) 247-3794
nicholl@oscars.org
www.oscars.org/nicholl
    Est. 1986. Film competition for
    screenwriters who haven't earned more
    than $5K in film or TV. Up to five
    $30K fellowships each year. Preferred
    Genre(s): Screenplays. Preferred
    Length: Full-length. Submission
    Materials: Application, full script. Fee:
    Yes. Deadline(s): 5/1/2011

**Electronic Arts Grant Program**
109 Lower Fairfield Rd., Newark Valley,
    NY 13811
Sherry Miller Hocking, Program Director
Tel: (607) 687-4341
Fax:(607) 687-4341
etc@experimentaltvcenter.org
www.experimentaltvcenter.org
    Specializing in moving image media,
    video, film and new media. Must be a
    New York state resident to be
    considered. Preferred Genre(s):
    Experimental. Preferred Length: Any
    length. Submission Materials: See
    website. Deadline(s): 3/15/2011

**Fulbright Program for US Scholars**
3007 Tilden St. NW, #5-L, Washington,
    DC 20008
Anne Clift Boris, Sr Program Officer,
    Recruitment
Tel: (202) 686-7859
Fax:(202) 362-3442
info@cies.iie.org
www.cies.org
    Est. 1947. Grants for US faculty or
    professionals to research or lecture
    abroad for 2-12 mos. in 140 countries.
    Submission Materials: See website.
    Deadline(s): August 2011

**Hodder Fellowship**
Lewis Center for the Arts, Princeton
    University. 6 New South, Princeton, NJ
    08542
Janine Braude, Council of the Humanities
Tel: (609) 258-4096
Fax:(609) 258-1178
jbraude@princeton.edu
www.princeton.edu/arts/lewis_center/
    society_of_fellows/
    1-yr fellowship for Academic Year
    2012-13 for individuals outside
    academia who have published one
    highly acclaimed book and are
    undertaking significant new work.
    Submission Materials: Project proposal,
    10 pg sample, resume. Deadline(s):
    11/1/2011

**Iowa Arts Council**
600 E. Locust, Des Moines, IA 50319
Linda Lee, Grants Manager
Tel: (515) 242-6194
Fax:(515) 242-6498
Linda.lee@iowa.gov
www.iowaartscouncil.org
    Deadlines: 2012 Major Grants - April
    1st, 2011; Mini Grants - 1st bus. day
    of each month. Application must be
    downloaded from website and sent.
    Applicant must be a resident of IA.
    Response: Appx. 4-6 wks. Deadline(s):
    4/1/2011 , Ongoing

**Jerome Playwright-in-Residence Fellowships**
Playwrights' Center (MN), 2301 Franklin Ave. E., Minneapolis, MN 55406
Kevin McLaughlin
Tel: (612) 332-7481
Fax:(612) 332-6037
info@pwcenter.org
www.pwcenter.org
    Fellowships to emerging playwrights for 1-yr residency (Jul-Jun) in MN using Center services. Apply online. Submission Materials: Application. Deadline(s): Refer to website

**John Simon Guggenheim Memorial Foundation**
90 Park Ave., New York, NY 10016
Keith B. Lewis, Program Assoc
Tel: (212) 687-4470
Fax:(212) 697-3248
fellowships@gf.org
www.gf.org
    Est. 1925. Fellowship to scholars and artists for research or creation. Submission Materials: query, application, sample. Deadline(s): 9/15/2010

**Jonathan Larson Performing Arts Foundation**
Box 672, Prince St. Sta., New York, NY 10012
Nancy Diekmann, Executive Director
Tel: (212) 529-0814
Fax:(212) 253-7604
jlpaf@aol.com
www.jlpaf.org
    Est. 1996. Annual grants to theater composers, lyricists, book writers and to theaters developing new musicals by former Larson award recipients. Response: 4 mos. Preferred Genre(s): Musical theatre. Preferred Length: Full-length. Submission Materials: Application, SASE. Deadline(s): 9/14/2010

**Kleban Award**
424 W. 44th St., New York, NY 10036
Tel: (212) 757-6960
Fax:(212) 265-4738
newdramatists@newdramatists.org
www.newdramatists.org/kleban_award.htm

Award to lyricists and librettists working in the American musical theater. Preferred Genre(s): Musical theatre. Preferred Length: Full-length. Submission Materials: Application. Deadline(s): 9/15/2011

**Louisiana Division of the Arts**
Box 44247, Baton Rouge, LA 70804
Danny Belanger, Director of Comm. & External Relations
Tel: (225) 342-8180
Fax:(225) 342-8173
dbelanger@crt.state.la.us
www.crt.state.la.us/arts
    Preferred Genre(s): Plays or Musicals. Preferred Length: Any length. Submission Materials: See website. Deadline(s): First Monday in March

**Marin Arts Council Fund for Artists**
555 Northgate Dr., #270, San Rafael, CA 94903
Argo Thompson, Executive Director
Tel: (415) 499-8350
Fax:(415) 499-8537
marinarts@marinarts.org
www.marinarts.org
    Est. 1985. Career Development Grants to individual artists for professional development. Preferred Genre(s): All genres. Preferred Length: Any length. Submission Materials: Application. Deadline(s): See website

**Massachusetts Cultural Council (MCC)**
10 St. James Ave., Fl. 3, Boston, MA 02116
Dan Blask, Program Coordinator
Tel: (617) 727-3668
Fax:(617) 727-0044
dan.blask@art.state.ma.us
www.massculturalcouncil.org
    Grants alternating between dance, drawing, prose, painting, poetry, traditional arts (even years) and crafts, film/video, music, photography, playwriting, sculpture (odd years). Submission Materials: Application. Deadline(s): See website

**McKnight National Playwriting Residency and Commission**
2301 Franklin Ave. E., Minneapolis, MN 55406
Kevin McLaughlin
Tel: (612) 332-7481
Fax:(612) 332-6037
info@pwcenter.org
www.pwcenter.org
Commissioning and production of new works from nationally recognized playwrights. Recipient in residence at Center while play is in development. Submission Materials: Agent only submissions. Deadline(s): Refer to website

**McKnight Theater Artist Fellowship**
2301 Franklin Ave. E., Minneapolis, MN 55406
Steve Moulds, Membership/Lit Assoc.
Tel: (612) 332-7481
Fax:(612) 332-6037
info@pwcenter.org
www.pwcenter.org
Fellowships to theater artists other than writers whose work demonstrates exceptional artistic merit and potential. Submission Materials: Application. Deadline(s): See website

**Michener Center for Writers**
702 E. Dean Keeton St., Austin, TX 78705
Debbie Dewees, Graduate Coordinator
Tel: (512) 471-1601
Fax:(512) 471-9997
mcw@www.utexas.edu
www.utexas.edu/academic/mcw
Est. 1993. Financial assistance for full-time students in MFA program. Author must have BA. Playwrights submit 1 full length or 2 one act plays. Preferred Genre(s): All genres. Preferred Length: One-act or Full-length. Submission Materials: Application. Fee: Yes. Deadline(s): 12/15/2010

**Mid Atlantic Arts Foundation**
201 N. Charles St., #401, Baltimore, MD 21201
Krista Bradley, Program Officer, Performing Arts
Tel: (410) 539-6656
Fax:(410) 837-5517
krista@midatlanticarts.org
www.midatlanticarts.org
Est. 1999. Artists & Communities program offers matching support for partnerships between artists in NJ, NY, PA with nonprofit orgs in DC, DE, MD, NJ, NY, PA, VA, VI, WV. Submission Materials: See website.

**Missouri Arts Council**
815 Olive Street, Suite 16, St. Louis, MO 63101
Beverly Strohmeyer, Executive Director
Tel: (314) 340-6845
Fax:(314) 340-7215
moarts@ded.mo.gov
www.missouriartscouncil.org
Submission Materials: Application. Deadline(s): Last Monday in February

**NEH Division for Research Prog./Collaborative Research**
1100 Pennsylvania Ave NW, Washington, DC 20506
NEH Admin
Tel: (202) 606-8461
Fax:(202) 606-8204
mhall@neh.gov
www.neh.gov/grants/guidelines/collaborative.html
Submission Materials: See website.

**New York Coalition of Professional Women in the Arts & Media**
Box 2537, Times Sq. Sta., New York, NY 10108
Deborah Savadge, Chair
Tel: (212) 592-4511
collaboration@nycwam.org
www.nycwam.org
Est. 1990. NYCWAM Collaboration Award is to encourage professional women in the arts and media to work collaboratively with other women on the creation of new works. Preferred Genre(s): Plays or Musicals. Preferred

Length: One-act or Full-length.
Submission Materials: 15 - 20 pg
writing sample. Deadline(s): See
website for biannual deadline

**New York State Council on the Arts
(NYSCA)**
175 Varick St., Fl. 3, New York, NY
10014
Heather Hitchens, Executive Director
Tel: (212) 627-4455
Fax:(212) 620-5911
www.nysca.org
Submission Materials: See website.

**New York Theatre Workshop (NYTW)
Playwriting Fellowship**
83 E. 4th St., New York, NY 10003
Geoffrey Scott, Literary Associate
Tel: (212) 780-9037
Fax:(212) 460-8996
www.nytw.org
Visit Website for list of Fellowships
and opportunities. Submission
Materials: See website.

**North Carolina Arts Council**
Department of Cultural Resources,
Raleigh, NC 27699
Mary B. Regan, Executive Director
Tel: (919) 807-6500
Fax:(919) 807-6532
ncarts@ncmail.net
www.ncarts.org
Submission Materials: See website.
Deadline(s): 3/1/2011 (orgs) ,
11/1/2011 (artists)

**North Dakota Council on the Arts**
1600 E. Century Ave., Suite 6, Bismarck,
ND 58503
Jan Webb, Executive Director
Tel: (701) 328-7590
Fax:(701) 328-7595
comserv@nd.gov
www.nd.gov/arts
Est. 1984. Fellowships for traditional
arts/dance/theatre (2011); visual/media
arts (2012); literary/musical artists

(2013). Response: 3 mos Submission
Materials: Application, SASE.
Deadline(s): 2/15/2011

**Page 73 Productions**
138 S. Oxford St. #5C, Brooklyn, NY
11217
Liz Jones, Producing Director
Tel: (718) 598-2099
Fax:(718) 398-2794
info@p73.org
www.p73.org
Est. 1997. Committed to developing
and producing the work of emerging
playwrights. See website for
requirements on what to submit and
who is eligible. Preferred Genre(s): All
genres. Preferred Length: Any length.
Submission Materials: See website.
Deadline(s): 5/1/2011

**Pew Fellowships in the Arts (PFA)**
Pew Center for Arts & Heritage, 1608
Walnut St., 18th Floor, Philadelphia,
PA 19103
Melissa Franklin, Director
Tel: (267) 350-4920
Fax:(267) 350-4997
pfa@pcah.us
www.pcah.us/fellowships
Est. 1991. As of 2010, a nomination
process determines who is invited to
apply. All disciplines are considered
each year. For more info, see website.
Submission Materials: Application.

**Pilgrim Project**
35 E. 21st. St. Floor 6, New York, NY
10010
Davida Goldman, Secretary
Tel: (212) 627-2288
Fax:(212) 627-2184
davida@firstthings.com
Est. 1987. Small grants for a reading,
workshop or full production of plays
that deal with questions of moral
significance. Grants are for production
of plays and not administrative costs.
Preferred Genre(s): Plays. Preferred
Length: Full-length. Submission
Materials: Complete script & SASE.

**Princess Grace Foundation USA
Playwriting Fellowship**
150 E. 58th St., Fl.25, New York, NY
    10155
Jelena Tadic, Program Associate
Tel: (212) 317-1470
Fax:(212) 317-1473
grants@pgfusa.org
www.pgfusa.org
    Est. 1982. 10-wk residency with New
    Dramatists; stipend; and
    publication/representation by Samuel
    French for 1 winning playwright.
    Preferred Genre(s): Comedy. Preferred
    Length: Full-length. Submission
    Materials: Application. Deadline(s):
    3/31/2011

**Radcliffe Institute Fellowships**
8 Garden Street, Cambridge, MA 02138
Radcliffe Application
Tel: (617) 496-1324
Fax:(617) 495-8136
fellowships@radcliffe.edu
www.radcliffe.edu/fellowships
    To support scholars, scientists, artists,
    and writers of exceptional promise and
    demonstrated accomplishments to
    pursue work in academic and
    professional fields and in the creative
    arts. Submission Materials: See
    website. Fee: Yes. Deadline(s):
    10/1/2011

**Rhode Island State Council on the Arts**
1 Capitol Hill, Fl. 3, Providence, RI 2908
Cristina DiChiera, Director, Individual
    Artists Program
Tel: (401) 222-3880
Fax:(401) 422-3018
cristina@arts.ri.gov
www.arts.ri.gov
    Annual fellowships in: film/video,
    play/screenwriting (April 1st);
    choreography and music composition
    (October 1st). Submission Materials:
    Application. Deadline(s): 4/1 and
    10/1/2011

**South Dakota Arts Council**
711 E. Wells Ave., Pierre, SD 57501
Michael Pangburn, Executive Director
Tel: (605) 773-3301
Fax:(605) 773-5657
sdac@state.sd.us
www.artscouncil.sd.gov
    Est. 1966. Must be a resident of SD.
    Submit application and sample online
    only. Response: 3 mos. Submission
    Materials: Application, sample .
    Deadline(s): 3/1/2011

**The Playwrights' Center Many Voices
Playwriting Residency**
The Playwrights' Center, 2301 Franklin
    Ave. E., Minneapolis, MN 55406
Kevin McLaughlin, Fellowships Manager
Tel: (612) 332-7481 Ext 15
Fax:(612) 332-6037
info@pwcenter.org
www.pwcenter.org
    Awards fellowship/grant for
    advancement of beginning/middle
    career writers living in MN. See
    website for details/award amounts and
    submissions guidelines. Preferred
    Genre(s): Plays or Musicals. Preferred
    Length: Full-length. Submission
    Materials: See website. Deadline(s):
    Refer to website

**The Playwrights' Center McKnight
Advancement Grants**
Playwrights' Center, 2301 Franklin Ave.
    E., Minneapolis, MN 55406
Kevin McLaughlin, Fellowships Manager
Tel: (612) 332-7481
Fax:(612) 332-6037
info@pwcenter.org
www.pwcenter.org
    Grants to advance a writer's art and
    career. Submission Materials:
    Application. Deadline(s): Refer to
    website

**The Public Theater/Emerging Writers
Group**
425 Lafayette Street, New York, NY
    10003
EWGquestions@publictheater.org
www.publictheater.org/ewg

Targets playwrights at the earliest stages in their careers. Preferred Genre(s): All genres. Preferred Length: Any length. Submission Materials: See website.

**U.S. Dept. of State Fulbright Program for US Students**
809 United Nations Plaza, New York, NY 10017
Walter Jackson
Tel: (212) 984-5330
us.fulbrightonline.org
Est. 1946. Funds for graduate study, research, or teaching. Students in US colleges must apply thru campus Fulbright Advisers. Those not enrolled in US may apply directly to IIE. Submission Materials: See website. Fee: Yes. Deadline(s): 3/1/2011

**Vermont Arts Council**
136 State St., Drawer 33, Montpelier, VT 05633
Sonia Rae, Artist & Community
  Programs Manager
Tel: (802) 828-3293
Fax:(802) 828-3363
srae@vermontartscouncil.org
www.vermontartscouncil.org

Est. 1994. Opportunity grants for programs (organizations) creation and for artist development. Submit via online only. Must be a VT resident. Response: 2 mos. Submission Materials: See website. Deadline(s): See website

**Wisconsin Arts Board**
101 E. Wilson St., Fl. 1, Madison, WI 53702
Mark Fraire, Grant Programs & Services
  Specialist
Tel: (608) 264-8191
Fax:(608) 267-9629
mark.fraire@wisconsin.gov
artsboard.wisconsin.gov
Artist Fellowship Awards of unrestricted funds to prof. WI artists. Rotating between Lit Arts, Music Comp, Choreog/Perf Art (even yrs), & Vis/Media Arts (odd yrs). Submission Materials: See website. Deadline(s): 9/17/2011

---

# Theaters

**16th St. Theater**
6420 16th. St., Berwyn, IL 60402
Ann Filmer, Artistic Director
Tel: (708) 795-6704
info@16thstreettheater.org
www.16thstreettheater.org
Preference for IL resident writers able to commit to being "playwright-in-residence". No musicals. Preferred Genre(s): Contemporary - comedy or drama. Preferred Length: Full-length. Submission Materials: Query and synopsis only.

**A Noise Within (ANW)**
234 S. Brand Blvd., Glendale, CA 91204
Geoff Elliot, Co-Artistic Dir.
Tel: (818) 265-7957
Fax:(818) 240-0826
boxoffice@anoisewithin.org
www.anoisewithin.org
Est. 1991. Response Time: 8 mos. Preferred Genre(s): Adapatation of Classics. Preferred Length: Full-length. Submission Materials: Complete script.

## A. D. Players

2710 W. Alabama St., Houston, TX
77098
Lee Walker, Literary Manager
Tel: (713) 526-2721
Fax:(713) 439-0905
lee@adplayers.org
www.adplayers.org
Est. 1967. Production cast limit 10
(mainstage)/8 (children's), piano only,
limited sets. Response Time: 3-6 mos.
Email professional recommendation.
Preferred Genre(s): All genres.
Preferred Length: One-act or Full-
length. Submission Materials: Query,
synopsis and 10-pg sample.

## Abingdon Theatre Company

312 W. 36th St., Fl. 6, New York, NY
10018
Kim T. Sharp, Literary Manager
Tel: (212) 868-2055
Fax:(212) 868-2056
ksharp@abingdontheatre.org
www.abingdontheatre.org
Est. 1993. Production: cast limit 8.
Response Time: 3 - 6 mos. Deadline is
ongoing. No musicals. Work must be
unproduced/unoptioned in NYC.
Preferred Genre(s): Comedy or Drama.
Preferred Length: Full-length.
Submission Materials: See website.

## About Face Theatre (AFT)

1222 W. Wilson Ave., Fl. 2, Chicago, IL
60640
Aurelia K. Fisher, Producing Director
Tel: (773) 784-8565
Fax:(773) 784-8557
aurelia@aboutfacetheatre.com
www.aboutfacetheatre.com
Est. 1995. New plays exploring gender
& sexuality. Production: no fly space.
Perf. art considered. Preferred
Genre(s): All genres. Special Interest:
LGBT. Preferred Length: One-act or
Full-length. Submission Materials: See
website.

## Absinthe-Minded Theatre Company

1484 Stadium Ave., Bronx, NY 10465
Ralph Scarpato, Producing Artistic Dir.
Tel: (212) 714-4696
rscarp@aol.com
myspace.com/absmind
Seeking edgy material. Preferred
Genre(s): All genres. Submission
Materials: See website.

## Act II Playhouse

56 E. Butler Pike, Ambler, PA 19002
Bud Martin, Producing Artistic Dir.
Tel: (215) 654-0200
Fax:(215) 654-5001
bud@act2.org
www.act2.org
Est. 1998. 130-seat SPT. Staff: Bud
Martin (Producing Artistic Director),
Harriet Power (Associate Artistic
Director) Preferred Genre(s): Comedy.

## ACT Theater (A Contemporary Theatre)

700 Union St., Seattle, WA 98101
Anita Montgomery, Literary Assoc.
Tel: (206) 292-7660
Fax:(206) 292-7670
www.acttheatre.org
Est. 1965. Authors from WA, OR, AK,
ID and MT only. Response Time: 6
mos. Preferred Genre(s): All genres.
Preferred Length: Full-length.
Submission Materials: Synopsis and
10-pg sample.

## Acting Company

Box 898, Times Square Station, New
York, NY 10108
Margot Harley, Producing Dir
Tel: (212) 258-3111
Fax:(212) 258-3299
mail@theactingcompany.org
www.theactingcompany.org
Est. 1972. Prefer solo one-acts on US
historical figures for HS tours and full-
length adaptations of classic novels.
Production: Cast limit 13. Preferred
Genre(s): Educational. Special Interest:
Theatre for Young Audiences. Preferred
Length: One-act or Full-length.
Submission Materials: Agent only
submissions.

**Actors Art Theatre (AAT)**
6128 Wilshire Blvd., #110, Los Angeles,
  CA 90048
Jolene Adams, Artistic Dir
Tel: (323) 969-4953
actorsart@actorsart.com
www.actorsart.com
   Est. 1994. 32-seat theater developing
   plays thru workshops and labs.
   Produces 1 original play each year,
   plus one-acts and solos under Equity
   99-seat. Production: no orchestra
   Response Time: 1 yr Preferred
   Genre(s): No musicals.

**Actors Collective**
447 W. 48th St., Ste. 1W, New York, NY
  10036
Catherine Russell, Managing Dir.
Tel: (212) 445-1016
Fax:(212) 445-1015
postarvis@aol.com
www.perfect-crime.com
   Est. 1981. Production: cast limit 8.
   Response time: 1 mo. Preferred
   Genre(s): All genres. Preferred Length:
   75 min. or longer. Submission
   Materials: Query letter, synopsis and
   S.A.S.E.. Deadline(s): September, 2012

**Actor's Express**
887 W. Marietta St. NW, #J-107, Atlanta,
  GA 30318
Freddie Ashley, Artistic Dir
Tel: (404) 875-1606
Fax:(404) 875-2791
freddie@actorsexpress.com
www.actors-express.com
   Est. 1988. Readings, workshops,
   production. Assistance:
   room/board,travel. Response Time: 6
   mos. Preferred Genre(s): Comedy,
   Drama or Musical. Preferred Length:
   Any length. Submission Materials:
   Complete script.

**Actors Theatre of Louisville [KY]**
316 W. Main St., Louisville, KY 40202
Amy Wegener, Literary Mgr.
Tel: (502) 584-1265
Fax:(502) 561-3300
awegener@actorstheatre.org
www.actorstheatre.org

Est. 1964. Best time to submit: April-
August. Response Time: 9 mos.
Preferred Length: Any length.
Submission Materials: Agent only
submissions.

**Actors Theatre of Phoenix**
P.O. Box 1924, Phoenix, AZ 85001
Matthew Wiener, Producing Artistic Dir.
Tel: (602) 253-6701
Fax:(602) 254-9577
info@actorstheatrePHX.org
www.actorstheatrePHX.org
   Est. 1985. Production: cast limit 8.
   Response Time: 10 mos. Preferred
   Genre(s): Political. Preferred Length:
   Full-length. Submission Materials:
   Professional referral only.

**Adventure Stage Chicago (ASC)**
1012 N. Noble St., Chicago, IL 60642
Tom Arvetis, Producing Artistic Dir
Tel: (773) 342-4141
Fax:(773) 278-2621
email@adventurestage.org
www.adventurestage.org
   Est. 1998. Production: ages 18 and
   older, cast limit 10. Response Time: 1
   mo. Preferred Genre(s): All genres.
   Special Interest: Theatre for Young
   Audiences. Preferred Length: One-act
   or Full-length. Submission Materials:
   Query, synopsis and character
   breakdowns.

**Allenberry Playhouse**
1559 Boiling Springs Road, Boiling
  Springs, PA 17007
Claude Giroux, Artistic Director
Tel: (717) 960-3211
Fax:(717) 960-5280
Aberry@allenberry.com
www.allenberry.com
   Production: age 20-60, cast of 6-10,
   orchestra limit 5. Preferred Genre(s):
   All genres. Preferred Length: One-act
   or Full-length. Submission Materials:
   Query and 20-pg sample.

**Alley Theatre**
615 Texas Ave. 18th Floor, Houston, TX
  77002
Mark Bly, Senior Dramaturg & Director
  of New Play Development
Tel: (713) 228-9341
Fax:(713) 222-6542
laurenh@alleytheatre.org
www.alleytheatre.org
  Est. 1947. Response Time: 3 months
  Preferred Genre(s): All genres.
  Preferred Length: Full-length.
  Submission Materials: Query letter
  only.

**Alliance Theatre**
1280 Peachtree St. NE, Atlanta, GA
  30309
Celise Kalke, Director of New Projects
Tel: (404) 733-4650
Fax:(404) 733-4625
allianceinfo@woodruffcenter.org
www.alliancetheatre.org
  Est. 1968. 11 shows in 2 spaces: 800-
  seat proscenium, 200-seat black box.
  Response Time: 1 yr. Agent submission
  only except from local writers w/10
  page sample. Preferred Genre(s): All
  genres. Special Interest: Theatre for
  Young Audiences. Preferred Length:
  Full-length. Submission Materials:
  Agent only submissions.

**American Folklore Theatre (AFT)**
Box 273, Fish Creek, WI 54212
Jeffrey Herbst, Artistic Director
Tel: (920) 854-6117
Fax:(920) 854-9106
dmaier@folkloretheatre.com
www.folkloretheatre.com
  Est. 1990. Original musical works for
  families. Production: cast of 3-10. Must
  have professional recommendation.
  Preferred Genre(s): Musical theatre.
  Preferred Length: One-Act. Submission
  Materials: Synopsis, character
  breakdowns, 10 pg sample, SASE.

**American Music Theater**
**Festival/Prince Music Theater**
100 S. Broad St., #650, Philadelphia, PA
  19110
Tel: (215) 972-1000
Fax:(215) 972-1020
www.princemusictheater.org
  Preferred Genre(s): Musical theatre.

**Amherst Players/Upstage NY**
56 Bright St., Lockport, NY 14094
Debra Cole, VP, Production
Tel: (716) 713-2649
Fax:(716) 833-1767
colebuffalo@aol.com
  Preferred Genre(s): All genres.
  Preferred Length: One-Act. Submission
  Materials: Query and full script.

**Animated Theaterworks Inc.**
240 Central Park S., #13-B, New York,
  NY 10019
Elysabeth Kleinhans, President
Tel: (212) 757-5085
Fax:(212) 247-3826
info@animatedtheaterworks.org
www.animatedtheaterworks.org
  Est. 1999. Readings and showcase
  productions of
  unpublished/unproduced, new and
  developing works. Production: cast
  limit 6, unit set. Response Time: 6
  mos. Preferred Genre(s): All genres.
  Preferred Length: One-act or Full-
  length. Submission Materials: Query,
  synopsis and 10-pg sample.

**Arden Theatre Company**
40 N. 2nd St., Philadelphia, PA 19106
Dennis Smeal, Literary Manager
Tel: (215) 992-8900
Fax:(215) 922-7011
dsmeal@ardentheatre.org
www.ardentheater.org
  Est. 1988. 7 shows/yr in 2 houses.
  Response Time: 10 wks. Preferred
  Genre(s): Adaptation. Preferred
  Length: Full-length. Submission
  Materials: Synopsis and 10-pg sample.

**Arena Players Repertory Theatre**
296 Rte. 109, East Farmingdale, NY
11735
Fred De Feis, Producer
Tel: (516) 293-0674
Fax:(516) 777-8688
arena109@aol.com
www.arenaplayers.org
    Est. 1950. Award. Production: cast of
    2-10. Response time: 6 mos.
    Unproduced/unpublished. Preferred
    Genre(s): Plays. Preferred Length:
    One-act or Full-length. Submission
    Materials: Query, synopsis, full script,
    SASE.

**Arena Stage**
1101 6th St. SW, Washington, DC 20024
Janine Sobeck, Senior Dramaturg
Tel: (202) 554-9066
Fax:(202) 488-4056
info@arenastage.org
www.arenastage.org
    Est. 1950. Response: 3 mos. Preferred
    Genre(s): All genres. Preferred Length:
    Full-length. Submission Materials:
    Agent only submissions.

**Arizona Theatre Company**
Box 1631, Tucson, AZ 85702
Jennifer Bazzell, Literary Manager
Tel: (520) 884-8210
Fax:(520) 628-9129
jbazzell@arizonatheatre.org
www.arizonatheatre.org
    Est. 1966. Response time: 6 mos. Non
    AZ residents must submit query before
    sending script. Preferred Genre(s):
    Plays or Musicals. Preferred Length:
    Full-length. Submission Materials:
    Query, synopsis, 10-pg sample &
    SASE.

**Arkansas Repertory Theatre**
Box 110, Little Rock, AR 72201
Robert Hupp, Literary Manager
Tel: (866) 6TH-EREP
Fax:(501) 378-0012
www.therep.org
    Production: small cast. Response Time:
    3 mos query, 6 mos script. Preferred
    Genre(s): All genres. Preferred Length:
    Full-length. Submission Materials:
    Query and synopsis only.

**Ars Nova**
511 W. 54th St., New York, NY 10019
Jason Eagan, Artistic Director
Tel: (212) 489-9800
Fax:(212) 489-1908
arsnovanyc.com
    Founded in memory of Gabe Weiner,
    Ars Nova develops/produces theatre,
    comedy, music melding disciplines and
    giving voice to new generation of
    artists. Preferred Genre(s): All genres.
    Preferred Length: Any length.
    Submission Materials: See website.

**ART Station**
Box 1998, Stone Mountain, GA 30086
Jon Goldstein, Literary Manager
Tel: (770) 469-1105
Fax:(770) 469-0355
jon@artstation.org
www.artstation.org
    Est. 1986. Work about Southern
    experience for Southern, suburban,
    senior audience. Production: cast limit
    6. Response time: 1 yr. Snail mail
    submission only. Preferred Genre(s):
    Comedy; Play or Musical. Preferred
    Length: Full-length. Submission
    Materials: Synopsis, 10-pg sample,
    SASE.

**Artists Repertory Theatre**
1515 SW Morrison Street, Portland, OR
97205
Stephanie Mulligan, Literary Manager
Tel: (503) 241-9807 Ext 110
Fax:(503) 241-8268
www.artistsrep.org
    Est. 1981. 7 shows per season on 2
    stages, plus staged readings. Response
    time: 2 mos query, 6 mos script
    Preferred Genre(s): Plays. Preferred
    Length: Full-length. Submission
    Materials: Query letter, synopsis and
    S.A.S.E..

**ArtsPower National Touring Theatre**
271 Grove Ave. Bldg. A, Velena, NJ
07044
Gary Blackman, Managing Director
Tel: (973) 239-0100
Fax:(973) 239-0165
gblackman@artspower.org
www.artspower.org

Tourable theater presenting unpublished one-act plays and musicals for young and family audiences. Production: cast limit 4. Preferred Genre(s): Plays or Musicals. Special Interest: Theatre for Young Audiences. Preferred Length: One-Act. Submission Materials: Synopsis, audio, SASE.

## Asolo Repertory Theatre
5555 N. Tamiami Tr., Sarasota, FL 34243
Sasso Lauryn, Assistant Managing Director
Tel: (941) 351-9010
Fax:(941) 351-5796
lit_intern@asolo.org
www.asolo.org
Est. 1960. Email preferred. Preferred Genre(s): All genres. Preferred Length: Any length. Submission Materials: Query letter only.

## Atlantic Theater Company
76 9th Ave., #537, New York, NY 10011
Abigail Katz, Literary Associate
Tel: (212) 691-5919
Fax:(212) 645-8755
literary@atlantictheater.org
www.atlantictheater.org
Est. 1985. 4-show mainstage season, 2-show second stage season. Response time: 6 mos. Submit through prof recommendation, agent or inquiry. Preferred Genre(s): Plays or Musicals. Preferred Length: Full-length. Submission Materials: query, synopsis, 20 pg sample, full script, audio, SASE.

## Axis Theatre Company
1 Sheridan Sq., New York, NY 10014
Brian Barnhart, Artistic Director
Tel: (212) 807-9300
Fax:(212) 807-9039
b@axiscompany.org
www.axiscompany.org
Est. 1997. Preferred Genre(s): Plays. Preferred Length: One-Act. Submission Materials: Query letter only.

## Bailiwick Repertory Theatre
3023 N. Clark #327, Chicago, IL 60657
Kevin Mays, Executive Director
Tel: (773) 883-1090
Fax:(773) 883-2017
Bailiwick@Bailiwick.org
www.bailiwick.org
Est. 1982. Mainstage Series; Deaf Bailiwick Artists; The Lesbian Initiative; College/University Playwriting Festival. Preferred Genre(s): Plays or Musicals. Special Interest: LGBT. Preferred Length: Full-length. Submission Materials: See website.

## Barksdale Theatre
114 W. Broad Street, Richmond, VA 23220
Janine Serresseque
Tel: (804) 783-1688
Fax:(804) 288-6470
TheatreIVandBarksdale@gmail.com
www.barksdalerichmond.org
Est. 1953. Production: small cast, no fly or wing space. Response time: 6 mos query, 1 yr script. Preferred Genre(s): Plays. Preferred Length: Full-length. Submission Materials: Query, synopsis, full script.

## Barrow Group
312 W. 36th St., #4-W, New York, NY 10018
Tel: (212) 760-2615
Fax:(212) 760-2962
lit@barrowgroup.org
www.barrowgroup.org
Est. 1986. Offers 1-2 mainstage shows/yr, plus readings and workshops. Response: 1 mo query, 4 mos script. Submission Materials: See website.

## Bay Street Theatre
Box 810, Sag Harbor, NY 11963
Murphy Davis
Tel: (631) 725-0818 Ext 108
Fax:(631) 725-0906
www.baystreet.org
Est. 1991. Mainstage season and play reading series. Production: cast limit 9, unit set, no fly/wing space. Response time: 6 mos. Preferred Genre(s): Plays.

Preferred Length: Full-length.
Submission Materials: Agent only
submissions.

## Berkeley Repertory Theatre
2025 Addison St., Berkeley, CA 94702
Madeleine Oldham, Dramaturg/Literary
  Manager
Tel: (510) 647-2900
Fax:(510) 647-2976
info@berkeleyrep.org
www.berkeleyrep.org
  Est. 1968. Response time: 8 mos.
  Preferred Genre(s): All genres.
  Preferred Length: Any length.
  Submission Materials: Complete script
  & SASE.

## Berkshire Public Theater
Box 860, 30 Union St., Pittsfield, MA
  01202
Frank Bessell, Artistic Director

## Berkshire Theatre Festival
P.O. Box 797, Stockbridge, MA 1262
Kate Maguire, Artistic Director
Tel: (413) 298-5536
Fax:(413) 298-3368
info@berkshiretheatre.org
www.berkshiretheatre.org
  Est. 1928. New works, small musicals.
  Production: cast of up to 8. Will
  respond only if interested. Submissions
  not returned. Preferred Genre(s): Plays
  or Musicals. Preferred Length: One-act
  or Full-length. Submission Materials:
  Agent only submissions.

## Black Dahlia Theatre Los Angeles
5453 W. Pico Blvd., Los Angeles, CA
  90019
Tel: (323) 525-0085
info@thedahlia.com
www.thedahlia.com
  Preferred Genre(s): All genres.
  Preferred Length: Any length.
  Submission Materials: See website.

## Black Rep
1717 Olive St., Fl. 4, St. Louis, MO
  63103
Ron Himes, Founder & Producing
  Director
Tel: (314) 534-3807
Fax:(314) 534-4035
www.theblackrep.org
  Est. 1976. Preferred Genre(s): Plays.
  Special Interest: African-American.
  Preferred Length: Full-length.
  Submission Materials: Query, synopsis,
  3-5 pages, resume.

## Black Spectrum Theatre
119-07 Merrick Boulevard, Jamaica, NY
  11434
Literary Manager
Tel: (718) 723-1800
Fax:(718) 723-1806
info@blackspectrum.com
www.blackspectrum.com
  Preferred Genre(s): All genres.
  Preferred Length: Full-length.
  Submission Materials: Complete script.

## Black Swan Theater
109 Roberts Street, Asheville, NC 28801
David B. Hopes, Artistic Director
Tel: (828) 254-6057
Fax:(828) 251-6603
swanthtre@aol.com
www.blackswan.org
  Est. 1988. Develops new scripts &
  revisits classics. Production: modest
  cast, simple set. Response time: 3 mos.
  Material must be unpublished.
  Preferred Genre(s): All genres.
  Preferred Length: Any length.
  Submission Materials: Complete script.

## Bond Street Theatre
2 Bond St., New York, NY 10012
Joanna Sherman, Artistic Director
Tel: (212) 254-4614
Fax:(212) 460-9378
info@bondst.org
www.bondst.org
  Response time: 1 mo. Specialize in
  non-verbal scripts (dance, masks,
  music, circus arts, gestural arts).
  Preferred Genre(s): Movement-based.
  Preferred Length: Any length.

Submission Materials: Query letter, synopsis and S.A.S.E..

**Boston Playwrights' Theatre**
949 Commonwealth Ave., Boston, MA 02215
Michael Duncan Smith, Program Coordinator
Tel: (617) 353-5443
Fax:(617) 353-6196
newplays@bu.edu
www.bu.edu/bpt
   Est. 1981. Production and workshop. Production: cast limit 8, black box set. Response time: 6 mos. Preferred Genre(s): All genres. Preferred Length: Any length. Submission Materials: Query letter and S.A.S.E..

**Brat Productions**
56 S. 2nd St., Philadelphia, PA 19106
Michael Altop, Producing Artistic Director
Tel: (215) 627-2577
Fax:(215) 627-4304
www.bratproductions.org
   Est. 1996. New work, experimental/immersive theatre ideas considered by query; invite to follow if interested. Production: cast limit 7, unit set. Response time: 1 mo query, 6 mos script. Preferred Genre(s): Plays or Musicals. Preferred Length: Full-length. Submission Materials: Query letter only.

**Break A Leg Productions**
Box 20503, Hammarskjold Ctr., New York, NY 10017
Elisa London, Literary Manager
Tel: (212) 330-0406
Fax:(212) 750-8341
breakalegproductionsnyc@yahoo.com
www.breakalegproductions.com
   Submission Materials: See website.

**Burning Coal Theatre Company**
Box 90904, Raleigh, NC 27675
Jerome Davis, Director, New Works
Tel: (919) 834-4001
Fax:(919) 834-4002
burning_coal@ipass.net
www.burningcoal.org

Est. 1995. 4 staged readings/yr, Response time: 6 mos. Author must be resident or connected to NC. Submit via mail only. Preferred Genre(s): Plays. Preferred Length: One-Act. Submission Materials: Complete script, SASE. Deadline(s): Dec. 16, 2011

**Caffeine Theatre**
PO Box 1904, Chicago, IL 60690
Jennifer Shook, Artistic Director
Tel: (312) 409-4778
info@caffeinetheatre.com
www.caffeinetheatre.com
   Not currently accepting unsolicited work. Preferred Genre(s): All genres.

**Caldwell Theatre Company**
7901 N. Federal Hwy., Boca Raton, FL 33487
Patricia Burdett
Tel: (561) 241-7432
Fax:(561) 997-6917
patricia@caldwelltheatre.com
www.caldwelltheatre.com
   Est. 1975. Playsearch series reads 4 plays annually. Production: cast up to 8. Response time varies. Preferred Genre(s): Plays or Musicals. Preferred Length: Full-length. Submission Materials: See website.

**Capital Repertory Theatre**
111 N. Pearl St., Albany, NY 12207
Maggie Mancinelli-Cahill
Tel: (518) 462-4531
Fax:(518) 465-0213
info@capitalrep.org
www.capitalrep.org
   Est. 1981. Submission Materials: See website.

**Celebration Theatre**
7985 Santa Monica Blvd., #109-1, Los Angeles, CA 90046
Jordana Oberman, Literary Manager
Tel: (323) 957-1884
Fax:(888) 898-9374
admin@celebrationtheatre.com
www.celebrationtheatre.com
   Est. 1982. Accepting unproduced scripts via mail for new works series. See website for guidelines. Production:

cast limit 12. Response if interested.
Preferred Genre(s): Plays or Musicals.
Special Interest: LGBT. Preferred
Length: One-act or Full-length.
Submission Materials: Synopsis,
complete script, bio. Deadline(s):
Rolling

**Center Stage [MD]**
700 N. Calvert St., Baltimore, MD 21202
Center Stage Literary Manager
Tel: (410) 986-4042
Fax:(410) 986-4046
dlichtenberg@centerstage.org
www.centerstage.org
  Est. 1963. Seeking unproduced scripts.
  Preferred Genre(s): Plays. Preferred
  Length: Full-length. Submission
  Materials: Query, synopsis, 10pg
  sample, audio, SASE.

**Center Stage Community Playhouse**
Box 138, Westchester Square Station,
  Bronx, NY 10461
Holland Renton
Tel: (212) 823-6434
info@centerstageplayhouse.org
www.centerstageplayhouse.org
  Est. 1969. Nonprofit community theater
  seeks unoptioned, unpublished,
  unproduced work. Response time: 2
  mos. Preferred Genre(s): Adaptation,
  Plays, Musicals. Preferred Length: Any
  length. Submission Materials: Query
  letter, SASE.

**Center Theatre Group (CTG)**
601 W. Temple St., Los Angeles, CA
  90012
Mike Sablone, Literary Manager/Resident
  Dramaturg
Tel: (213) 972-8033
Fax:(213) 972-0746
scriipts@ctgla.org
www.centertheatregroup.org
  Est. 1967. Incl. Ahmanson Theatre and
  Mark Taper Forum at Music Center in
  L.A. and Kirk Douglas Theatre in
  Culver City. Response time: 6 wks.
  Preferred Genre(s): All genres.
  Preferred Length: One-act or Full-
  length. Submission Materials: Query,
  synopsis, sample, SASE.

**Charleston Stage**
Box 356, Charleston, SC 29402
Julian Wiles, Producing Artistic Director
Tel: (843) 577-5967
Fax:(843) 577-5422
www.charlestonstage.com
  Est. 1977. In residence at the Historic
  Dock Street Theater. Not accepting
  new work at this time. Preferred
  Genre(s): All genres. Special Interest:
  Latino. Preferred Length: Full-length.
  Submission Materials: See website.
  Deadline(s): May 21. 2011, June 15,
  2011

**Charter Theatre**
Box 3505, Reston, VA 20195
Tel: (202) 333-7009
www.chartertheatre.org
  Submission Materials: See website.

**Cherry Lane Theatre**
38 Commerce St., New York, NY 10014
Dave Batan, Operations Manager
Tel: (212) 989-2020
Fax:(212) 989-2867
company@cherrylanetheatre.org
www.cherrylanetheatre.org
  Submission Materials: See website.

**Chicago Theater Company**
500 E. 67th St., Chicago, IL 60637
Tel: (773) 493-5360
Fax:(773) 493-0360
www.chicagotheatrecompany.com

**Children's Theatre Company (CTC)
[MN]**
2400 3rd Ave. S., Minneapolis, MN
  55404
Elissa Adams, Director New Play
  Development
Tel: (612) 874-0500 Ext 134
Fax:(612) 874-8119
eadams@childrenstheatre.org
www.childrenstheatre.org
  Est. 1965. Preferred Genre(s): Plays or
  Musicals. Special Interest: Theatre for
  Young Audiences. Preferred Length:
  Full-length. Submission Materials:
  Agent only submissions.

**Children's Theatre of Cincinnati [OH]**
2106 Florence Ave., Cincinnati, OH
45206
Jack Louiso, Artistic Director
Tel: (513) 569-8080
www.thechildrenstheatre.com
Submission Materials: See website.

**Childsplay**
900 S. Mitchell Dr., Tempe, AZ 85281
David Saar, Artistic Director
Tel: (480) 921-5700
Fax:(480) 921-5777
info@childsplayaz.org
www.childsplayaz.org
Est. 1977. 6 mainstage and 3 touring
productions/yr. Opportunities incl
Whiteman New Plays Program.
Production: cast of 2-12. Preferred
Genre(s): Plays or Musicals. Special
Interest: Theatre for Young Audiences.
Preferred Length: One-act or Full-
length. Submission Materials:
Synopsis, 10-pg sample, SASE.

**Cider Mill Playhouse**
2 S. Nanticoke Ave., Endicott, NY 13760
Tel: (607) 748-7363
www.cidermillplayhouse.com
Est. 1976. Production: small cast, unit
set, no fly space. Response time: 6
months. Preferred Genre(s):
Adaptation. Submission Materials:
Agent only submissions.

**Cincinnati Playhouse in the Park**
Box 6537, Cincinnati, OH 45206
Tel: (513) 345-2242
Fax:(513) 345-2254
Anita.Trotta@cincyplay.com
www.cincyplay.com
Est. 1960. Response: 8 mos. Include
audio tape or CD of selections from
score for musicals. Preferred Genre(s):
Plays or Musicals. Preferred Length:
Full-length. Submission Materials: See
website.

**Cincinnati Shakespeare Festival**
719 Race St., Cincinnati, OH 45202
Brian Isaac Phillips, Artistic Director
Tel: (513) 381-2289
Fax:(513) 381-2298
csfed@cincyshakes.com
www.cincyshakes.com

Est. 1993. Preferred Genre(s):
Adaptation. Preferred Length:
Full-length. Submission Materials:
Query, synopsis, 20pg sample.

**Cinnabar Theater**
3333 Petaluma Blvd. N., Petaluma, CA
94952
Elly Lichenstein, Exec/Artistic Director
Tel: (707) 763-8920
Fax:(707) 763-8929
elly@cinnabartheater.org
www.cinnabartheater.org
Est. 1970. Will consider operas.
Submission Materials: See website.

**Circle Theatre [TX]**
230 W. Fourth St., Ft. Worth, TX 76102
Dorothy Sanders
Tel: (817) 877-3040
Fax:(817) 877-3536
plays@circletheatre.com
www.circletheatre.com
Est. 1981. Professional contemporary
theater in an intimate setting. Please
note theme addressed in query letter.
Preferred Genre(s): Plays or Musicals.
Preferred Length: One-act or Full-
length. Submission Materials: Query,
synopsis, audio, SASE.

**Circle Theatre of Forest Park [IL]**
7300 W. Madison St., Forest Park, IL
60130
Circle Theatre Submissions
Tel: (708) 771-0700
Fax:(708) 771-1826
circletheatre@gmail.com
www.circle-theatre.org
Est. 1985. Opportunities incl new play
fest of shorts and full-lengths.
Preferred Genre(s): All genres.
Preferred Length: Any length.
Submission Materials: See website.

**Citizen Pell Theater Group**
30 The Hamlet, Pelham, NY 10803
Jeffrey Menaker, Artistic Director
Tel: (917) 428-1955
citizenpell@yahoo.com
www.citizenpell.com
Submission Materials: See website.

**City Garage**
Box 2016, Santa Monica, CA 90406
Paul Rubenstein, Literary Manager
Tel: (310) 396-5871
Fax:(310) 396-1040
citygarage@citygarage.net
www.citygarage.org
  Est. 1987. Material must be highly
  experimental, social and political work.
  Production: unit set. Response time: 2
  weeks letter, 6 weeks script. Preferred
  Genre(s): Experimental. Preferred
  Length: Full-length. Submission
  Materials: Query and synopsis only.

**City Theatre [FL]**
444 Brickell Ave., #229, Miami, FL
  33131
Stephanie Norman, Executive Director
Tel: (305) 755-9401
Fax:(305) 755-9404
www.citytheatre.com
  Est. 1996. Summer Shorts fest/guest
  artist residency , Short Cuts
  educational tours, Festival Reading
  Series and Kid Shorts Project.
  Submissions not returned. Preferred
  Genre(s): Plays. Preferred Length:
  One-Act. Submission Materials:
  Complete script.

**City Theatre Company [PA]**
1300 Bingham St., Pittsburgh, PA 15203
Carlyn Aquiline, Literary
  Manager/Dramaturg
Tel: (412) 431-4400
Fax:(412) 431-5535
caquiline@citytheatrecompany.org
www.citytheatrecompany.org
  Est. 1974. Produces new and
  contemporary full-length solo work,
  translations, adaptations with emphasis
  on under-represented voices.
  Production: cast limit 6, prefer 4 or
  fewer. See website for list of materials
  to submit. Preferred Genre(s): Plays or
  Musicals. Preferred Length:
  Full-length. Submission Materials:
  Query by mail.

**Cleveland Play House**
8500 Euclid Ave., Cleveland, OH 44106
Laura Kepley, Director New Play
  Development
Tel: (216) 795-7000
Fax:(216) 795-7005
www.clevelandplayhouse.com
  Est. 1916. Response time: 2 mos query,
  6 mos script. Preferred Genre(s): Plays.
  Preferred Length: Full-length.
  Submission Materials: Query, synopsis,
  10-pg sample, resume & SASE.

**Cleveland Public Theatre**
6415 Detroit Ave., Cleveland, OH 44102
Raymond Bobgan, Executive Artistic
  Director
Tel: (216) 631-2727
Fax:(216) 631-2575
rbobgan@cptonline.org
www.cptonline.org
  Est. 1983. Looking for experimental,
  poetic, political,
  intellectually/spiritually challenging
  work. Response time: 9-12 mos.
  Preferred Genre(s): Experimental.
  Preferred Length: Any length.
  Submission Materials: Query, synopsis,
  10-pg sample, SASE.

**Clubbed Thumb**
141 E. 3rd Street, #11H, New York, NY
  10009
Clubbed Thumb Info
Tel: (212) 802-8007
Fax:(212) 228-0153
info@clubbedthumb.org
www.clubbedthumb.org
  See website for details. Submission
  Materials: See website.

**Colony Theatre Company**
555 N. Third St., Burbank, CA 91502
Barbara Beckley, Artistic Director
Tel: (818) 558-7000
Fax:(818) 558-7110
barbarabeckley@colonytheatre.org
www.colonytheatre.org
  Est. 1975. Production: cast limit 4.
  Preferred Genre(s): Plays. Preferred
  Length: Full-length. Submission
  Materials: Agent only submissions.

**Congo Square Theatre Company**
2936 N. Southport #210, Chicago, IL 60657
Derrick Sanders, Artistic Director
Tel: (773) 296-0968
www.congosquaretheatre.org
Submission Materials: See website.

**Contemporary American Theatre Company (CATCO) - Phoenix, Inc**
55 East State Street, Columbus, OH 43215
Joe Bishara, Assistant Artistic Director
Tel: (614) 645-7558
jputnam@catco.org
www.catco.org
Est. 1984. 5-6 plays/season. Merged w/Phoenix Theatre for Children www.phoenix4kids.org. Production: cast limit 10, set limit 2. Response: 6 mos. Preferred Genre(s): Plays or Musicals. Special Interest: Theatre for Young Audiences. Preferred Length: Any length. Submission Materials: Synopsis and 10-pg sample. Deadline(s): Year round

**Cornerstone Theater Company**
708 Traction Ave., Los Angeles, CA 90013
Laurie Woolery
Tel: (213) 613-1700
Fax:(213) 613-1714
lwoolery@cornerstonetheater.org
www.cornerstonetheater.org
Est. 1986. Collaborating with playwrights to develop new work. Response : 6 mos. Preferred Length: Any length. Submission Materials: Query, 5 pages of script.

**Coterie Theatre**
2450 Grand Blvd., #144, Kansas City, MO 64108
Jeff Church, Artistic Director
Tel: (816) 474-6785 Ext 232
Fax:(816) 474-7112
jefchurch@aol.com
www.coterietheatre.org
Est. 1979. Production: cast limit 10, orchestra limit 3, no fly/wing space. Response : 1 mo query. Preferred Genre(s): Adaptation. Special Interest:

Theatre for Young Audiences. Preferred Length: One-Act. Submission Materials: See website.

**Crossroads Theatre Company [NJ]**
P.O. Box 238, 7 Livingston Ave., New Brunswick, NJ 08901
Marshall Jones, Executive Director
Tel: (732) 545-8100
Fax:(732) 907-1864
membership@crossroadstheatrecompany.org
www.crossroadstheatrecompany.org
Est. 1978. Submission Materials: See website.

**Curan Repertory Company**
561 Hudson St., #88, New York, NY 10014
Ken Terrell, Artistic Director
Tel: (212) 479-0821
Fax:(212) 645-7495
kenatcuran@hotmail.com
www.curan.org
Est. 1990. 5 original full-length plays and one-act fest each season. Production: cast of 2-15, small set. Response: 4 mos. Preferred Genre(s): Plays. Preferred Length: One-Act. Submission Materials: Query, 10pg sample, SASE.

**Dad's Garage Theatre Co.**
280 Elizabeth St., #C-101, Atlanta, GA 30307
Scott Warren, Artistic Director
Tel: (404) 523-3141
Fax:(404) 688-6644
scott@dadsgarage.com
www.dadsgarage.com
Est. 1995. Preferred Genre(s): Adaptation. Preferred Length: Any length. Submission Materials: Query, synopsis, sample.

**Dallas Children's Theater**
5938 Skillman St., Dallas, TX 75231
Artie Olaisen, Artistic Associate
Tel: (214) 978-0110
Fax:(214) 978-0118
artie.olaisen@dct.org
www.dct.org
Est. 1984. Professional family theater. Preferred Genre(s): Plays or Musicals.

Special Interest: Theatre for Young Audiences. Preferred Length: Full-length. Submission Materials: Query, synopsis, cast list. Deadline(s): rolling

**Dallas Theater Center**
3636 Turtle Creek Blvd., Dallas, TX 75219
Kevin Moriarty, Artistic Director
Tel: (214) 526-8210
Fax:(214) 521-7666
www.dallastheatercenter.org
   Est. 1959. Response: 1 yr Preferred Genre(s): All genres. Preferred Length: One-act or Full-length. Submission Materials: Synopsis and 10-pg sample.

**Danisarte**
PO Box 286146, 1617 Third Ave., New York, NY 10128
Alicia Kaplan, Producing Artistic Director
Tel: (212) 561-0191
Danisarte@aol.com
www.danisarte.org
   Est. 1992. Seeking unpublished/unproduced works. Production: cast limit 6 Preferred Genre(s): All genres. Special Interest: Theatre for Young Audiences. Preferred Length: Any length. Submission Materials: Query letter, SASE.

**Deaf West Theatre (DWT)**
5114 Lankershim Blvd., North Hollywood, CA 91601
Ed Waterstreet, Artistic Director
Tel: 818-508-8389 TTY
Fax:(818) 762-2981
www.deafwest.org
   Est. 1991.

**Delaware Theatre Company**
200 Water St., Wilmington, DE 19801
Anne Marie Cammarato, Artistic. Associate
Tel: (302) 594-1104
Fax:(302) 594-1107
literary@delawaretheatre.org
www.delawaretheatre.org
   Est. 1978. Season usually 5-6 readings/productions. Production: cast limit 10, small orchestra, unit set.

Response: 6 mos. Preferred Genre(s): All genres. Preferred Length: Full-length. Submission Materials: See website.

**Detroit Repertory Theatre**
13103 Woodrow Wilson St., Detroit, MI 48238
Barbara Busby, Literary Mgr.
Tel: (313) 868-1347
Fax:(313) 868-1705
detreph@aol.com
www.detroitreptheatre.com
   Est. 1957. Production: age 18-65, cast of 5-7, non-traditional casting. Response: 6 mos Preferred Genre(s): Plays or Musicals. Preferred Length: Any length. Submission Materials: Complete script & SASE.

**Dicapo Opera Theatre**
184 E. 76th St., New York, NY 10021
Michael Capasso, General Director
Tel: (212) 288-9438
Fax:(212) 744-1082
mcdicapo@aol.com
www.dicapo.com
   Limited run performances. Preferred Genre(s): Opera. Submission Materials: See website.

**Directors Company**
311 W. 43rd St., #307, New York, NY 10036
Tel: (212) 246-5877
directorscompany@aol.com
mysite.verizon.net/directorscompany
   Submission Materials: See website.

**Diversionary Theatre**
4545 Park Blvd., #101, San Diego, CA 92116
Dan Kirsch, Executive/Artistic Director
Tel: (619) 220-6830
Fax:(619) 220-0148
boxoffice@diversionary.org
www.diversionary.org
   Est. 1986. 3rd oldest LGBT theater in US. 6-show season and new-work readings in 106-seat space. Apply online. Response: 6 mos. Preferred Genre(s): All genres. Special Interest: LGBT. Preferred Length: Any length.

Submission Materials: Application, synopsis, 15 pg sample.

## Dixon Place
161A Christie Street, New York, NY 10002
Ellie Covan, Executive Director
Tel: (212) 219-0736
Fax:(212) 219-0761
submissions@dixonplace.org
www.dixonplace.org
Est. 1986. Nonprofit laboratoty theater for NY- based performing and literary artists to create and develop new works in front of a live audience. Preferred Genre(s): All genres. Preferred Length: Any length. Submission Materials: See website.

## Do Gooder Productions
359 W. 54th St., #4FS, New York, NY 10019
Mark Robert Gordon, Founding Artistic/Executive Director
Tel: (212) 581-8852
Fax:(212) 541-7928
www.dogooder.org
Not accepting unsolicited scripts at this time.

## Dorset Theatre Festival
Box 510, Dorset, VT 5251
Carl Forsman, Artistic Director
Tel: (802) 867-2223
Fax:(802) 867-0144
theatre@sover.net
www.dorsettheatrefestival.org
Dorset only accepts scripts of writers in residence or by invitation. Submission Materials: See website.

## Dream Theatre
484 W. 43rd St., #14-Q, New York, NY 10036
Andrea Leigh, Artistic Director
Tel: (212) 564-2628
andrealeigh88@hotmail.com
Est. 2001. New works, esp. by/for women, that have not been optioned or produced in NYC. Mailed submissions not returned. Email preferred. Response: 6 mos. Preferred Genre(s): Plays. Preferred Length: Any length.

Submission Materials: Synopsis and full script. Deadline(s): Ongoing

## Drilling Company
236 W. 78th Street, 3rd floor, New York, NY 10024
Hamilton Clancy, Artistic Director
Tel: (212) 877-4234
Fax:(212) 877-0099
DrillingCompany@aol.com
www.drillingcompany.org
Est. 1999. Commissions and workshops new work. Response: 3 mos. Preferred Genre(s): Plays or Musicals. Preferred Length: Any length. Submission Materials: See website.

## East West Players
120 N. Judge John Aiso St., Los Angeles, CA 90012
Jeff Liu, Literary Manager
Tel: (213) 625-7000
Fax:(213) 625-7111
jliu@eastwestplayers.org
www.eastwestplayers.org
Est. 1965. 4 mainstage productions/season in addition to readings. Submissions by US mail only. Response: 9 mos. Preferred Genre(s): Plays or Musicals. Special Interest: Asian-American. Preferred Length: Full-length. Submission Materials: Synopsis, full script, resume, SASE.

## Electric Theatre Company
LIterary Manager, PO Box 854, Scranton, PA 18501
John Beck, Literary Manager
Tel: (570) 558-1520
jbeck@electrictheatre.org
www.electrictheatre.org
Est. 1992. Seeking unproduced work. Production: cast limit 6. Response: 3 mos. Preferred Genre(s): Plays. Preferred Length: Full-length. Submission Materials: Synopsis and 10-pg sample. Deadline(s): September 1st

**Emelin Theatre for the Performing Arts**
153 Library Lane, Mamaroneck, NY 10543
Lisa Reilly, Executive Director
Tel: (914) 698-3045
Fax:(914) 698-1404
www.emelin.org
Est. 1972. Production: small cast, no fly. Response: 6 mos. Preferred Genre(s): All genres. Preferred Length: Any length. Submission Materials: Professional referral only.

**Emerging Artists Theatre (EAT)**
15 West 28th St., 3rd Floor, New York, NY 10001
Paul Adams, Artistic Director
Tel: (212) 247-2429
eattheatre@gmail.com
www.eatheatre.org
Develop and produce new work. Submit by email. Production: age 20-70, cast 2-10. Response: 3-6 mos. Preferred Genre(s): All genres. Special Interest: LGBT. Preferred Length: Any length. Submission Materials: Query letter, synopsis and S.A.S.E.. Deadline(s): Eatfest June 1st, New Works Nov. 15th

**Enrichment Works**
5605 Woodman Ave., # 207, Valley Glen, CA 91401
Abraham Tetenbaum, Executive Director
Tel: (818) 780-1400
Fax:(818) 780-0300
atetenbaum@enrichmentworks.org
www.enrichmentworks.org
Est. 1999. Tours in L.A. schools, libraries, museums and community venues. Production: cast limit 3, touring set. Response: 6 mos. Preferred Genre(s): Musical theatre. Preferred Length: One-Act. Submission Materials: Complete script & SASE.

**Ensemble Studio Theatre (EST)**
549 W. 52nd St., New York, NY 10019
EST Literary Manager, Literary Manager
Tel: (212) 247-4982
Fax:(212) 664-0041
est@ensemblestudiotheatre.org
www.ensemblestudiotheatre.org

Est. 1972. Preferred Genre(s): All genres. Preferred Length: Any length. Submission Materials: See website.

**First Stage Children's Theater [WI]**
325 W. Walnut St., Milwaukee, WI 53212
Jeff Frank
Tel: (414) 267-2929
Fax:(414) 267-2930
jfrank@firststage.org
www.firststage.org
Est. 1987. Response : 3 mo query, 9 mos script. Preferred Genre(s): All genres. Special Interest: Theatre for Young Audiences. Preferred Length: Any length. Submission Materials: Query, synopsis, resume.

**Flat Rock Playhouse**
Box 310, Flat Rock, NC 28731
Vincent Marini, Producing Artistic Director
Tel: (828) 693-0403
Fax:(828) 693-6795
frp@flatrockplayhouse.org
www.flatrockplayhouse.com
Preferred Genre(s): Plays or Musicals. Preferred Length: Full-length. Submission Materials: Complete script.

**Florida Repertory Theatre**
2267 1st St., Fort Myers, FL 33901
Jason Parrish, Associate Director
Tel: (239) 332-4665
Fax:(239) 332-1808
jason.parrish@floridarep.org
www.floridarep.org
Est. 1989. 8 mainstage plays Sep-Jun. Production: cast limit 10, orchestra 4-5, sets limit 2. Response: 1 yr. Preferred Genre(s): All genres. Preferred Length: Full-length. Submission Materials: Agent only submissions.

**Florida Stage**
701 Okeechobee Blvd. Ste 300, West Palm Beach, FL 33401
Andrew Rosendorf, Artistic Assoc
Tel: (561) 585-3404
Fax:(561) 588-4708
andrew@floridastage.org
www.floridastage.org
Est. 1987. New work specializing in thought-provoking, issue-oriented material. Submit via email. Production:

cast of 2-6, unit set. Response: 4 mos. Preferred Genre(s): Plays. Preferred Length: Full-length. Submission Materials: Agent only submissions.

## Folger Theatre
201 E. Capitol St., SE, Washington, DC 20003
Tel: (202) 675-0340
Fax:(202) 608-1719
Est. 1986. Submission Materials: See website.

## Ford's Theatre Society
511 10th St., NW, Washington, DC 20004
Paul Tetreault, Producing Director
Tel: (202) 638-2941
Fax:(202) 638-6269
www.fordstheatre.org
Est. 1968. 4-5 shows/yr, incl. perhaps 1 original play or musical. Production: orchestra limit 7. Response: 1 yr. Preferred Genre(s): All genres. Preferred Length: Full-length. Submission Materials: See website.

## Fountain Theatre
5060 Fountain Ave., Los Angeles, CA 90029
Simon Levy, Producing Director/Dramaturg
Tel: (323) 663-2235
Fax:(323) 663-1629
fountaintheatre1@aol.com
www.fountaintheatre.com
Submit work w/professional recommendation. Production: cast limit 12, unit set, no fly. Response: 3 mos. Preferred Genre(s): Plays. Preferred Length: One-act or Full-length. Submission Materials: Query and synopsis only.

## Freed-Hardeman University
Theater Dept., 158 E. Main St., Henderson, TN 38340
Cliff Thompson, Director of Theater
Tel: (731) 989-6780
Fax:(731) 989-6938
cthompson@fhu.edu
www.fhu.edu
Preferred Genre(s): Plays. Preferred Length: One-act or Full-length. Submission Materials: Synopsis, 30pg sample, SASE.

## GableStage
1200 Anastasia Ave., Coral Gables, FL 33134
Joseph Adler, Producing Artistic Director
Tel: (305) 446-1116
Fax:(305) 445-8645
jadler@gablestage.org
www.gablestage.org
Est. 1979. 6 productions/yr. Preferred Genre(s): Plays. Preferred Length: Full-length. Submission Materials: Query letter only.

## Geffen Playhouse
10886 LeConte Ave, Los Angeles, CA 90024
Amy Levinson Millan, Literary Mgr/Dramaturg
Tel: (310) 208-6500
Fax:(310) 208-0341
www.geffenplayhouse.com
Est. 1995. Response Time: 6 mos
Submission Materials: Agent only submissions.

## George Street Playhouse
9 Livingston Ave., New Brunswick, NJ 08901
Jeremy Stoller, Literary Apprentice
Tel: (732) 846-2895
Fax:(732) 247-9151
www.georgestplayhouse.org
Est. 1974. Productions, readings, tours of issue-oriented 40-min one-acts for schools, Next Stage Fest workshops. Production: cast limit 7. Response: 10 mos. Preferred Genre(s): No translation. Special Interest: Theatre for Young Audiences. Preferred Length: Any length. Submission Materials: See website.

## Geva Theatre Center
75 Woodbury Blvd., Rochester, NY 14607
Marge Betley, Literary Mgr/Dramaturg
Tel: (585) 232-1366
Fax:(585) 232-4031
mbetley@gevatheatre.org
www.gevatheatre.org
Est. 1972. Productions, readings, workshops of classics, musicals, new works. Response: 3 mos query; 6 mos

script. Preferred Genre(s): Plays or
Musicals. Preferred Length: Any
length. Submission Materials: Query,
synopsis, 10-pg sample, SASE.

**Goodman Theatre**
170 N. Dearborn St., Chicago, IL 60601
Tanya Palmer, Literary Manager
Tel: (312) 443-3811
Fax:(312) 443-3821
info@goodman-theatre.org
www.goodmantheatre.org
   Est. 1925. Response: 6 - 8 wks.
   Preferred Genre(s): All genres.
   Preferred Length: Full-length.
   Submission Materials: Agent only
   submissions.

**Goodspeed Musicals**
6 Main St, P.O. Box A, East Haddam, CT
   06423-0281
Donna Lynn Cooper Hilton, Line
   Producer
Tel: (860) 873-8664
Fax:(860) 873-2329
info@goodspeed.org
www.goodspeed.org
   Est. 1959. Preferred Genre(s): Musical
   theatre. Preferred Length: Full-length.
   Submission Materials: Agent only
   submissions.

**Great Lakes Theater Festival**
1501 Euclid Ave., # 300, Cleveland, OH
   44115
Charles Fee, Producing Artistic Director
Tel: (216) 241-5490
Fax:(216) 241-6315
mail@greatlakestheater.org
www.greatlakestheater.org
   Est. 1961. Response: 3 mos. Preferred
   Genre(s): Plays. Preferred Length:
   Full-length. Submission Materials:
   Professional referral only.

**Greenbrier Valley Theatre**
113 E. Washington St., Lewisburg, WV
   24901
Cathey Sawyer, Artistic Director
Tel: (304) 645-3838
Fax:(304) 645-3818
cathey@gvtheatre.org
www.gvtheatre.org

Est. 1967. Production: age 7 and older,
cast of 6-10, orchestra of 1-4, set limit
1. Submissions not returned. Response:
6 mos. Preferred Genre(s): Plays or
Musicals. Preferred Length:
Full-length. Submission Materials:
Agent only submissions.

**Guthrie Theater**
818 S. 2nd St., Minneapolis, MN 55415
Jo Holcomb, Literary Manager
Tel: (612) 225-6000
Fax:(612) 225-6004
www.guthrietheater.org
   Est. 1963. New 3-theater complex
   opened 2006, incl. 1100-seat thrust,
   700-seat proscenium and 199-seat
   studio. Response : varies. Preferred
   Genre(s): All genres. Preferred Length:
   Full-length. Submission Materials:
   Agent only submissions.

**Halcyon Theatre**
3334 W. Wilson #1, Chicago, IL 60625
Tony Adams
Tel: (312) 458-9170
submissions@halcyontheatre.org
www.halcyontheatre.org
   We are not currently accepting
   submissions. For submissions policies
   go to halcyontheatre.org/submissions
   Preferred Genre(s): Plays or Musicals.
   Preferred Length: Any length.
   Submission Materials: Agent only
   submissions.

**Harlequin Productions of Cayuga
Community College**
197 Franklin St., Auburn, NY 13021
Robert Frame, Director of Theater
Tel: (315) 255-1743
Fax:(315) 255-2117
framer@cayuga-cc.edu
www.cayuga-cc.edu
   Est. 1958. 6 perfs over 2 weekends
   (fall and spring) with college students
   in high-quality extracurricular program.
   Production: age 16-35, cast of 7-14.
   Response: 1 yr. Preferred Genre(s):
   Plays. Preferred Length: One-act or
   Full-length. Submission Materials:
   Complete script & SASE.

**Hartford Stage**
50 Church St., Hartford, CT 06103
Jeremy B. Cohen, Assoc Artistic
  Director/New Play Development
Tel: (860) 525-5601
Fax:(860) 224-0183
litman@hartfordstage.org
www.hartfordstage.org
  Est. 1963. Author must be CT resident.
  Preferred Genre(s): All genres.
  Preferred Length: Full-length.
  Submission Materials: Agent only
  submissions.

**Harwich Junior Theatre (HJT)**
Box 168, 105 Division St., West
  Harwich, MA 02671
Nina Schuessler, Artistic Director
Tel: (508) 432-2002
Fax:(508) 432-0726
hjt@capecod.net
www.hjtcapecod.org
  Est. 1951 New plays for
  intergenerational casts and audiences.
  Production: intergenerational, no fly.
  Response: 6 mos. Preferred Genre(s):
  All genres. Special Interest: Theatre for
  Young Audiences. Preferred Length:
  Any length. Submission Materials:
  Synopsis, SASE.

**Hedgerow Theatre**
64 Rose Valley Rd., Media, PA 19063
Penelope Reed, Producing Artistic
  Director
Tel: (610) 565-4211
Fax:(610) 565-1672
preed@hedgerowtheatre.org
www.hedgerowtheatre.org
  Est. 1923. Readings of new plays by
  Delaware Valley writers in readings
  and workshops. Production: cast of 2-8.
  Response: 2 mos query, 4 mos script.
  Preferred Genre(s): All genres.
  Preferred Length: Any length.
  Submission Materials: Query and
  synopsis only.

**Hip Pocket Theatre**
Box 136758, Ft. Worth, TX 76136
Diane Simons, Producer
Tel: (817) 246-9775
Fax:(817) 246-5651
hippockettheatre@aol.com
www.hippocket.org
  Est. 1977. Production: simple set,
  outdoor amphitheater. Response: 2
  mos. Preferred Genre(s): Plays or
  Musicals. Preferred Length:
  Full-length. Submission Materials:
  Synopsis, sample, audio.

**Hobo Junction Productions**
2526 West Argyle Avenue, Apt 2,
  Chicago, IL 60625
Tel: (773) 820-2732
hobojunction@sbcglobal.net
www.hobojunctionproductions.com
  Established in 2008. Focus on
  innovative, imaginative and original
  approaches to comedy. See website for
  details. Preferred Genre(s): Comedy.
  Preferred Length: Full-length.
  Submission Materials: Query, synopsis,
  full script, SASE. Deadline(s): rolling.

**Honolulu Theatre for Youth**
229 Queen Emma Sq., Honolulu, HI
  96813
Eric Johnson, Artistic Director
Tel: (808) 839-9885
Fax:(808) 839-7018
htyeric@gmail.com
www.htyweb.org
  Est. 1955. Commissioning and
  producing new plays, Sep-May.
  Production: cast limit 5 Preferred
  Genre(s): Plays or Musicals. Special
  Interest: Theatre for Young Audiences.
  Preferred Length: Any length.
  Submission Materials: Query letter
  only.

**Horizon Theatre Rep [NY]**
41 E. 67th St., New York, NY 10021
Rafael De Mussa, Artistic Director
Tel: (212) 737-3357
Fax:(212) 737-5103
info@htronline.org
www.htronline.org

Est. 2000. Unproduced/unoptioned
only. Submissions not returned.
Production: ages 16-75,cast size 4-15.
Response: 1 mo. Preferred Genre(s):
Plays. Preferred Length: One-act or
Full-length. Submission Materials:
Synopsis only.

**Horse Trade Theater Group**
85 E. 4th St., New York, NY 10003
Erez Ziv, Associate Producer
Tel: (212) 777-6088
Fax:(212) 777-6120
office@horsetrade.info
www.horsetrade.info
  Horse Trade is a self-sustaining theater
  development group; with a focus on
  new work featuring a resident artist
  program. Preferred Genre(s): All
  genres. Preferred Length: Any length.
  Submission Materials: Complete script.

**Hubris Productions**
724 W. Roscoe Street, #3S, Chicago, IL
  60657
Lorraine Freund
Tel: (773) 398-3273
lorraine@hubrisproductions.com
hubrisproductions.com
  Looking for new work; unoptioned,
  unproduced, unpublished. Email
  submissions only. Preferred Genre(s):
  Plays or Musicals. Preferred Length:
  Full-length. Submission Materials:
  Query, synopsis, full script, cover
  letter. Deadline(s): Ongoing

**Hudson Theatres**
6539 Santa Monica Blvd., Los Angeles,
  CA 90038
Elizabeth Reilly, Artistic Director
Tel: (323) 856-4252
Fax:(323) 856-4316
ereilly@hudsontheatre.com
www.hudsontheatre.com
  Est. 1991. Response: 6 mos query, 1 yr
  script. Preferred Genre(s): All genres.
  Preferred Length: Full-length.
  Submission Materials: Query, synopsis
  and 10-pg sample.

**Huntington Theatre Company**
264 Huntington Ave., Boston, MA 02115
Charles Haugland, Literary Associate
Tel: (617) 273-1503
Fax:(617) 353-8300
chaugland@huntingtontheatre.bu.edu
www.huntingtontheatre.org
  Est. 1981. MA, RI writers send
  unsolicited, others, must have agent
  submit. Response: 1 year. Preferred
  Genre(s): All genres. Preferred Length:
  Any length. Submission Materials:
  Complete script & SASE.

**Hypothetical Theatre Company**
P.O. Box 944, New York, NY 10009
Amy Feinberg, Producing Artistic
  Director
Tel: (212) 780-0800
Fax:(212) 780-0859
htc@hypotheticaltheatre.org
www.hypotheticaltheatre.org
  Est. 1986. Work must be unproduced
  in NYC. Response: 6 mos. Preferred
  Genre(s): Plays. Preferred Length:
  Full-length. Submission Materials:
  Agent only submissions.

**Idaho Repertory Theatre (IRT)**
University of Idaho - Box 442008,
  Moscow, ID 83844
Dean Panttaja, Artistic Director
Tel: (208) 885-6465
Fax:(208) 885-2558
theatre@uidaho.edu
www.idahorep.org
  Seeking work from new/emerging
  unpublished writer. Submit via email
  only. Production: ages 13-35, cast of
  2-10. Response: 4 mos. Preferred
  Genre(s): All genres. Preferred Length:
  Any length. Submission Materials:
  Query letter only.

**Illusion Theater**
528 Hennepin Ave., #704, Minneapolis,
  MN 55403
Michael Robins, Executive Producing
  Director
Tel: (612) 339-4944
Fax:(612) 337-8042
info@illusiontheater.org
www.illusiontheater.org

Est. 1974. Submit via email. Response: 1 yr. Preferred Genre(s): All genres. Preferred Length: Any length. Submission Materials: Professional referral only.

## Imagination Stage
4908 Auburn Ave., Bethesda, MD 20814
Janet Stanford, Artistic Director
Tel: (301) 961-6060
Fax:(301) 718-9526
kbryere@imaginationstage.org
www.imaginationstage.org
Est. 1979. Production: cast of 4-10. Preferred Genre(s): All genres. Preferred Length: Any length. Submission Materials: Query, 10pg sample, outline.

## Indiana Repertory Theatre
140 W. Washington St., Indianapolis, IN 46204
Richard J. Roberts, Resident Dramaturg
Tel: (317) 635-5277
Fax:(317) 236-0767
rroberts@irtlive.com
www.irtlive.com
Est. 1972.Interested in material w/cross-generational appeal from authors w/ Midwest voice (but not exclusively). Production: cast limit 10. Submit via email. Response: 6 mos Preferred Genre(s): Plays. Special Interest: Theatre for Young Audiences. Preferred Length: One-act or Full-length. Submission Materials: Query, synopsis, resume.

## Infamous Commonwealth Theatre
600 South Dearborn Street, Unit 905, Chicago, IL 60605
Chris Maher, Artistic Director
Tel: (312) 458-9780
cmaher@infamouscommonwealth.org
www.infamouscommonwealth.org
est. 2001. Submission Materials: See website.

## InterAct Theatre Company [PA]
2030 Sansom St., Philadelphia, PA 19103
Rebecca Wright, Literary Director & Dramaturg
Tel: (215) 568-8077
Fax:(215) 568-8095
bwright@interacttheatre.org
www.interacttheatre.org
Est. 1988. Looking for work that explores specific social/political themes/issues. Production: 1-8. Response: 6-12 mos. Preferred Genre(s): Plays. Preferred Length: Full-length. Submission Materials: Query, 10pg sample, resume.

## Irish Arts Center
553 W. 51st St., New York, NY 10019
Pauline Turley, Executive Director
Tel: (212) 757-3318
Fax:(212) 247-0930
info@irishartscenter.org
www.irishartscenter.org
Est. 1972. Submission Materials: See website.

## Irish Repertory Theatre
132 W. 22nd St., New York, NY 10011
Kara Manning, Literary Manager
Tel: (212) 255-0270
Fax:(212) 255-0281
kara@irishrep.org
www.irishrep.org
Ongoing new works reading series reflecting the Irish and Irish American experience. Female playwrights and writers of color encouraged. Preferred Genre(s): All genres. Preferred Length: Any length. Submission Materials: See website.

## Jewish Theater of New York
Box 845, Times Sq. Sta., New York, NY 10108
Liz Lauren
Tel: (212) 494-0050
Fax:(212) 494-0050
thejtny@aol.com
www.jewishtheater.org
Est. 1994. Seeking unproduced/unpublished/unoptioned work. Submissions not returned. Response: 3 mos. Preferred Genre(s):

Musical theatre. Preferred Length: Full-length. Submission Materials: Synopsis only.

**Judith Shakespeare Company NYC**
367 Windsor Hwy., #409, New Windsor, NY 12553
Joanne Zipay, Artistic Director/Producer
Tel: (212) 592-1885
judithshakes@gmail.com
www.judithshakespeare.org
Est. 1995. Offers RESURGENCE concert reading series and full productions of new plays with heightened language and significant roles for women. Submit by US mail only. Preferred Genre(s): Plays. Preferred Length: One-act or Full-length. Submission Materials: Synopsis and 10-pg sample.

**Kairos Italy Theater (KIT)**
60 E. 8th Street, #12B, New York, NY 10003
Laura Caparrotti, Artistic Director
Tel: (212) 254-4025
Fax:(801) 749-6727
info@kitheater.com
www.kitheater.com
Est. 2002. Produces plays by and about Italian authors and Italian themes. Submit by email. Preferred Genre(s): Plays. Preferred Length: Any length. Submission Materials: Synopsis and 10-pg sample.

**Kansas City Repertory Theatre**
4949 Cherry St., Kansas City, MO 64110
Kyle Hatley, Artistic Director
Tel: (816) 235-2727
Fax:(816) 235-5367
prestonem@kcrep.org
www.kcrep.org
Est. 1964. Formerly Missouri Repertory Theatre. Preferred Genre(s): All genres. Preferred Length: Full-length.

**Kidworks Touring Theatre Co.**
5215 N. Ravenswood Ave., #307, Chicago, IL 60640
Andrea Salloum, Artistic Director
Tel: (773) 907-9932
Fax:(773) 907-9933
kidworkstheatre@aol.com
www.kidworkstheatre.org
Est. 1987. Preferred Genre(s): All genres. Special Interest: Theatre for Young Audiences.

**Killing Kompany**
21 Turn Ln., Levittown, NY 11756
Jon Avner, Artistic Director
Tel: (212) 772-2590
Fax:(212) 202-6495
killingkompany@killingkompany.com
www.killingkompany.com
Interactive shows for dinner theater. Preferred Genre(s): Interactive. Preferred Length: Full-length.

**L.A. Theatre Works (LATW)**
681 Venice Blvd., Venice, CA 90291
Susan Lowenberg, Producer, Director
Tel: (310) 827-0808
Fax:(310) 827-4949
www.latw.org
Est. 1974. Live performances and studio recordings for broadcast over public radio. Response: 6 mos. Preferred Genre(s): Radio plays. Preferred Length: Any length. Submission Materials: Agent only submissions.

**La Jolla Playhouse**
Box 12039, La Jolla, CA 92039
Gabriel Greene, Literary Manager
Tel: (858) 550-1070
Fax:(858) 550-1075
www.lajollaplayhouse.org
Est. 1947. Commissions playwrights and provides developmental support thru Page to Stage readings (est. 2001). Response: 2 mos query, 1 yr script. Preferred Genre(s): Plays or Musicals. Preferred Length: Full-length. Submission Materials: See website.

**La MaMa Experimental Theater Club**
74-A E. 4th St., New York, NY 10003
Ellen Stewart, Artistic Director
Tel: (212) 254-6468
Fax:(212) 254-7597
web@lamama.org
www.lamama.org
  Est. 1961. Response: 6 mos. Preferred
  Genre(s): Plays. Preferred Length: Any
  length. Submission Materials:
  Professional referral only.

**LAByrinth Theater Company**
307 W. 38th Street, Suite 1605, New
  York, NY 10018
John Ortiz, Co-Artistic Dir.
Tel: (212) 513-1080
Fax:(212) 513-1123
lab@labtheater.org
www.labtheater.org
  Preferred Genre(s): All genres.
  Preferred Length: Any length.

**LaMicro Theater**
Box 20019, London Ter., New York, NY
  10011
Pietro Gonzalez, Artistic Director
Tel: (212) 979-5744
Fax:(775) 205-5453
info@lamicrotheater.org
www.lamicrotheater.org
  Est. 2003. Production: cast of 2-4.
  Submission Materials: See website.

**Lincoln Center Theater**
150 W. 65th St., New York, NY 10023
Anne Cattaneo, Dramaturg
Tel: (212) 362-7600
www.lct.org
  Est. 1966. Response: 2 mos. Preferred
  Genre(s): All genres. Preferred Length:
  Full-length. Submission Materials:
  Agent only submissions.

**Literally Alive**
The Players Theatre, 115 MacDougal St.,
  New York, NY 10012
Brenda Bell, Artistic Director
Tel: (212) 866-5170
brenda@literallyalive.com
www.literallyalive.com
  Preferred Genre(s): Plays or Musicals.
  Special Interest: Theatre for Young
  Audiences. Preferred Length: Any
  length.

**Little Fish Theatre (LFT)**
777 Centre St., San Pedro, CA 90731
Melanie Jones, Artistic Director
Tel: (310) 512-6030
Fax:(310) 507-0269
melanie@littlefishtheatre.org
www.littlefishtheatre.org
  Est. 2002. No longer accepting full
  length plays, see website for annual
  Pick of the Vine short play festival.
  Preferred Genre(s): Plays. Preferred
  Length: 10-min./10pgs.. Submission
  Materials: See website. Deadline(s):
  8/1/2010

**Looking Glass Theatre [NY]**
422 W. 57th St., New York, NY 10019
Erica Nilson, Literary Manager
Tel: (212) 307-9467
lgtlit@yahoo.com
www.lookingglasstheatrenyc.com
  est. 1993. Submit work via US mail
  AND email. Author must be female.
  Production: minimal. Response: 6
  mos-1 yr. Preferred Genre(s): Plays.
  Preferred Length: 10 min and one-acts.
  Submission Materials: Complete script.
  Deadline(s): ongoing

**Lookingglass Theatre [IL]**
2936 N. Southport Ave., Fl. 3, Chicago,
  IL 60657
Margot Bordelon, Literary Associate
Tel: (773) 477-9257
info@lookingglasstheatre.org
www.lookingglasstheatre.org
  Ensemble-based theater producing
  primarily company-developed projects.
  Shows are highly physical with strong
  narrative. No kitchen sink or talking
  heads. Preferred Genre(s): Plays.
  Preferred Length: Any length.
  Submission Materials: Query, synopsis,
  SASE.

**Lost Nation Theater**
City Hall, 39 Main St., Montpelier, VT
  05602
Mr. Kim Bent, Founding Artistic Director
Tel: (802) 229-0492
Fax:(802) 223-9608
info@lostnationtheater.org
www.lostnationtheater.org

Est. 1977. Production: cast limit 8, unit set, no fly. Response: 2 mo query, 4 mos script. Submission Materials: Query, synopsis, sample, resume. Deadline(s): 11/1/2010

**Magic Theatre**
Ft. Mason Ctr., Bldg. D, San Francisco, CA 94123
Jayne Benjulian, Director of New Play Development
Tel: (415) 441-8001
Fax:(415) 771-5505
jayneb@magictheatre.org
www.magictheatre.org
Magic produces world premieres and 2nd and 3rd productions of new work. Production: cast limit 8. Response: 3-9 mos script. Preferred Genre(s): Comedy. Preferred Length: Any length. Submission Materials: See website. Deadline(s): Rolling

**Marin Theater Company (MTC)**
397 Miller Ave., Mill Valley, CA 94941
Margot Melcon, Literary Manager
Tel: (415) 388-5200
Fax:(415) 388-1217
margot@marintheatre.org
www.marintheatre.org
Est. 1966. Response: 6 - 9 mos. Preferred Genre(s): Plays. Preferred Length: One-act or Full-length. Submission Materials: See website.

**Ma-Yi Theatre Company**
520 8th Ave, #309, New York, NY 10018
Ralph B. Pena, Artistic Director
Tel: (212) 971-4862
Fax:(212) 971-4862
info@ma-yitheatre.org
www.ma-yitheatre.org
Est. 1989. Submissions not returned. Preferred Genre(s): Plays. Special Interest: Asian-American. Preferred Length: Full-length. Submission Materials: Query and synopsis only.

**MCC Theater**
311 W. 43rd St., #206, New York, NY 10036
Stephen Willems, Literary Manager
Tel: (212) 727-7722
Fax:(212) 727-7780
literary@mcctheater.org
www.mcctheater.org
Est. 1986. Production: cast limit 10. Response: 2 mos. Preferred Genre(s): All genres. Preferred Length: Full-length. Submission Materials: Query, synopsis, 10-pg sample, SASE.

**McCarter Theater Center**
91 University Pl., Princeton, NJ 8540
Carrie Hughes, Literary Manager
Tel: (609) 258-6500
Fax:(609) 497-0369
chughes@mccarter.org
www.mccarter.org
Response: 6 mos. Preferred Genre(s): Plays. Preferred Length: Full-length. Submission Materials: Agent only submissions.

**Merrimack Repertory Theatre**
132 Warren St., Lowell, MA 01852
Merrimack Literary Dept
Tel: (978) 654-7550
Fax:(978) 654-7575
info@merrimackrep.org
www.merrimackrep.org
Est. 1979. Production: cast limit 8. Prefer digital scripts. Response: 12 mos. Preferred Genre(s): Plays. Preferred Length: Full-length. Submission Materials: Agent only submissions.

**Metro Theater Company**
8308 Olive Blvd., St. Louis, MO 63132
Carol North, Artistic Director
Tel: (314) 997-6777
Fax:(314) 997-1811
carol@metrotheatercompany.org
www.metrotheatercompany.org
Est. 1973. Mainstage shows, tours and commissions of theater for children and family audiences. Production: cast limit 10. Response: 3 mos. Preferred Genre(s): Plays or Musicals. Special Interest: Theatre for Young Audiences.

Preferred Length: One-Act. Submission Materials: Synopsis, sample, SASE.

**MetroStage**
1201 N. Royal St., Alexandria, VA 22314
Carolyn Griffin, Producing Artistic
  Director
Tel: (703) 548-9044
Fax:(703) 548-9089
info@metrostage.org
www.metrostage.org
  Est. 1984. Production: cast limit 6 - 8, orchestra limit 5, unit set. Musicals must be already be workshopped and have a demo cd. Author must have agent. Preferred Genre(s): Plays or Musicals. Preferred Length: Full-length. Submission Materials: Synopsis, 10-pg sample, SASE.

**Milwaukee Chamber Theatre**
158 N. Broadway, Milwaukee, WI 53202
Jacque Troy, Literary Manager
Tel: (414) 276-8842
Fax:(414) 277-4477
jacque@chamber-theatre.com
www.chamber-theatre.com
  Est. 1975. Production: small cast, unit set. Response: 6 mos. Preferred Genre(s): All genres. Preferred Length: Full-length. Submission Materials: Query, synopsis, 10-pg sample & SASE. Deadline(s): Accepting all year round

**Milwaukee Repertory Theater**
108 E. Wells St., Milwaukee, WI 53202
Literary Director, Literary Director
Tel: (414) 224-1761
Fax:(414) 224-9097
www.milwaukeerep.com
  Est. 1954. Response: 4 mos. Preferred Genre(s): Plays. Preferred Length: Full-length. Submission Materials: See website.

**Miracle Theatre Group**
425 SE 6th Ave., Portland, OR 97214
Olga Sanchez, Artistic Director
Tel: (503) 236-7253
Fax:(503) 236-4174
olga@milagro.org
www.milagro.org

Est. 1985. Author must be Hispanic. Production: cast limit 10, no fly. Response: 1 yr. Seeking plays but will consider musicals. Preferred Genre(s): Plays. Special Interest: Latino. Preferred Length: Full-length. Submission Materials: Complete script.

**Missouri Repertory Theatre**
4949 Cherry St., Kansas City, MO 64110
Peter Altman, Producing Artistic Director
Tel: (816) 235-2727
Fax:(816) 235-6562
theatre@umkc.edu
www.missourireptheatre.org
  Est. 1964. Preferred Genre(s): Plays. Preferred Length: Full-length. Submission Materials: Agent only submissions.

**Mixed Blood Theatre Company**
1501 S. 4th St., Minneapolis, MN 55454
Aditi Kapil, Resident Artist
Tel: (612) 338-0937
Fax:(612) 338-1851
literary@mixedblood.com
www.mixedblood.com
  Est. 1976. Response: 4 mos. Preferred Genre(s): All genres. Preferred Length: Full-length. Submission Materials: See website.

**Moving Arts**
Box 481145, Los Angeles, CA 90048
Steve Lozier, Managing Director
Tel: (323) 666-3259
Fax:(323) 666-2841
info@movingarts.org
www.movingarts.org
  Est. 1992. Currently not accepting submissions. Preferred Genre(s): Plays. Preferred Length: Full-length.

**National Theatre of the Deaf**
139 N. Main St., West Hartford, CT 06107
Aaron M. Kubey, Executive
  Director/President
Tel: (860) 236-4193
Fax:(860) 236-4163
akubey@ntd.org
www.ntd.org
  Est. 1967. Looking for work unproduced professionally. Production: cast limit 10, touring set. Response: 1

mo query, 6 mos script. Preferred
Genre(s): Plays. Special Interest: Deaf.
Preferred Length: Full-length.
Submission Materials: Query, synopsis,
sample, SASE.

**National Yiddish Theater—Folksbiene**
135 W. 29th St. , Room 504, New York,
NY 10001
Zalmen Mlotek, Artistic Director
Tel: (212) 213-2120
Fax:(212) 213-2186
info@folksbiene.org
www.folksbiene.org
Seeking material in Yiddish or based
on Yiddish source material. Preferred
Genre(s): Plays or Musicals. Preferred
Length: One-act or Full-length.
Submission Materials: See website.

**Near West Theatre (NWT)**
6514 Detroit Avenue, Cleveland, OH
44102
Carole L. Hedderson, Artistic Director
Tel: (216) 961-9750
Fax:(216) 961-6381
nearwesttheatre.org

**New Conservatory Theatre Center**
25 Van Ness Ave., Lower Lobby, San
Francisco, CA 94102
Ed Decker, Artistic Director
Tel: (415) 861-4914
Fax:(415) 861-6988
ed@nctcsf.org
www.nctcsf.org
Est. 1981. Material must be
unoptioned. Response: 3-6 mos.
Preferred Genre(s): No translation.
Preferred Length: One-act or Full-
length. Submission Materials: See
website.

**New Federal Theatre**
292 Henry St., New York, NY 10002
Woodie King Jr., Producing Director
Tel: (212) 353-1176
Fax:(212) 353-1088
newfederal@aol.com
www.newfederaltheatre.org
Est. 1970. Production: cast limit 5, unit
set. Response: 6 mos. Preferred
Genre(s): Plays. Preferred Length:

Full-length. Submission Materials:
Complete script & SASE.

**New Georges**
109 W. 27th St., #9-A, New York, NY
10001
Kara-Lynn Vaeni, Literary Manager
Tel: (646) 336-8077
Fax:(646) 336-8051
info@newgeorges.org
www.newgeorges.org
Est. 1992. Seeking highly
theatrical/experimental work from
female authors only. US mail only.
Response: 6 - 9 mos. Preferred
Genre(s): Plays. Preferred Length:
Full-length. Submission Materials:
Complete script.

**New Ground Theatre**
2113 E. 11th St., Davenport, IA 52803
Chris Jansen, Artistic Director
Tel: (563) 326-7529
Fax:(563) 359-7576
cjansen@hotmail.com
www.newgroundtheatre.org
Est. 2001. Author must be resident of
IA, IL or quad city area. Production:
cast limit 6, unit set, no fly. Response:
6 mos. Preferred Genre(s): All genres.
Preferred Length: Full-length.
Submission Materials: Complete script.

**New Jersey Repertory Company**
179 Broadway, Long Branch, NJ 07740
Suzanne Barabas, Artistic Director
Tel: (732) 229-3166
Fax:(732) 229-3167
info@njrep.org
www.njrep.org
Est. 1997. Seeking
unproduced/unpublished via email only.
US mail submits not returned.
Production: cast limit 4 for plays and
musicals. 6-7 Full length plays
produced each year. Preferred Genre(s):
Plays or Musicals. Preferred Length:
Full-length, 10 min. Submission
Materials: Full Script, cast breakdown,
synopsis, audio. Deadline(s): ongoing

**New Repertory Theatre**
200 Dexter Ave., Watertown, MA 02472
Bridget Kathleen O'Leary, Artistic
  Associate
Tel: (617) 923-7060
Fax:(617) 923-7625
bridgetoleary@newrep.org
www.newrep.org
  Est. 1984. Author must have agent or
  be a local playwright. Production: cast
  limit 12. Preferred Genre(s): Plays or
  Musicals. Preferred Length:
  Full-length. Submission Materials:
  Complete script.

**New Theatre**
4120 Laguna St., Coral Gables, FL 33146
Steven Chambers, Literary Manager
Tel: (305) 443-5373
Fax:(305) 443-1642
schambers@new-theatre.org
www.new-theatre.org
  Est. 1986. New works and new
  adaptations of Shakespeare sought.
  Production: cast limit 6, minimal set.
  Response: 2-3 mos. Preferred Genre(s):
  All genres. Preferred Length:
  Full-length. Submission Materials: See
  website. Deadline(s): Preferably Late
  December

**New Works/Vantage Theatres**
1251 W. Muirlands Dr., La Jolla, CA
  92037
Dori Salois, Artistic Manager
Tel: (858) 456-9664
VantageTheatre@bigfoot.com
home.san.rr.com/vantagetheatre
  Seeking work with big
  political/spiritual ideas. Preferred
  Genre(s): Plays. Preferred Length:
  One-act or Full-length. Submission
  Materials: Synopsis, full script, SASE.

**New WORLD Theater (NWT)**
100 Hicks Way, #16 Curry Hicks,
  Amherst, MA 01003
Andrea Assaf, Artistic Director
Tel: (413) 545-1972
Fax:(413) 545-4414
nwt@admin.umass.edu
www.newworldtheater.org

Hosts "New Works for a New World"
every summer & invite up to 4 artists
for a development residency. Preferred
Genre(s): All genres. Preferred Length:
Any length. Submission Materials:
Query letter only.

**New York Stage and Film (NYSAF)**
315 W. 36th St., #1006, New York, NY
  10018
Johanna Pfaelzea, Artistic Director
Tel: (212) 736-4240
Fax:(212) 736-4241
info@newyorkstageandfilm.org
www.newyorkstageandfilm.org
  Est. 1985. Summer season (Jun-Aug)
  in residence as part of Powerhouse
  program at Vasser Coll. Response: 6
  mos. Preferred Genre(s): Plays.
  Preferred Length: Full-length.
  Submission Materials: Complete script
  & SASE.

**New York Theatre Workshop (NYTW)**
83 E. 4th St., New York, NY 10003
Linda S. Chapman, Associate Artistic
  Director
Tel: (212) 780-9037
Fax:(212) 460-8996
info@nytw.org
www.nytw.org
  Est. 1979. Works of innovative form &
  language about socially relevant issues.
  Response: 3 mos query, 8 mos script.
  Preferred Genre(s): Plays. Preferred
  Length: Full-length. Submission
  Materials: Query, synopsis, sample,
  resume, SASE.

**Next Theater Company**
927 Noyes St., Suite 108, Evanston, IL
  60201
Jason Southerland, Artistic Director
Tel: (847) 475-1875
Fax:(847) 475-6767
info@nexttheatre.org
www.nexttheatre.org
  Est. 1981. Commissions 1 world
  premiere per season. Production: cast
  limit 10 Preferred Genre(s): Plays.
  Preferred Length: Full-length.
  Submission Materials: Query, synopsis,
  10-pg sample, SASE.

**Northern Stage**
Box 4287, White River Junction, VT
05001
Brooke Ciardelli, Artistic Director
Tel: (802) 291-9009
info@northernstage.org
www.northernstage.org
  Est. 1997. Preferred Genre(s): All
  genres. Preferred Length: Full-length.
  Submission Materials: Query letter and
  S.A.S.E..

**Northlight Theatre**
9501 N. Skokie Blvd., Skokie, IL 60077
Meghan Beals McCarthy, Literary
  Manager
Tel: (847) 679-9501
Fax:(847) 679-1879
bjjones@northlight.org
www.northlight.org
  Est. 1975. Response: 1 mo query, 8
  mos script. Preferred Genre(s): All
  genres. Preferred Length: Any length.
  Submission Materials: Query, 10pg
  sample, SASE.

**Obsidian Theatre Company**
50 Carroll St. #215, Toronto, ON M4M-
  3G3 Canada
Philip Akin, Artistic Director
Tel: (416) 463-8444
obsidiantheatre@bellnet.ca
www.obsidian-theatre.com
  Check website for submission details.
  Preferred Genre(s): Plays. Preferred
  Length: Full-length. Submission
  Materials: See website.

**Omaha Theater Company at The Rose**
2001 Farnam St., Omaha, NE 68102
James Larson, Artistic Director
Tel: (402) 502-4618
Fax:(402) 344-7255
jamesl@rosetheater.org
www.rosetheater.org
  Est. 1949. Production: cast limit 10,
  unit set. Response: 6 mos. Preferred
  Genre(s): Plays. Preferred Length:
  One-Act. Submission Materials: See
  website.

**Open Eye Theater**
Box 959, Margaretville, NY 12455
Amie Brockway, Producing Artistic
  Director
Tel: (845) 586-1660
Fax:(845) 586-1660
openeye@catskill.net
www.theopeneye.org
  Est. 1972. Readings and productions
  for a multigenerational audience.
  Production: small cast, modest set.
  Response: 6 mos. Preferred Genre(s):
  All genres. Preferred Length: Any
  length. Submission Materials: Query
  and synopsis only.

**OpenStage Theatre & Company**
Box 617, Fort Collins, CO 80522
Denise Burson Freestone, Artistic
  Director
Tel: (970) 484-5237
Fax:(970) 482-0859
denisef@openstagetheatre.org
www.openstagetheatre.org
  Est. 1973. Staged workshops, minimal
  tech. Response: 1 year. Preferred
  Genre(s): Plays. Preferred Length:
  Full-length. Submission Materials: See
  website.

**Opera Cleveland**
1422 Euclid Ave, #1052, Cleveland, OH
  44115
Dean Williamson, Artistic Director
Tel: (216) 575-0903
Fax:(216) 575-1918
williamson@operacleveland.org
www.operacleveland.org
  Est. 2006 (merger of Lyric Opera
  Cleveland, Cleveland Opera). Spring-
  fall season and summer fest of 3 full-
  length operas. Response: 1 mo.
  Preferred Genre(s): Opera. Preferred
  Length: Full-length. Submission
  Materials: Query, synopsis, full script,
  audio, SASE.

**Oregon Shakespeare Festival**
Box 158, Ashland, OR 97520

Lue Morgan Douthit, Dir, Literary
Development/Dramaturgy
Tel: (541) 482-2111
Fax:(541) 482-0446
literary@osfashland.org
www.osfashland.org
Est. 1935. Response: 6 mos. Preferred
Genre(s): Plays. Preferred Length:
Full-length. Submission Materials:
Query letter only.

**Passage Theatre**
P.O. Box 967, Trenton, NJ 08605
Tel: (609) 392-0766
Fax:(609) 392-0318
info@passagetheatre.org
www.passagetheatre.org
Est. 1985. Seeks boundary-pushing &
stylistically adventurous new works.
Production: Modest cast size 4-6
actors, no fly. Response: 5 mos.
Preferred Genre(s): Plays or Musicals.
Preferred Length: One-act or Full-
length. Submission Materials: See
website. Deadline(s): Ongoing

**PCPA Theatrefest**
800 S. College Dr., Santa Maria, CA
93454
Patricia M. Troxel, Literary Manager
Tel: (805) 928-7731
Fax:(805) 928-7506
literary@pcpa.org
www.pcpa.org
Est. 1964. Response: 3 mos query, 6
mos script. Preferred Genre(s): Plays.
Preferred Length: Full-length.
Submission Materials: Query and
synopsis only.

**Pegasus Theater Company**
Box 942, Monte Rio, CA 95462
Tel: (707) 522-9043
www.pegasustheater.com
Est. 1998. Submission Materials: See
website.

**Penguin Repertory Company**
Box 91, Stony Point, NY 10980
Staci Swedeen, Literary Manager
Tel: (845) 786-2873
Fax:(845) 786-3638
samanthacarlin@penguinrep.org
www.penguinrep.org

Est. 1977. Full length plays, small sets,
four characters or fewer. Response: Up
To One Year. Preferred Genre(s):
Plays. Preferred Length: Full-length.
Submission Materials: Complete script.

**Penumbra Theatre Company**
270 N. Kent St., St. Paul, MN 55102
Dominic Taylor, Assoc. Artistic Director
Tel: (651) 288-6795
Fax:(651) 224-3180
dominic.taylor@penumbratheatre.org
www.penumbratheatre.org
Est. 1976. Response: 9 mos Preferred
Genre(s): Plays. Preferred Length:
One-act or Full-length. Submission
Materials: See website.

**People's Light and Theatre Company**
39 Conestoga Rd., Malvern, PA 19355
Alda Cortese, Literary Manager
Tel: (610) 647-1900
cortese@peopleslight.org
www.peopleslight.org
Est. 1974. Preferred Genre(s): Plays.
Preferred Length: Full-length.
Submission Materials: Query, synopsis,
sample, full script.

**Performance Network Theatre**
120 E. Huron St., Ann Arbor, MI 48104
David Wolber, Artistic Dir.
Tel: (734) 663-0696
Fax:(734) 663-7396
www.performancenetwork.org
Est. 1981. Production: cast limit 10, no
fly. Response: 6 mos. Preferred
Genre(s): Plays. Preferred Length:
Full-length. Submission Materials:
Synopsis, 10-pg sample, SASE.

**Philadelphia Theatre Company (PTC)**
230 S. Broad St., Ste. 1105, Philadelphia,
PA 19102
Jacqueline Goldfinger, Literary Manager
Tel: (215) 985-1400
Fax:(215) 985-5800
jgoldfinger@philadelphiatheatrecompany.org
www.philadelphiatheatrecompany.org
Est. 1974. Agent submissions or local
writers only. 4 contemporary US
plays/season (Sep-July). Production:
cast limit 10. Response: 6 mos. to 1

year. Preferred Genre(s): Musical
theatre. Preferred Length: Full-length.
Submission Materials: Complete script.

**Phoenix Arts Association Theatre [CA]**
414 Mason St. #601, New York, NY
94102
Linda Ayres-Frederick
Tel: (415) 759-7696
Fax:(415) 664-5001
www.phoenixtheatresf.org
　　Est. 1985. NOTE: Due to economics,
we have taken a hiatus in 2011 from
receiving new scripts. Production: cast
limit 7, unit set. Response: 6 wks
query, 6 mos script. Preferred Genre(s):
Plays. Preferred Length: One-act or
Full-length.

**Phoenix Theatre [IN]**
749 N. Park Ave., Indianapolis, IN 46202
Bryan Fonseca, Literary Manager
Tel: (317) 635-7529
bfonseca@phoenixtheatre.org
www.phoenixtheatre.org
　　Est. 1983. Production: cast limit 6.
Response: 6 mos. Preferred Length:
One-act or Full-length. Submission
Materials: Query, synopsis, sample,
SASE.

**Pier One Theatre**
Box 894, Homer, AK 99603
Lance Petersen, Artistic Director
Tel: (907) 235-7333
Fax:(907) 235-7333
info@pieronetheatre.net
www.pieronetheatre.org
　　Est. 1973. Non-Equity community
theater. Response: 6 mos. Preferred
Genre(s): Plays or Musicals. Preferred
Length: Full-length. Submission
Materials: Complete script & SASE.

**Pillsbury House Theatre**
3501 Chicago Ave. S., Minneapolis, MN
55407
Neal Spinler
Tel: (612) 825-0459
Fax:(612) 827-5818
theatre@pillsburyhousetheatre.org
www.pillsburyhousetheatre.org
　　Est. 1992. Submit by invitation only.
Production: cast limit 10. Response: 5
mos query, 6 mos script. Preferred

Genre(s): Plays. Preferred Length:
Full-length. Submission Materials:
Agent only submissions.

**Pioneer Theatre Company**
300 South 1400 East, #205, Salt Lake
City, UT 84112
Elizabeth Williamson, Literary Manager
Tel: (801) 581-6356
Fax:(801) 581-5472
elizabeth.williamson@PTC.utah.edu
www.pioneertheatre.org
　　Est. 1962. Response: 1 mo query, 6
mos script. Preferred Genre(s): Plays.
Preferred Length: Full-length.
Submission Materials: Agent only
submissions.

**Pittsburgh Public Theater**
621 Penn Ave., Pittsburgh, PA 15222
Margie Romero, Communications
Manager
Tel: (412) 316-8200
Fax:(412) 316-8216
mromero@ppt.org
www.ppt.org
　　Est. 1975. Not accepting submissions
at this time.

**Plan-B Theatre Company**
138 W. 300 S., Salt Lake City, UT 84101
Jerry Rapier, Producing Director
Tel: (801) 297-4200
Fax:(801) 466-3840
jerry@planbtheatre.org
www.planbtheatre.org
　　Est. 1995. Submit script via email in
PDF format. Preference given to work
by UT playwrights. Production: cast
limit 5, minimal set. Response: 3 mos.
Preferred Genre(s): Plays. Preferred
Length: One-Act. Submission
Materials: Complete script & SASE.

**Play With Your Food**
PO Box 2161, Westport, CT 06880
Carole Schweid
Tel: (203) 247-4083
carole@playwithyourfood.org
www.playwithyourfood.org
　　Looking for first rate one-act plays for
popular lunchtime play-reading series.
Preferred Genre(s): Plays. Preferred

Length: One-Act. Submission
Materials: Complete script.

**Playhouse on the Square**
51 S. Cooper St., Memphis, TN 38104
Jackie Nichols, Executive Producer
Tel: (901) 725-0776
www.playhouseonthesquare.org
  Est. 1968. No longer accepting
  submissions.

**Playwrights Horizons**
416 W. 42nd St., New York, NY 10036
Adam Greenfield, Director, New Play
  Development
Tel: (212) 564-1235
Fax:(212) 594-0296
literary@playwrightshorizons.org
www.playwrightshorizons.org
  Est. 1971. Offering 6
  productions/season and numerous
  readings to new American voices. See
  website for material preferences.
  Production: cast limit 10. Response: 6
  mos for plays; 9 mos for musicals.
  Preferred Genre(s): Plays or Musicals.
  Preferred Length: Full-length.
  Submission Materials: Full Script,
  audio, bio, SASE.

**Playwrights Theatre of New Jersey**
Box 1295, Madison, NJ 07940
Peter Hays, Director New Play
  Development
Tel: (973) 514-1787
Fax:(973) 514-2060
phays@ptnj.org
www.ptnj.org
  Est. 1986. Works accepted through
  New Play Development Program.
  Production: ages 10 and above; casts
  up to 6. Response: 1 year. Preferred
  Genre(s): Plays. Preferred Length:
  Full-length. Submission Materials:
  Synopsis, sample, SASE.

**Playwrights/Actors Contemporary
Theatre (PACT)**
105 W. 13th St., #5-G, New York, NY
  10011
Juel Wiese, Managing Director
Tel: (212) 242-5888
Fax:(212) 242-5888
juelwiese@msn.com

Production: cast of up to 8, unit set.
Preferred Genre(s): Comedy.

**Polarity Ensemble Theatre**
135 Asbury Ave., Evanston, IL 60202
Richard Engling
Tel: (847) 475-1139
richard@petheatre.com
www.petheatre.com
  Visit our website and register on our
  auditions list to be notified when we
  accept/read scripts. Preferred Genre(s):
  Plays. Preferred Length: Full-length.
  Submission Materials: Complete script.

**Poplar Pike Playhouse (PPP)**
7653 Old Poplar Pike, Germantown, TN
  38138
Frank Bluestein, Director
Tel: (901) 755-7775
Fax:(901) 755-6951
elfbluestein@gmail.com
www.ppp.org
  Est. 1976. Occasionally produce
  original work. Production: ages 14-19,
  full orchestra. Response: 3 mos.
  Preferred Genre(s): Plays or Musicals.
  Special Interest: Theatre for Young
  Audiences. Preferred Length: Any
  length. Submission Materials:
  Complete script, SASE.

**Porchlight Music Theatre Chicago**
2814 N. Lincoln Ave., Chicago, IL 60657
L. Walter Stearns, Artistic Director
Tel: (773) 325-9884
info@porchlighttheatre.com
www.porchlighttheatre.com
  Est. 1994. Response: 6 mos. Preferred
  Genre(s): Musical theatre. Preferred
  Length: Full-length. Submission
  Materials: Synopsis, bio, audio, SASE.

**Portland Center Stage [OR]**
128 NW 11th Ave., Portland, OR 97209
Kelsey Tyler, Literary Director
Tel: (503) 445-3793
Fax:(503) 445-3721
kelseyt@pcs.org
www.pcs.org
  Est. 1988. At this time, not accepting
  unsolicited script submission for
  general season consideration. Preferred

Genre(s): All genres. Preferred Length:
Full-length. Submission Materials:
Query, sample, resume.

**Portland Stage Company [ME]**
PO Box 1458, Portland, ME 04104
Daniel Burson, Literary Manager
Tel: (207) 774-1043
Fax:(207) 774-0576
dburson@portlandstage.com
www.portlandstage.com
    Est. 1970. Response: 3 mos query, 6
    mos script. Preferred Genre(s): Plays.
    Preferred Length: Full-length.
    Submission Materials: Agent only
    submissions. Deadline(s): Rolling

**Premiere Stages at Kean University**
Hutchinson Hall, 1000 Morris Ave.,
    Union, NJ 7083
Tel: (908) 737-5526
Fax:(908) 737-4636
premiere@kean.edu
www.kean.edu/premierestages

**Primary Stages**
307 W. 38th St, #1510, New York, NY
    10018
Tessa LaNeve, Literary Manager
Tel: (212) 840-9705
Fax:(212) 840-9725
www.primarystages.org
    Est. 1984. Founded to produce new
    plays and develop playwrights.
    Response: 1 yr. Preferred Genre(s): All
    genres. Preferred Length: Full-length.
    Submission Materials: Agent only
    submissions.

**Prime Stage Theatre**
Box 99446, Pittsburgh, PA 15233
Wayne Brinda, Artistic Director
Tel: (724) 371-0447
wbrinda@primestage.com
www.primestage.com
    Literature based youth and adult
    theatre. Production: age 12 - senior
    citizen Preferred Genre(s): Adaptation.
    Special Interest: Theatre for Young
    Audiences. Preferred Length:
    Full-length. Submission Materials:
    Query, synopsis, 30-pg sample, SASE.

**Public Theater [NY]**
425 Lafayette St., New York, NY 10003
Liz Frankel, Literary Assoc
Tel: (212) 539-8530
Fax:(212) 539-8505
lfrankel@publictheater.org
www.publictheater.org
    Est. 1954. Response: 6 mos. Preferred
    Genre(s): Plays or Musicals. Preferred
    Length: Full-length. Submission
    Materials: Query, synopsis and 10-pg
    sample.

**Puerto Rican Traveling Theatre**
304 W. 47th St., New York, NY 10036
Allen Davis, Playwrights Unit Supervisor
Tel: (212) 354-1293
Fax:(212) 307-6769
allen@prtt.org
www.prtt.org
    est. 1977.
    Readings/workshops/productions for
    beginning and professional playwrights.
    Prefer author to be Latino/minority.
    Preferred Genre(s): All genres. Special
    Interest: Latino. Preferred Length:
    Full-length. Submission Materials:
    Complete script, SASE.

**Pulse Ensemble Theatre**
266 W 37th St., Fl. 22, New York, NY
    10018
Alexa Kelly, Artistic Director
Tel: (212) 695-1596
Fax:(212) 594-4208
theatre@pulseensembletheatre.org
www.pulseensembletheatre.org
    Est. 1989. Only developing new works
    in Playwrights' Lab. Response: up to 1
    year. Preferred Genre(s): Plays.
    Preferred Length: Full-length.
    Submission Materials: Synopsis, 10-pg
    sample, SASE.

**Purple Rose Theatre Company**
137 Park St., Chelsea, MI 48118
Guy Sanville, Artistic Director
Tel: (734) 433-7782
Fax:(734) 475-0802
info@purplerosetheatre.org
www.purplerosetheatre.org
    Est. 1991. Prefer comedy. Must be
    unoptioned/unpublished/unproduced.

Production: ages 18-80, cast of 2-10.
Response: 8 mos. Preferred Genre(s):
Plays. Preferred Length: Full-length.
Submission Materials: Synopsis, 15-pg
sample, character breakdowns, SASE.

**Queens Theatre in the Park**
Box 520069, Flushing, NY 11352
Rob Urbinati, Director, New Play
  Development
Tel: (718) 760-0064
Fax:(718) 760-1972
urbinati@aol.com
www.queenstheatre.org
  Est. 2001. New play development
  series. Production: cast limit 6.
  Response: 6 mos. Preferred Genre(s):
  All genres. Preferred Length:
  Full-length. Submission Materials: See
  website.

**Rainbow Dinner Theatre**
3065 Lincoln Hwy East, Box 56,
  Paradise, PA 17562
David DiSavino, Executive Producer
Tel: (717) 687-4300
Fax:(717) 687-8280
david@rainbowdinnertheatre.com
www.rainbowdinnertheatre.com
  Est. 1984. Professional non-Equity
  dinner theater. Production: ages 18 and
  older, cast of 2-12, set limit 2.
  Response: 6 mos. Preferred Genre(s):
  Plays. Preferred Length: Full-length.
  Submission Materials: Synopsis,
  sample, SASE.

**Rattlestick Playwrights Theatre**
244 Waverly Pl., New York, NY 10014
Lou Moreno, Associate Artistic Director
Tel: (212) 627-2556
Fax:(630) 839-8352
info@rattlestick.org
www.rattlestick.org
  Yearlong development program,
  culminating in annual spring Exposure
  Fest. Production: cast of up to 8.
  Preferred Genre(s): All genres.
  Preferred Length: Full-length.
  Submission Materials: See website.

**Red Bull Theater**
Literary Submission, P.O. Box 250863,
  New York, NY 10025
Red Bull Theatre, Literary Submissions
Tel: (212) 414-5168
info@redbulltheater.com
www.redbulltheater.com
  Est. 2003. Interested in new full-length
  plays and adaptations that relate to our
  mission of exploring Jacobean
  themes/heightened language. US mail
  only. Response: six mos. Preferred
  Genre(s): Plays or Musicals. Preferred
  Length: One-act or Full-length.
  Submission Materials: See website.

**Repertorio Espanol**
138 E. 27th St., New York, NY 10016
Robert Federico, Executive Director
Tel: (212) 889-2850
Fax:(212) 225-9085
info@repertorio.org
www.repertorio.org
  Est. 1968. Production: small cast.
  Response: 6 mos. Preferred Genre(s):
  Plays or Musicals. Preferred Length:
  One-act or Full-length. Submission
  Materials: Query and synopsis only.

**Riverside Theatre [FL]**
3250 Riverside Park Dr., Vero Beach, FL
  32963
Allen D. Cornell, Artistic Director
Tel: (772) 231-5860
Fax:(772) 234-5298
www.riversidetheatre.com
  Est. 1985. Production: cast limit 10.
  Preferred Genre(s): Plays or Musicals.
  Special Interest: Theatre for Young
  Audiences. Preferred Length:
  Full-length. Submission Materials:
  Query and synopsis only.

**Riverside Theatre [IA]**
213 N. Gilbert St., Iowa City, IA 52245
Jody Hovland, Artistic Director
Tel: (319) 887-1360
Fax:(319) 887-1362
artistic@riversidetheatre.org
www.riversidetheatre.org
  Est. 1981. Also accepts submissions for
  annual monologue Festival. Production:
  small cast, simple set. Response only if

interested. Preferred Genre(s): Plays or Musicals. Preferred Length: Full-length. Submission Materials: Synopsis, first 10pgs, bio.

**Round House Theatre**
Box 30688, Bethesda, MD 20824
Tel: (240) 644-1099
Fax:(240) 644-1090
productionstaff@roundhousetheatre.org
www.roundhousetheatre.org
   Est. 1978. Literary Works Project in Bethesda, and New Works Series in Silver Spring. Production: cast limit 8, piano only, unit set. Response: 2 mos query, 1 yr script. Preferred Genre(s): All genres. Preferred Length: Any length. Submission Materials: Query letter only.

**Royal Court Theatre**
Sloane Sq., London, SW1W 8AS United Kingdom
www.royalcourttheatre.com
   Est. 1956. Production /development for both international writers and young writers. See website for details. US mail material only. Preferred Genre(s): All genres. Preferred Length: Full-length. Submission Materials: Synopsis, SASE.

**Salt Lake Acting Company**
168 West 500 North, Salt Lake City, UT 84103
Jason Bruffy, Aristic Director
Tel: (801) 363-7522
Fax:(801) 532-8513
jbruffy@saltlakeactingcompany.org
www.saltlakeactingcompany.org
   Est. 1970. SLAC works w/writers to workshop new pieces and produces new works (plays/musicals/adaptations). Preferred Genre(s): Plays or Musicals. Preferred Length: One-act or Full-length. Submission Materials: Query, synopsis, 20pg sample, bio.

**San Diego Repertory Theatre**
79 Horton Plz., San Diego, CA 92101-6144
Angela Rasbeary
Tel: (619) 231-3586
Fax:(619) 235-0939
arasbeary@sdrep.org
www.sdrep.org
   Est. 1976. Preferred Genre(s): All genres. Preferred Length: Full-length. Submission Materials: Complete script.

**Santa Monica Playhouse**
1211 4th St., Suite #201, Santa Monica, CA 90401
Cydne Moore, Dramaturg
Tel: (310) 394-9779
Fax:(310) 393-5573
theatre@SantaMonicaPlayhouse.com
www.santamonicaplayhouse.com
   Est. 1960. Production: cast limit 10. Response: 9 mos query, 12 mos script. Preferred Genre(s): Plays. Preferred Length: Full-length. Submission Materials: Query, synopsis and 10-pg sample, resume.

**Seacoast Repertory Theatre**
125 Bow St., Portsmouth, NH 03801
Craig Faulkner, Artistic Director
Tel: (603) 433-4793
Fax:(603) 431-7818
craig@seacoastrep.org
www.seacoastrep.org
   Est. 1986. Offers 8 mainstage and 6 youth works each year. Submissions must be unoptioned. Response: 6 mos. Preferred Genre(s): All genres. Special Interest: Theatre for Young Audiences. Preferred Length: Any length. Submission Materials: Synopsis, sample, SASE.

**Seattle Repertory Theatre**
155 Mercer St., Box 900923, Seattle, WA 98109
Braden Abraham, Literary Manager
Tel: (206) 443-2210
Fax:(206) 443-2379
bradena@seattlerep.org
www.seattlerep.org
   Est. 1963. 8-9 plays/yr on 2 proscenium stages: 850-seat Bagley

Wright; 300-seat Leo K. Staff:
Response: 6 mos. Preferred Genre(s):
Plays. Preferred Length: One-act or
Full-length. Submission Materials:
Complete script & SASE.

**Second Stage Theatre**
305 W. 43rd St., New York, NY 10036
Sarah Steele, Literary Manager
Tel: (212) 787-8302
Fax:(212) 397-7066
ssteele@2st.com
www.2st.com
Est. 1979. 2 Off-Broadway theaters, 6
shows per season; work featuring
heightened realism and sociopolitical
issues. Response : 1 mo query, 6 mos
script. Preferred Genre(s): Plays or
Musicals. Preferred Length:
Full-length. Submission Materials:
Agent only submissions.

**Seventh Street Playhouse, LLC**
PO Box 15414, Washington, DC 20003
Anthony Gallo, Producing Director
Tel: (202) 544-6973
seventheatre@verizon.net
webspace.webring.com/people/ta/agallo2368/
Email unpublished submissions only.
Prior professional recommendations
only. Preferred Genre(s): Plays.
Preferred Length: One-act or Full-
length. Submission Materials: Synopsis
and 10-pg sample.

**Shadowlight Productions**
22 Chattanooga St., San Francisco, CA
94114
Larry Reed, Artistic Director
Tel: (415) 648-4461
Fax:(415) 641-9734
info@shadowlight.org
www.shadowlight.org
Est. 1972. Production: cast limit 15.
Response: 1 mo. Preferred Genre(s):
Plays. Preferred Length: Full-length.
Submission Materials: See website.

**Shakespeare & Company**
70 Kemble St., Lenox, MA 01240
Tony Simotes, Artistic Director
Tel: (413) 637-1199 Ext 111
Fax:(413) 637-4274
tsimotes@shakespeare.org
www.shakespeare.org

Est. 1978. Not accepting submissions
at this time. Production: cast of 2-8.
Response: 3 mos. Preferred Genre(s):
Plays. Preferred Length: Full-length.
Submission Materials: Query, synopsis,
10-pg sample & SASE.

**Shakespeare Theatre Company**
516 8th St. SE, Washington, DC 20003-
2834
Akiva Fox, Literary Associate
Tel: (202) 547-3230
Fax:(202) 547-0226
afox@shakespearetheatre.org
www.shakespearetheatre.org
Est. 1986. Classical theatre dedicated
to works of Shakespeare and other
classical writers in new translations and
adaptations. Preferred Genre(s): Plays.
Preferred Length: Full-length.
Submission Materials: Query letter and
S.A.S.E..

**Shotgun Productions Inc.**
165 E. 35 St., #7-J, New York, NY 10016
Patricia Klausner, Managing Director
Tel: (212) 689-2322
Fax:(212) 689-2322
literary@shotgun-productions.org
www.shotgun-productions.org
Est. 1989. 3-step development, incl.
staged readings, workshops and full
productions for unoptioned/unproduced
work. Response: 1 yr. Preferred
Genre(s): Plays. Preferred Length:
One-act or Full-length. Submission
Materials: Query and synopsis only.

**Signature Theatre Company [NY]**
630 9th Ave., #1106, New York, NY
10036
Kirsten Bowen, Literary Associate
Tel: (212) 967-1913
Fax:(212) 967-2957
kbowen@signaturetheatre.org
www.signaturetheatre.org
Est. 1990. Premieres and revivals
produced in a season of work by
current and past playwrights in
residence. Submission Materials: See
website.

**SignStage**
11206 Euclid Ave., Cleveland, OH 44106
William Morgan, Artistic
  Director/Producer
Tel: (216) 231-8787
Fax:(216) 231-7141
wmorgan@chsc.org
www.signstage.org
  Est. 1975. In-school residencies,
  educational performances about deaf
  awareness. Response only if interested.
  Special Interest: Deaf. Submission
  Materials: Synopsis, SASE.

**Silk Road Theatre Project**
680 S. Federal, Ste 301, Chicago, IL
  60605
Jamil Khoury
Tel: (312) 857-1234 Ext 202
Fax:(312) 577-0849
jamil@srtp.org
www.srtp.org
  We accept full-length scripts only by
  US mail. Work must be from
  playwrights and about protagonists of
  Asian, Middle Eastern, and
  Mediterranean descent. Preferred
  Genre(s): Plays. Special Interest:
  Multi-Ethnic. Preferred Length:
  One-Act. Submission Materials: Query,
  synopsis and 15-pg sample.

**Six Figures Theatre Company**
Box 88, Planetarium Sta., New York, NY
  10024
Loren Ingrid Noveck, Literary Manager
Tel: (212) 946-1737
info@sixfigures.com
www.sixfigures.com
  Not accepting submissions at this time.
  Preferred Genre(s): Musical theatre.
  Preferred Length: Full-length.
  Submission Materials: See website.

**Society Hill Playhouse**
507 S. 8th St., Philadelphia, PA 19147
Deen Kogan
Tel: (215) 923-0210
Fax:(215) 923-1789
shp@erols.com
www.societyhillplayhouse.org
  Submit by US mail only. Production:
  cast of up to 8. Response: 3 mos.

Preferred Genre(s): Plays. Preferred
Length: Full-length. Submission
Materials: Query letter and S.A.S.E..

**SoHo Repertory Theatre Inc.**
86 Franklin St, Fl. 4, New York, NY
  10013
Sarah Benson, Artistic Dir.
Tel: (212) 941-8632
Fax:(212) 941-7148
sohorep@sohorep.org
www.sohorep.org
  Est. 1975. Seeking writers working on
  contemporary plays who are available
  to meet in NYC twice a month.
  Preferred Genre(s): Contemporary.
  Preferred Length: Any length.
  Submission Materials: See website.

**Sonoma County Repertory Theater**
104 N. Main St., Sebastopol, CA 95472
Scott O. Phillips
Tel: (707) 823-0177
the-rep.com
  Est. 1993. Preferred Genre(s): All
  genres. Preferred Length: Full-length.
  Submission Materials: Synopsis, full
  script, cast list, SASE.

**South Coast Repertory Theatre**
Box 2197, Costa Mesa, CA 92628
South Coast Lit Mgr, Literary Manager
Tel: (714) 708-5500
john@scr.org
www.scr.org
  Est. 1964. Mainstage programming,
  family programming, reading series,
  playwrights new work fest. Response:
  2 mos query; 6 mos script. Preferred
  Genre(s): Plays or Musicals. Preferred
  Length: Full-length. Submission
  Materials: Query, synopsis, sample,
  SASE.

**Stage One: The Louisville Children's
Theater**
323 W. Broadway, Suite #609, Louisville,
  KY 40202
Peter Holloway, Artistic Director
Tel: (502) 498-2436
Fax:(502) 588-4344
stageone@stageone.org
www.stageone.org

Est. 1946. Classic and contemporary tales of childhood with strong social and emotional content. Production: cast limit 12, touring set. Response: 3 mos. Preferred Genre(s): Plays or Musicals. Special Interest: Theatre for Young Audiences. Preferred Length: Any length. Submission Materials: Query, sample.

**Stages Repertory Theatre [TX]**
3201 Allen Pkwy., #101, Houston, TX 77019
Tel: (713) 527-0220
Fax:(713) 527-8669
www.stagestheatre.com
Est. 1978. Production cast limit: 6. Response: 9 mos. Preferred Genre(s): Plays. Preferred Length: Full-length. Submission Materials: Complete script.

**Stages Theatre Company [MN]**
1111 Main St., Hopkins, MN 55343
Bruce Rowan, Mgr, New Play Development
Tel: (952) 979-1120
Fax:(952) 979-1124
brow@stagestheatre.org
www.stagestheatre.org
Est. 1984. Material must be 60 - 70 min. Production: ages 10-21 in primary roles. Response: 3 mos. Preferred Genre(s): Plays. Special Interest: Theatre for Young Audiences. Preferred Length: One-Act. Submission Materials: Query, synopsis, full script, SASE.

**Stageworks/Hudson [NY]**
41-A Cross St., Hudson, NY 12534
Laura Margolis, Executive Artistic Director
Tel: (518) 828-7843
Fax:(518) 828-4026
contact@stageworkstheater.org
www.stageworkstheater.org
Est. 1993. Production: cast limit 8, unit set, no fly. Response: 8 mos. Preferred Genre(s): Adaptation. Preferred Length: Full-length. Submission Materials: Query and synopsis only.

**Statement Productions**
Box 496, Kittredge, CO 80457
Robin Freeman, Artistic Director
Tel: (303) 670-8397
Fax:(303) 670-1897
freerobbie@aol.com
Not accepting work at this time. Usually, productions mostly of 2-women plays. Production: age 30-50, cast of up to 10. Response: 90 days. Preferred Genre(s): Musical theatre. Preferred Length: Any length. Submission Materials: Complete script & SASE.

**Steppenwolf Theatre Company**
758 W. North Ave., 4th Fl., Chicago, IL 60610
Joy Meads, Director, New Play Development
Tel: (312) 335-1888
Fax:(312) 335-0808
theatre@steppenwolf.org
www.steppenwolf.org
Est. 1976. Actor's collective performing in three spaces. Production: cast limit 10. Response: 6-8 mos. Preferred Genre(s): Plays. Preferred Length: Full-length. Submission Materials: Query, synopsis, sample, resume.

**Sundog Theatre**
Box 10183, Staten Island, NY 10301
Susan Fenley, Artistic Director
Tel: (718) 816-5453
sfenley@sundogtheatre.org
www.SundogTheatre.org
SI Series: looking for six 12 - 20 minute unproduced/unoptioned plays with Staten Island Ferry as setting. Full Length work: cast of 2-10, orchestra limit 4, minimal set. Preferred Genre(s): Plays or Musicals. Preferred Length: Any length. Submission Materials: See website. Deadline(s): 1/18/2011, 12/15/2011

**Sweetwood Productions**
3406 Riva Ridge Rd., Austin, TX 78746
Pat Hazell, Chief Creative Officer
Tel: (512) 383-9498
Fax:(512) 383-1680
pat@sweetwoodproductions.com
www.sweetwoodproductions.com
　　Not accepting submissions at this time.

**Synchronicity Performance Group**
Box 6012, Atlanta, GA 31107
Rachel May, Producing Artistic Director
Tel: (404) 523-1009
Fax:(404) 325-5168
www.synchrotheatre.com
　　Est. 1997. Dedicated to strong women
　　characters, scripts with depth, meaning
　　and social content and powerful stories.
　　Production: cast limit 12, no fly.
　　Response only if interested. Preferred
　　Genre(s): No musicals. Preferred
　　Length: Full-length. Submission
　　Materials: Query, synopsis, sample,
　　SASE.

**Syracuse Stage**
820 E. Genesee St., Syracuse, NY 13210
Kyle Bass, Dramaturg
Tel: (315) 443-4008
Fax:(315) 443-9846
kebass@syr.edu
www.syracusestage.org
　　Est. 1974. Production: small cast
　　Preferred Genre(s): Plays. Preferred
　　Length: Full-length. Submission
　　Materials: Agent only submissions.

**TADA! Youth Theater**
15 W 28th St, Fl. 3, New York, NY
　10001
Emmanuel Wilson, Artistic
　　Assoc./Literary Mgr.
Tel: (212) 252-1619
Fax:(212) 252-8763
jgreer@tadatheater.com
www.tadatheater.com
　　Est. 1984. Production: teenage cast
　　(limit 2 adults). Response: 6 mos.
　　Preferred Genre(s): Musical theatre.
　　Special Interest: Theatre for Young
　　Audiences. Preferred Length:
　　Full-length. Submission Materials: See
　　website.

**Teatro Vista**
3712 N Broadway, #275, Chicago, IL
　60613
Sandra Marquez, Associate
Tel: (312) 666-4659
Fax:(312) 666-4659
info@teatrovista.org
www.teatrovista.org
　　We focus on works by, about or for
　　Latinos. Preferred Genre(s): Plays or
　　Musicals. Special Interest: Latino.
　　Preferred Length: Full-length.
　　Submission Materials: Synopsis,
　　character breakdown.

**Tectonic Theater Project**
204 W 84th St, New York, NY 10024
Jimmy Maize, Literary Manager
Tel: (212) 579-6111
Fax:(212) 579-6112
literary@tectonictheaterproject.org
www.tectonictheaterproject.org
　　Est. 1992. Lab led by Moises
　　Kaufman. Response: 1 month.
　　Preferred Genre(s): All genres.
　　Preferred Length: Full-length.
　　Submission Materials: Synopsis, full
　　script, SASE.

**Ten Grand Productions**
123 E 24th Street, New York, NY 10010
Jason Hewitt, Managing Director
Tel: (212) 253-2058
Fax:(917) 591-9398
jhewitt@tengrand.org
www.tengrand.org
　　Est. 2003. Preferred Genre(s): Drama.
　　Preferred Length: Full-length.
　　Submission Materials: Sample (20pg),
　　SASE.

**Tennessee Repertory Theatre**
161 Rains Ave., Nashville, TN 37203
Rene D. Copeland, Prod. Artistic Director
Tel: (615) 244-4878
Fax:(615) 782-4001
www.tennesseerep.org
　　Est. 1985. Production: small cast, small
　　orchestra. Response: 1 yr. Preferred
　　Genre(s): Plays or Musicals. Preferred
　　Length: Full-length. Submission
　　Materials: See website.

**The Bridge Theatre Company**
244 W. 54th St., 12th Fl., New York, NY
10019
Esther Barlow
Tel: (212) 246-6655
www.thebridgetheatrecompany.com
Development through reading,
workshops, moving towards off-off
Broadway production. Author must be
Canadian or the work about Canada in
some way. Preferred Genre(s): Plays.
Preferred Length: One-act or Full-
length. Submission Materials: Query,
synopsis and 10-pg sample.

**The Ensemble Theatre [TX]**
3535 Main St., Houston, TX 77002
Eileen J. Morris, Artistic Director
Tel: (713) 807-4316
Fax:(713) 520-1269
ejmorris@ensemblehouston.com
www.ensemblehouston.com
Est. 1976. Produces contemporary and
classical works devoted to the portrayal
of the African-American experience.
Production: cast limit 5, touring set.
Response: 3 mos. Preferred Genre(s):
Plays or Musicals. Special Interest:
African-American. Preferred Length:
One-act or Full-length. Submission
Materials: Query, synopsis, sample,
audio, resume, SASE. Deadline(s):
March , April

**The Lark Theatre Company**
939 8th Ave., #301, New York, NY
10019
Miles Lott, Literary Manager
Tel: (212) 246-2676
Fax:(212) 246-2609
submissions@larktheatre.org
www.larktheatre.org
Preferred Genre(s): All genres.
Preferred Length: Full-length.
Submission Materials: See website.

**The New Group**
410 W. 42nd St., New York, NY 10036
Ian Morgan, Assoc Artistic Director
Tel: (212) 244-3380
Fax:(212) 244-3438
info@thenewgroup.org
www.thenewgroup.org

Est. 1991. Workshops and readings. US
mail submissions only. Response: 2
mos for samples, 9 mos for full scripts.
Preferred Genre(s): Plays. Preferred
Length: Full-length. Submission
Materials: See website.

**The Pearl Theatre Company, Inc.**
307 West 38th St., Suite 1805, New York,
NY 10018
Kate Farrington, Asst. to Artistic Director
Tel: (212) 505-3401
Fax:(212) 505-3404
kfarrington@pearltheatre.org
www.pearltheatre.org
Est. 1982. Focusing on classical
adaptations/translations or based on
classical themes/characters only.
Production: age 18-75, cast size 6-13, 1
set. Response: 4-6 mos. Preferred
Genre(s): Adaptation. Preferred
Length: One-act or Full-length.
Submission Materials: Character
breakdowns, synopsis.

**The York Shakespeare Company**
Box 720, JAF Sta., New York, NY 10116
Seth Duerr, Artistic Director
Tel: (646) 623-7117
Fax:(866) 380-7510
www.yorkshakespeare.org
Est. 2001. Seeking Classical-oriented,
unoptioned work. Need professional
recommendation. Preferred Genre(s):
Plays. Preferred Length: Full-length.
Submission Materials: Complete script.

**Theater at Monmouth**
Box 385, Monmouth, ME 04259
David Greenham, Producing Director
Tel: (207) 933-2952
Fax:(207) 933-2952
TAMOffice@TheaterAtMonmouth.org
www.theateratmonmouth.org
Est. 1970. Only adaptations of popular
classics for adults and children.
Response: 2 mos. Preferred Genre(s):
Plays. Special Interest: Theatre for
Young Audiences. Preferred Length:
One-act or Full-length. Submission
Materials: Query and synopsis only.

**Theater Breaking Through Barriers**
306 W. 18th St. #3A, New York, NY
  10011
Ike Schambelan, Co-Artistic Director
Tel: (212) 243-4337
Fax:(212) 243-4337
ischambelan@nyc.rr.com
www.tbtb.org
  Est. 1979. Work must be about
  disability or by a disabled writer.
  Production: cast of 1-6. Response: 2
  mos. Preferred Genre(s): All genres.
  Special Interest: Disabled. Preferred
  Length: Any length. Submission
  Materials: Complete script & SASE.

**Theater for the New City (TFNC)**
155 1st Ave., New York, NY 10003
Crystal Field, Executive Artistic Director
Tel: (212) 254-1109
Fax:(212) 979-6570
crystalfield@theaterforthenewcity.net
www.theaterforthenewcity.net
  Est. 1970. Experimental new works.
  Preferred Genre(s): Experimental.
  Preferred Length: Any length.
  Submission Materials: Synopsis, 10-pg
  sample, SASE.

**Theater IV**
114 Broad St., Richmond, VA 23220
Janine Serresseque
Tel: (804) 783-1688
TheatreIVandBarksdale@gmail.com
www.theatreiv.org
  Est. 1975. Fairy tales, folk tales, fables,
  history, African American history,
  safety, outreach, science. Production:
  cast of 3-5, touring set. Audience:
  Grades K - 12. Response: 2 mos query,
  2 yrs script. Preferred Genre(s): Plays
  or Musicals. Special Interest: Theatre
  for Young Audiences. Preferred
  Length: One-Act. Submission
  Materials: Query and synopsis only.

**Theater J**
1529 16th St. NW, Washington, DC
  20036
Shirley Serotsky, Artistic Director
Tel: (202) 777-3228
Fax:(202) 518-9421
shirleys@washingtondcjcc.org
www.theaterj.org
  Est. 1991. Offers readings, workshops,
  and productions of work that celebrates
  the distinctive urban voice and social
  vision of the Jewish culture. Response:
  6 mos. Preferred Genre(s): Plays or
  Musicals. Preferred Length:
  Full-length. Submission Materials:
  Synopsis and 10-pg sample.

**Theater of the First Amendment, First
Light Discovery Progra**
George Mason University, 4400
  University Dr., MS 3E6, Fairfax, VA
  22030
Suzanne Maloney, Asst Dramaturg
Tel: (703) 993-2195
Fax:(703) 993-2191
smaloney@gmu.edu
www.theateroffirstamendment.org
  New play developmental workshops
  and readings throughout the year.
  Response: 2 wks query, 6 mos script.
  Preferred Genre(s): Plays. Preferred
  Length: Full-length. Submission
  Materials: Query, sample . Deadline(s):
  Nov. 15, 2011

**Theatre at the Center / Lawrence Arts
Center**
940 New Hampshire St., Lawrence, KS
  66044
Ric Averill, Artistic Director
Tel: (785) 843-2787
Fax:(785) 843-6629
ricaverill@lawrenceartscenter.org
www.lawrenceartscenter.com
  Est. 1973. Submit by email.
  Production: cast limit 6 adults or 30
  youth. Response: 6 wks query, 3 mos
  script. Preferred Genre(s): Plays or
  Musicals. Special Interest: Theatre for
  Young Audiences. Preferred Length:
  Full-length. Submission Materials:
  Synopsis and 10-pg sample.

**Theatre for a New Audience**
154 Christopher St. #3-D, New York, NY
    10014
Jeffrey Horowitz, Artistic Director
Tel: (212) 229-2819
Fax:(212) 229-2911
info@tfana.org
www.tfana.org
    Submission Materials: See website.

**Theatre of Yugen**
2840 Mariposa St., San Francisco, CA
    94110
Jubilith Moore, Co-Artistic Director
Tel: (415) 621-0507
Fax:(415) 621-0223
www.theatreofyugen.org
    Est. 1978. Traditional and new works
    of East-West fusion primarily based on
    Noh forms. Preferred Genre(s):
    Experimental. Preferred Length:
    One-Act. Submission Materials: Query
    letter and S.A.S.E..

**Theatre Rhinoceros**
1360 Mission St. Ste #200, San
    Francisco, CA 94103
John Fisher, Executive Director
Tel: (415) 552-4100
Fax:(415) 558-9044
www.therhino.org
    Est. 1977. Response: 6 mos. Preferred
    Genre(s): Plays or Musicals. Special
    Interest: LGBT. Preferred Length:
    Full-length. Submission Materials:
    Agent only submissions.

**Theatreworks/USA [NY]**
151 W. 26th St., Fl. 7, New York, NY
    10001
Michael Alltop, Literary Manager
Tel: (212) 647-1100
Fax:(212) 924-5377
info@theatreworksusa.org
www.theatreworksusa.org
    Est. 1961. Production: age 20-50, cast
    of up to 6, piano only, touring set.
    Preferred Genre(s): All genres. Special
    Interest: Theatre for Young Audiences.
    Preferred Length: Full-length.
    Submission Materials: Agent only
    submissions.

**Touchstone Theatre**
321 E. 4th St., Bethlehem, PA 18015
Lisa Jordan, Producing Director
Tel: (610) 867-1689
lisa@touchstone.org
www.touchstone.org
    Est. 1981. We only accept proposals
    for collaborative work with movement-
    based company ensemble. Response: 8
    mos. Preferred Genre(s): Ensemble
    theatre. Submission Materials: Query
    letter only.

**Transport Group**
520 Eighth Ave., Ste. 305, New York, NY
    10018
Jack Cummings, Artistic Director
Tel: (212) 564-0333
Fax:(212) 564-0331
info@transportgroup.org
www.transportgroup.org
    Preferred Genre(s): All genres.
    Preferred Length: Any length.
    Submission Materials: See website.

**TriArts at the Sharon Playhouse**
Box 1187, Sharon, CT 06069
Michael Berkeley, Artistic Director
Tel: (860) 364-7469
Fax:(860) 364-8043
info@triarts.net
www.triarts.net
    Est. 1989. Submit between January -
    July. Production: no fly. Response: 2
    mos query, 6 mos. Preferred Genre(s):
    Plays or Musicals. Preferred Length:
    Any length. Submission Materials:
    Query, synopsis, audio. Deadline(s):
    January - July is best submission
    period

**Trinity Repertory Company**
201 Washington St., Providence, RI
    02903
Craig Watson, Literary Manager
Tel: (401) 351-4242
cwatson@trinityrep.com
www.trinityrep.com
    Est. 1964. Response: 4 mos. Preferred
    Genre(s): Plays. Preferred Length:
    Full-length. Submission Materials:
    Query, synopsis and 10-pg sample.

**Turtle Shell Productions**
300 W. 43rd St., #403, New York, NY
  10036
John Cooper
Tel: (646) 765-7670
lacoopster@aol.com
www.turtleshellproductions.com
  Preferred Genre(s): All genres.
  Preferred Length: Any length.
  Submission Materials: Complete script.
  Deadline(s): April 9, 2011

**Two River Theatre Company (TRTC)**
21 Bridge Ave., Red Bank, NJ 07701
Aaron Posner, Artistic Director
Tel: (732) 345-1400
Fax:(732) 345-1414
info@trtc.org
www.trtc.org
  Est. 1994. Does not accept unsolicited
  material. Preferred Genre(s):
  Adaptation.

**Valley Youth Theatre (VYT)**
807 N. 3rd St., Phoenix, AZ 85004
Bobb Cooper, Producing Artistic Director
Tel: (602) 253-8188 Ext 305
Fax:(602) 253-8282
bobb@vyt.com
www.vyt.com
  Est. 1989. Response: 2 wks query, 2
  mos script. Preferred Genre(s): Plays or
  Musicals. Special Interest: Theatre for
  Young Audiences. Preferred Length:
  Full-length. Submission Materials:
  Query, synopsis, audio.

**Victory Gardens Theater**
2257 N. Lincoln Ave., Chicago, IL 60614
Aaron Carter
Tel: (773) 549-5788
Fax:(773) 549-2779
acarter@victorygardens.org
www.victorygardens.org
  Est. 1974. 6 productions/season.
  Submissions Jan - June ONLY.
  Response: 6 mos. Preferred Genre(s):
  Plays. Preferred Length: Full-length.
  Submission Materials: See website.
  Deadline(s): January - June

**Victory Theatre Center**
3326 W. Victory Blvd., Burbank, CA
  91505
Maria Gobetti, Artistic Director
Tel: (818) 841-4404
Fax:(818) 841-6328
thevictory@mindspring.com
www.thevictorytheatrecenter.org
  Est. 1979. Incl. 99-seat Big Victory and
  50-seat Little Victory theaters.
  Production: unit set. Response: 1 yr.
  Preferred Genre(s): Plays or Musicals.
  Preferred Length: Full-length.
  Submission Materials: Complete script
  & SASE.

**Village Theatre**
303 Front St. N., Issaquah, WA 98027
Robb Hunt, Executive Producer
Tel: (425) 392-1942 Ext 113
Fax:(425) 391-3242
rhunt@villagetheatre.org
www.villagetheatre.org
  Est. 1979. Readings, workshops and
  productions of new musicals.
  Production: cast limit 20. Response: 6
  mos. Preferred Genre(s): Musical
  theatre. Preferred Length: One-act or
  Full-length. Submission Materials: Full
  Script, audio, SASE.

**Vineyard Theatre**
108 E. 15th St.., New York, NY 10003
Sarah Stern, Assoc Artistic Director
Tel: (212) 353-3366
Fax:(212) 353-3803
literary@vineyardtheatre.org
www.vineyardtheatre.org
  Est. 1981. Response: 1 yr query.
  Submissions not returned. Preferred
  Genre(s): All genres. Preferred Length:
  Full-length. Submission Materials:
  Query, synopsis, sample, audio,
  resume.

**Virginia Stage Company (VSC)**
Box 3770, Norfolk, VA 23514
Patrick Mullins, Artistic Assoc
Tel: (757) 627-6988
Fax:(757) 628-5958
pmullins@vastage.com
www.vastage.com

Est. 1979. Production: cast limit 8.
Response: 1 mo query, 6 mos script.
Preferred Genre(s): Plays. Preferred
Length: Full-length. Submission
Materials: Query and synopsis only.

**Vital Theatre Company**
2162 Broadway, Fl. 4, New York, NY
  10024
Kerry McGuire, Literary Manager
Tel: (212) 579-0528
Fax:(212) 579-0646
office@vitaltheatre.org
www.vitaltheatre.org
  Not accepting unsolicited scripts at this
  time.

**VS. Theatre Company**
Box 2293, Los Angeles, CA 91610
Johnny Clark, Artistic Director
Tel: (323) 816-2471
Fax:(323) 850-6045
www.vstheatre.org
  Est. 2003. Production: cast limit 6.
  Response: 6 mos. Preferred Genre(s):
  Plays. Preferred Length: Full-length.
  Submission Materials: Agent only
  submissions.

**Walnut Street Theatre**
825 Walnut St., Philadelphia, PA 19103
Beverly Elliott, Literary Manager
Tel: (215) 574-3550
Fax:(215) 574-3598
literary@walnutstreettheatre.org
www.walnutstreettheatre.org
  Est. 1809. Looking for scripts based on
  literature. Production: cast limit 4
  (studio), 14 (Mainstg play) or 20
  (Mainstg musical). Response: 3 mos
  query, 6 mos script. Preferred Genre(s):
  Plays or Musicals. Preferred Length:
  Full-length. Submission Materials: See
  website.

**Wellfleet Harbor Actors Theater**
Box 797, Wellfleet, MA 02667
Daniel Lombardo, Literary Manager
Tel: (508) 349-3011 Ext 107
Fax:(508) 349-9082
lombardo.what@gmail.com
www.what.org

Est. 1985. Cast size: 6 maximum.
Response: 3 mos query, 6 mos script.
Preferred Genre(s): Plays. Preferred
Length: Full-length. Submission
Materials: Synopsis, sample, bio.

**Western Stage**
156 Homestead Ave., Salinas, CA 93901
Jon Selover, Artistic Director
Tel: (831) 755-6987
Fax:(831) 755-6954
artistic@westernstage.com
www.westernstage.com
  Preferred Genre(s): Plays. Special
  Interest: Theatre for Young Audiences.
  Preferred Length: Full-length.
  Submission Materials: Query, synopsis,
  audio.

**Westport Arts Center**
51 Riverside Ave., Westport, CT 06880
Tel: (203) 222-7070
Fax:(203) 222-7999
www.westportartscenter.org
  Programs in visual and performing arts.
  Preferred Genre(s): All genres.
  Preferred Length: Any length.
  Submission Materials: See website.

**Westport Country Playhouse**
25 Powers Ct., Westport, CT 06880
David Kennedy, Artistic Dir.
Tel: (203) 227-5137
Fax:(203) 221-7482
www.westportplayhouse.org
  Est. 1931. Production: ages 12 and
  older, cast of 2-10, orchestra of 4-8.
  Response: 9 mos. Preferred Genre(s):
  Plays or Musicals. Preferred Length:
  Full-length. Submission Materials:
  Complete script & SASE.

**White Horse Theater Company**
205 3rd Ave., #6-N, New York, NY
  10003
Cyndy A. Marion, Producing Artistic
  Director
Tel: (212) 592-3706
cymarion@whitehorsetheater.com
www.whitehorsetheater.com
  Est. 2002. Work must be unproduced.
  Response: 4 mos. Preferred Genre(s):
  Plays. Preferred Length: Full-length.
  Submission Materials: See website.

**Williamstown Theatre Festival**
229 W. 42nd St., #801, New York, NY
  10036
Michael Ritchie, Producer
Tel: (212) 395-9090
Fax:(212) 395-9099
www.wtfestival.org
  Est. 1955. New Play Staged Reading
  Series offers 7 works/season. Preferred
  Genre(s): Plays. Preferred Length:
  Full-length. Submission Materials:
  Query letter and S.A.S.E..

**Wilma Theater**
265 S. Broad St., Philadelphia, PA 19107
Walter Bilderback, Dramaturg/Literary
  Manager
Tel: (215) 893-9456
Fax:(215) 893-0895
wcb@wilmatheater.org
www.wilmatheater.org
  Est. 1979. Highly theatrical, poetic,
  imaginative, politically evocative (not
  provocative), arousing, artful, bold,
  inventive. Production: cast limit 8.
  Response: 1 yr. Preferred Genre(s):
  Plays or Musicals. Preferred Length:
  Full-length. Submission Materials: See
  website.

**Woolly Mammoth Theatre Company**
641 D St. NW, Washington, DC 20004
Miriam Weisfeld, Director of New Play
  Development
Tel: (202) 289-2443
submissions@woollymammoth.net
www.woollymammoth.net
  Est. 1980. Production: cast limit 6.
  Response: 1 yr. Preferred Genre(s):
  Plays. Preferred Length: Full-length.
  Submission Materials: Query, synopsis
  and 10-pg sample.

**Writers' Theatre**
376 Park Ave., Glencoe, IL 60022
Jimmy McDermott, Artistic Asst
Tel: (847) 242-6001
Fax:(847) 242-6011
info@writerstheatre.org
www.writerstheatre.org

Est. 1992. Response: 6 mos. Preferred
Genre(s): Plays. Preferred Length:
Full-length. Submission Materials:
Synopsis, sample, SASE.

**Yale Repertory Theatre**
Box 208244, New Haven, CT 06520
Amy Boratko, Literary Manager
Tel: (203) 436-9098
literary.office@yale.edu
www.yalerep.org
  Est. 1965. Response: 2 mos query, 4
  mos script. Preferred Genre(s): Plays or
  Musicals. Preferred Length:
  Full-length. Submission Materials:
  Agent only submissions.

**Yangtze Repertory Theatre of America**
22 Howard St., #3-B, New York, NY
  10013
Dr. Joanna Chan, Artistic Director
Tel: (914) 941-7575
Fax:(914) 923-0733
joannawychan@juno.com
www.yangtze-rep-theatre.org
  Est. 1985. Opportunities incl.
  developmental reading series.
  Production: cast of 3-6, piano only.
  Submit via US mail. Response: 6 mos.
  Preferred Genre(s): Musical theatre.
  Preferred Length: Full-length.
  Submission Materials: Full Script,
  audio, SASE.

**York Theatre Company**
619 Lexington Ave., New York, NY
  10022
Tel: (212) 935-5820
Fax:(212) 832-0037
mail@yorktheatre.org
www.yorktheatre.org

## Theaters (Fee Charged)

**Attic Ensemble**
The Barrow Mansion, Jersey City, NJ
07302
Mary Anne Murphy
Tel: (201) 413-9200
www.atticensemble.org
Est. 1970. Production: cast 4-8,
character ages 15-65, unit set or
conceptual. Preferred Genre(s):
Comedy. Preferred Length: Full-length.
Submission Materials: Complete script
& SASE.

**Patrick's Cabaret**
3010 Minnesota Ave., Minneapolis, MN
55406
Patrick Scully, Artistic Dir.
Tel: (612) 724-6273
amy@patrickscabaret.org
www.patrickscabaret.org
Est. 1986. Primarily a rental house for
shared evenings of short works (up to
15 minutes). Production: all ages,cast
2-20, minimal sets. Response: 1 month
Preferred Genre(s): All genres.
Preferred Length: 15 min.. Submission
Materials: Query letter only.

**Teatro Dallas**
1331 Record Crossing Rd., Dallas, TX
75235
Cora Cordona
Tel: (214) 689-6492
Fax:(214) 670-3243
teatro@airmail.net
www.teatrodallas.org
Est. 1985. Work (in English or
Spanish) about Latino issues; priority

given to Latino or Iberian playwrights.
US mail. Production: cast limit 6, unit
set. Response if interested. Preferred
Genre(s): Plays. Special Interest:
Latino. Preferred Length: One-act or
Full-length. Submission Materials:
Query, synopsis, SASE. Deadline(s):
December 15th

**The Present Company**
520 Eighth Ave., #311, New York, NY
10018
Elena K. Holy, Artistic Director
Tel: (212) 279-4488
Fax:(212) 279-4466
info@presentcompany.org
www.fringenyc.org
Creators and producers of the New
York International Fringe Festival
featuring 200+ shows every August in
NYC. Preferred Genre(s): All genres.
Preferred Length: Any length.
Submission Materials: See website.
Deadline(s): February 14th, 2011

**Urban Stages**
555 8th Ave., New York, NY 10018
Frances Hill, Artistic Director
Tel: (212) 421-1380
Fax:(212) 421-1387
urbanstage@aol.com
www.urbanstages.org
Production: cast size 7 or less.
Response: 6 mos. Preferred Genre(s):
Plays. Preferred Length: Full-length.
Submission Materials: Query, synopsis,
sample, full script.

# Educational Opportunities

## Colleges and Universities

**Academy of Art University**
79 New Montgomery Street, San
Francisco, CA 94119
Tel: (800) 544-2787
Fax:(415) 618-6287
info@academyart.edu
www.academyart.edu
Rolling admissions. Undergraduate and
Graduate degree programs. Certificates,
Continuing Art Education, and Pre-
college programs available online and
on campus. Est. 1929. Fees: $670/unit
(undergrad), $770/unit (grad)

**Angelo State University (ASU)**
Box 10895, ASU Station, San Angelo,
76909
Bill Doll, Chair, Theater
Tel: (325) 942-2146 Ext 246
Fax:(325) 942-2033
bill.doll@angelo.edu
www.angelo.edu
Preferred Genre(s): Plays or Musicals.
Preferred Length: Full-length.
Submission Materials: Complete script.

**Arizona State University (ASU)**
School of Theatre and Film, Box 872002,
Tempe, AZ 85287
Guillermo Reyes, Head of Playwriting
Tel: (480) 965-0519
Fax:(480) 965-5351
Guillermo.Reyes@asu.edu
www.asu.edu/clas/english/creativewriting/
Fee: Yes.

**Artistic New Directions**
250 W. 90th St. #15G, New York, NY
10024
Kristine Niven
Tel: (212) 875-1857
www.artisticnewdirections.org
Summer Playwright's Retreat.
Preferred Genre(s): All genres. Fee:
Yes.

**Bard College**
Box 5000, Annandale-on-Hudson, NY
12504
JoAnne Akalaitis, Chair, Theater
Department
Tel: (845) 758-7957
rbangiola@bard.edu
www.bard.edu

**Bates College**
Schaeffer Theater, #302, Lewiston, ME
04238
Martin Andrucki, Chair, Theater/Rhetoric
Dept.
Tel: (207) 786-8294
mandruc@bates.edu
www.bates.edu

**Boston University**
855 Commonwealth Ave., #470, Boston,
MA 02215
Jim Petosa, Director, School of Theatre
Tel: (617) 353-3390
theatre@bu.edu
www.bu.edu/but
Fee: Yes.

**Bowling Green State University
(BGSU)**
338 South Hall, Bowling Green, OH
43403
Ronald E. Shields, Chair, Theater and
Film Dept.
Tel: (419) 372-2222
Fax:(419) 372-7186
theatrefilm@bgsu.edu
www.bgsu.edu/theatrefilm
Fee: Yes.

**Brigham Young University**
Dept. of Theatre and Media Arts, D-581
  HFAC, Provo, UT 84602
Elizabeth Funke
Tel: (801) 422-7768
Fax:(801) 422-0654
tmaweb@byu.edu
www.byu.edu
  Fee: Yes.

**Brooklyn College**
English Dept., 2900 Bedford Ave.,
  Brooklyn, NY 11210
Nancy Black, Professor of English
www.brooklyn.cuny.edu
  Fee: Yes.

**Brown University**
Box 1852, Waterman St., Providence, RI
  02912
Spencer Golub, Chair, Theater Dept.
Tel: (401) 863-1955
spencer_golub@brown.edu
www.brown.edu
  Degrees offered: AB, BA, MA, MFA.
  Submission Materials: See website.
  Fee: Yes.

**California Institute of the Arts (Cal
Arts)**
24700 McBean Pkwy., Valencia, CA
  91355
Ellen McCartney, Dean, Theater School
Tel: (661) 253-7853
EMcCartney@calarts.edu
www.calarts.edu
  Submission Materials: See website.
  Fee: Yes.

**Campbell University**
Box 128, Buries Creek, NC 27506
Stephen J. Larson, Chair, Theater Arts
Tel: (910) 893-1507
www.campbell.edu/coas/theatre
  Degree offered: B.A. Submission
  Materials: See website. Fee: Yes.

**Carnegie Mellon University**
Purnell Center A32, Pittsburgh, PA 15213
Dick Block, Coordinator, Graduate
  Admissions
Tel: (412) 268-7219
rblock@andrew.cmu.edu
www.cmu.edu/cfa/drama

MFA, Dramatic Writing. 4 students
admitted annually plus 2 students
admitted in screenwriting. Applicants
unable to visit are interviewed by
phone. Submission Materials: See
website. Fee: Yes.

**Catholic University of America**
Catholic University, Dept. of Drama, 620
  Michigan Ave. NE, Washington, DC
  20064
Jon Klein, Head of MFA Writing Program
Tel: (202) 319-5360
kleinj@cua.edu
drama.cua.edu/MFAPlaywriting/MFAplay.html
  Degrees Offered: MFA in Playwriting.
  Staged readings to full thesis
  production in mainstage season,
  directed by guest professional director.
  Submission Materials: See website.
  Fee: Yes. Deadline(s): 3/31/2011

**Central Washington University (CWU)**
CWU Theater Dept., 400 E. University
  Way, MS: 7460, Ellensburg, WA 98926
Scott Robinson, Department Chair
Tel: (509) 963-2020
scott.robinson@cwu.edu
www.cwu.edu/~theatre
  Biannual Theatre for Youth
  competition. Submission Materials: See
  website.

**College of Charleston (CofC)**
66 George St., Charleston, SC 29424
Franklin Ashley
Tel: (843) 849-8287
Fax:(843) 953-8210
ashleyf@cofc.edu
www.cofc.edu
  Submission Materials: See website.
  Fee: Yes.

**College of the Holy Cross**
1 College St., Worcester, MA 01610
Edward Isser, Chair, Theater Dept.
Tel: (508) 793-3490
eisser@holycross.edu
www.holycross/edu
  Submission Materials: See website.
  Fee: Yes.

**Columbia College [IL]**
72 E. 11th St., Chicago, IL 60605
Sheldon Patinkin, Chair, Theater Dept.
Tel: (312) 344-6100
theatre@colum.edu
www.colum.edu
    Submission Materials: See website.
    Fee: Yes.

**Columbia University School of the Arts Theatre Program**
2960 Broadway MC 1807, 601 Dodge
    Hall, New York, NY 10027-7021
Julie Rossi, Program Assistant
Tel: (212) 854-3408
Fax:(212) 854-3344
arts.columbia.edu/theatre
    Submission Materials: See website.
    Fee: Yes.

**DePaul University**
2135 N. Kenmore Ave., Chicago, IL
    60614
Dean Corrin, Head, Playwriting
Tel: (773) 325-7932
dcorrin@depaul.edu
theatreschool.depaul.edu
    Fee: Yes.

**Drexel University, Westphal College**
3141 Chestnut St., Philadelphia, PA
    19104
Nick Anselmo, Program Director
Tel: (215) 895-1920
Fax:(215) 895-2452
nick.anselmo@drexel.edu
www.drexel.edu/westphal
    Submission Materials: See website.
    Fee: Yes.

**Duke University**
Box 90680, Durham, NC 27708
Sarah Beckwith, Chair, Theater Studies
Tel: (919) 660-3343
theater@duke.edu
www.duke.edu/web/drama
    We do not accept unsolicited scripts of
    any kind. Fee: Yes.

**Emerson College**
10 Boylston Pl., 5th Floor, Department of

Performing Arts, Boston, MA 02116
Melia Bensussen, Chair, Performing Arts
Tel: (617) 824-8780
stagedoor@emerson.edu
www.emerson.edu/performing-
arts/index.cfm
    Degree offered: BA. Submission
    Materials: See website. Fee: Yes.

**Florida State University (FSU)**
239 Fine Arts Bldg., Tallahassee, FL
    32306
Barbara Thomas, Program Assistant
Tel: (850) 644-7234
Fax:(850) 644-7246
bgthomas@admin.fsu.edu
theatre.fsu.edu
    Est. 1973. Undergrad and graduate
    degree programs. Scholarships and
    graduate grants available. Submission
    Materials: Application. Fee: Yes.

**Hollins University**
PO Box 9603, Roanoke, VA 24020
Todd Ristau, Program Director
Tel: (540) 362-6386
tristau@hollins.edu
www.hollins.edu/grad/playwriting/
    60 credit hour MFA in Playwriting can
    be completed in 4-5 annual 6-wk
    summer sessions (Jun-Jul). Production
    opportunities at affiliated theatres. Aid
    available, see website. Submission
    Materials: See website. Fee: Yes.

**Indiana University**
257 N. Jordan Ave., Rm. A300U,
    Bloomington, IN 47405
Catherine Richards, Academic Secretary
Tel: (812) 855-4535
Fax:(812) 856-0698
theatre@indiana.edu
www.indiana.edu
    Degrees offered: BA, MA, MFA, PhD.
    Submission Materials: See website.
    Fee: Yes.

**Johnson County Community College**
12345 College Blvd., Overland Park, KS
    66210
Beatte Pettigrew, Director, Theater Dept.
Tel: (913) 469-8500
Fax:(913) 469-2585
bpettigr@jccc.net
www.jccc.net

No original play submissions accepted.
Fee: Yes.

**Juilliard School**
Playwrights Program, 60 Lincoln Center
  Plaza, New York, NY 10023
Tanya Barfield
Tel: (212) 799-5000
Fax:(212) 875-8437
www.juilliard.edu
  Submission Materials: See website.
  Fee: Yes.

**Louisiana Tech University**
PO Box 8608, Ruston, LA 71272
Cherrie Schiro, Director, School of
  Performing Arts
Tel: (318) 257-2711
Fax:(318) 257-4571
lulu@latech.edu
stoneplaywritingaward@yahoo.com
performingarts.latech.edu
  Degree offered: BA, MA, Submission
  Materials: See website. Fee: Yes.

**Loyola University New Orleans**
6363 St. Charles Ave., Box 155, New
  Orleans, LA 70118
Cheryl Conway
Tel: (504) 865-3840
Fax:(504) 865-2284
theatre@loyno.edu
www.loyno.edu/theatrearts
  Degree offered: BA. Submission
  Materials: See website. Fee: Yes.

**Montclair State University**
1 Normal Ave., MSU LI-126G, Montclair,
  NJ 07043
Eric Diamond, Dept. Chair
Tel: (973) 655-7343
www.montclair.edu/Pages/theatredance
  Degrees offered: BA, BFA, MA.
  Submission Materials: See website.
  Fee: Yes.

**Mount Holyoke College**
50 College St., South Hadley, MA 01075
Vanessa James, Chair, Theater Arts
Tel: (413) 538-2118
Fax:(413) 538-2838
theatre@mtholyoke.edu
www.mtholyoke.edu/acad/theat/

Degree offered: BA. Submission
Materials: See website. Fee: Yes.

**Nebraska Wesleyan University**
500 St. Paul Ave., Lincoln, NE 68504
Jay Scott Chipman, Professor of Theatre
Tel: (402) 465-2386
jsc@nebrwesleyan.edu
www.nebrwesleyan.edu
  Degrees offered: BA in Theatre
  Education; BFA in Acting, Directing,
  Musical Theatre, Theatre Design and
  Technology, Theatre Studies.
  Submission Materials: See website.
  Fee: Yes.

**New School University**
151 Bank St., New York, NY 10014
Frank Pugliese, Chair, Playwriting
Tel: (212) 229-5859
studentinfo@newschool.edu
www.drama.newschool.edu
  Offers 3-yr MFA. Each year,
  playwrights work with at least two
  teachers, completing at least one full-
  length play and one screenplay by
  graduation. Preferred Genre(s): All
  genres. Preferred Length: Any length.
  Submission Materials: See website.
  Fee: Yes. Deadline(s): See website

**New York University (NYU) Dramatic
Writing**
721 Broadway, Fl. 7, New York, NY
  10003
David Ranghelli, Dramatic Writing
  Director
Tel: (212) 998-1940
ddw.tisch.nyu.edu/page/home.html
  BFA, MFA from Playwriting Div.,
  Goldberg Dept. of Dramatic Writing, at
  Tisch School of the Arts. Submission
  Materials: See website.

**New York University (NYU) Musical
Theater Writing**
113-A 2nd Ave., Fl. 1, New York, NY
  10003
Sarah Schlesinger, Chair, Dept. Musical
  Theater Writing
Tel: (212) 998-1830
Fax:(212) 995-4873
muscial.theatre@nyu.edu
gmtw.tisch.nyu.edu/page/home.html

Est. 1981. MFA for composers, lyricists and bookwriters from Inst. of Performing Arts at Tisch School of the Arts. Response: Decisions are made in april for class starting in Sept. Preferred Genre(s): Musical theatre. Submission Materials: See website. Fee: Yes. Deadline(s): April

**Northern Kentucky University**
NKU, FA 205-A, Highland Heights, KY 41099
Ken Jones, Chair, Theater Dept.
Tel: (859) 572-6362
Fax:(859) 572-6057
www.nku.edu/~theatre
Degrees offered: BA, BFA. Submission Materials: Application. Fee: Yes.

**Northwestern University**
Theatre Interpertation Building, 1949 Campus Drive, Evanston, IL 60208
Laura Schelhardt
Tel: (847) 491-3170
Fax:(847) 467-2019
v-valliere@northwestern.edu
www.communication.northwestern.edu/
Degrees offered: BA, MFA, PhD. Submission Materials: Application. Fee: Yes.

**Oakland University**
Music, Theater, Dance, Rochester, MI 48309
Kerro Knox, Head, Theater
Tel: (248) 370-2030
Fax:(248) 370-2041
knox@oakland.edu
www.oakland.edu/mtd
BA, BFA. Meadow Brook Theater is on campus. Submission Materials: Application.

**Palm Beach Atlantic University**
Box 24708, West Palm Beach, FL 33416
Deborah McEniry, Director, Theatre
Tel: (561) 803-2000
timothy_cox@pba.edu
www.pba.edu
Submission Materials: See website. Fee: Yes.

**Purdue Univ.**
552 W. Wood Street, West Lafayette, IN 47907
Richard Stockler Rand, Chair
Tel: (765) 494-3074
Fax:(765) 496-1766
theatre@purdue.edu
www.purdue.edu/theatre
Degree offered: BA, MA, MFA. Submission Materials: See website. Fee: Yes.

**Radford University**
Dance and Theatre, RU Station, Radford, VA 24142
Carl Lefko, Chair, Theater Dept.
Tel: (540) 831-5207
Fax:(540) 831-6313
clefko@radford.edu
theatre.asp.radford.edu
Degree offered: BA. Submission Materials: See website. Fee: Yes.

**Rutgers University (State University of New Jersey)**
Rutgers University/Mason Gross School of the Arts, Theatre Arts Department, 2 Chapel Drive, New Brunswick, NJ 08901
Barbara Harwanko, Head of Playwriting
Tel: (732) 932-4891
mgsa.rutgers.edu/theater/thea.html
Degree offered: MFA. Submission Materials: See website. Fee: Yes.

**San Francisco State University (SFSU)**
Creative Writing Dept., 1600 Holloway Ave., San Francisco, CA 94132
Roy Conboy, Head of Playwriting
Tel: (414) 338-1614
rconboy@sfsu.edu
www.sfsu.edu
Degrees offered: MA, MFA. Shares resources with El Teatro de la Esperanza. Submission Materials: Application. Fee: Yes.

**Smith College**
Theatre Dept., Mendenhall Ctr., Northampton, MA 01063
Len Berkman, Professor of Theatre
Tel: (413) 585-3206
lberkman@email.smith.edu
www.smith.edu/theatre

Est. 1969. Degrees offered: BA, MFA, DFA. Submission Materials: See website. Fee: Yes.

**Southern Illinois University, Carbondale (SIU)**
Comm. Bldg, #2238, Carbondale, IL 62901
David Rush, Head, Playwriting Program
Tel: (618) 453-5747
darush@siu.edu
www.siu.edu/~mcleod
   Est. 1952. Degrees offered: BA, MFA, PhD. Preferred Genre(s): Plays or Musicals. Preferred Length: Full-length. Submission Materials: See website. Deadline(s): March

**Southern Methodist University (SMU)**
Box 750369, Dallas, TX 75275
Gretchen Elizabeth Smith
Tel: (214) 768-2937
gesmith@mail.smu.edu
www.smu.edu
   Degrees offered: BFA, MFA. Submission Materials: See website.

**SUNY Purchase**
735 Anderson Hill Rd., Purchase, NY 10577
Howard Enders, Chair, Dramatic Writing Program
Tel: (914) 251-6833
www.purchase.edu
   Submission Materials: See website. Fee: Yes.

**Texas State University, San Marcos**
601 University Dr., San Marcos, TX 78666
John Fleming
Tel: (512) 245-2147
Fax:(512) 245-8440
jf18@txstate.edu
www.theatreanddance.txstate.edu
   Degrees offered: BA, BFA. Submission Materials: See website. Fee: Yes.

**University of California, Riverside (UCR)**
The Department of Theatre, 900 University Ave., ARTS 121, University of California, Riverside, Riverside, CA 92521
Eric Barr, Chair, Theater Dept.
Tel: (951) 827-4602
Fax:(951) 827-4651
Chrisy@ucr.edu
www.theatre.ucr.edu
   Degrees offered: BA, MFA Submission Materials: See website. Fee: Yes.

**University of California, San Diego (UCSD)**
9500 Gilman Dr., MC0509, La Jolla, CA 92093
Allan Havis, Provost/Head, MFA Playwriting
Tel: (858) 534-4004
Fax:(858) 534-8931
ahavis@ucsd.edu
theatre.ucsd.edu
   Degrees offered: BA, MFA, PhD. Submission Materials: See website. Fee: Yes.

**University of California, Santa Barbara (UCSB)**
552 University Rd., Santa Barbara, CA 93106
Ellen K. Anderson, Playwriting Program
Tel: (805) 893-8303
ellena@silcom.com
www.dramadance.ucsb.edu
   Degrees offered: BA., BFA, MA, PhD. Submission Materials: See website. Fee: Yes.

**University of Idaho (UI)**
Box 442008, Moscow, ID 83844
Robert Caisley, Head, Dramatic Writing
Tel: (208) 885-6465
rcaisley@uidaho.edu
www.uitheatre.com
   Home of Idaho Repertory Theater. MFA in Dramatic Writing offered. Submission Materials: See website. Fee: Yes.

**University of Iowa**
200 N. Riverside Dr., #107 TB, Iowa
    City, IA 52242
Art Borreca, Head, Playwrights Workshop
Tel: (319) 353-2407
Fax:(319) 335-3568
art-borreca@uiowa.edu
www.uiowa.edu/~theatre/programs/
    playwrighting/playwritinginfo.htm
Est. 1971. Degrees offered: BA and
    MFA. Submission Materials: See
    website. Fee: Yes.

**University of Michigan (UM)**
1226 Murfin Ave., 2230 Walgreen Drama
    Center, Ann Arbor, MI 48109
Tel: (734) 764-5350
Fax:(734) 647-2297
theatre.info@umich.edu
www.music.umich.edu/departments/theatre
    Submission Materials: See website.
    Fee: Yes.

**University of Minnesota Duluth (UMD)**
Dept. of Theatre, 141 MPAC, 1215
    Ordean Ct., Duluth, MN 55812
Patricia Dennis
Tel: (218) 726-8778
pdennis@d.umn.edu
www.d.umn.edu/finearts/theatre.htm
    Degrees offered: BFA, BA. Submission
    Materials: See website. Fee: Yes.

**University of Missouri**
129 Fine Arts Bldg., Columbia, MO
    65211
Clyde Ruffin, Associate Professor,
    Playwriting
Tel: (573) 882-2021
Fax:(573) 884-4034
ruffinc@missouri.edu
theatre.missouri.edu
    Degrees offered: BA, MA, PhD.
    Submission Materials: See website.
    Fee: Yes.

**University of Missouri, Kansas City**
4949 Cherry St., Kansas City, MO 64110
Frank Higgins, Professor of Playwriting
Tel: (816) 235-2702
fhwriter@aol.com
cas.umkc.edu/theatre/
    Submission Materials: See website.
    Fee: Yes.

**University of Nevada, Las Vegas
(UNLV)**
Department of Theatre, 4505 Maryland
    Pkwy., Box 455036, Las Vegas, NV
    89154
Brackley Frayer, Chair, Theater Dept
Tel: (702) 895-3666
Fax:(702) 895-0833
theatre@unlv.edu
theatre.unlv.edu
    Est. 1967. Home of Nevada
    Conservatory Theatre. Submission
    Materials: See website. Fee: Yes.

**University of New Mexico (UNM)**
1 UNM, MSC04-2570, Department of
    Theatre & Dance, Albuquerque, NM
    87131
Bill Liotta, Professor
Tel: (505) 277-4332
Fax:(505) 277-8921
wliotta@unm.edu
www.unm.edu/~theatre
    University est. 1892. Theater Dept. est.
    1930. Degree offered: MFA, dramatic
    writing. Submission Materials: See
    website. Fee: Yes.

**University of New Orleans (UNO)**
Film, Theatre and Communication Arts,
    2000 Lake Shore Drive-PAC 307, New
    Orleans, LA 70148
David Hoover, Director, CWW
Tel: (504) 280-6317
Fax:(504) 280-6318
dhoover@uno.edu
www.uno.edu
    Degrees offered: BA, MFA.
    Submission Materials: See website.
    Fee: Yes.

**University of South Florida (USF)**
4202 E. Fowler Ave., FAH 110, Tampa,
    FL 33620
Denis Calandra, Chair, Theater Dept.
Tel: (813) 974-2701
theatreanddance.arts.usf.edu/theatre
    Degree offered: BA. Submission
    Materials: See website. Fee: Yes.

**University of Southern California (USC)**
University Park, DRC 107, Los Angeles, CA 90089
Velina Hasu Houston, Director, Playwriting
Tel: (213) 821-2744
Fax:(213) 740-8888
thtrinfo@usc.edu
theatre.usc.edu
  Est. 1945. Submission Materials: See website. Fee: Yes.

**University of Texas, Austin**
Department of Theater and Dance, The Unversity of Texas At Austin, 1 University Station, D3900, Austin, TX 78712
Suzan Zeder, Chair, Playwriting
Tel: (512) 232-5325
suzanz@mail.utexas.edu
www.utexas.edu/cofa/theatre
  Degrees offered: BA, MFA. Submission Materials: See website. Fee: Yes.

**University of Texas, El Paso (UTEP)**
Fox Fine Arts, Rm. 371, 500 W. Univ. Ave., El Paso, TX 79968
Tel: (915) 747-5746
jmurray@utep.edu
www.theatredance.utep.edu
  Submission Materials: See website. Fee: Yes.

**University of Tulsa (TU)**
Kendall Hall, 600 S. College Ave., Tulsa, OK 74104
Michael Wright, Director, Creative Writing
Tel: (918) 631-2566
Fax:(918) 631-5155
michael-wright@utulsa.edu
www.cas.utulsa.edu/writing
  Degree offered: BA. Submission Materials: See website. Fee: Yes.

**University of Wyoming**
1000 E. University Ave., Dept. 3951,
Laramie, WY 82071
William Missouri Downs
Tel: (307) 766-2198
www.uwyo.edu/th&d
  Degrees offered: BA, BFA. Submission Materials: See website. Fee: Yes.

**Villanova Theatre**
800 Lancaster Ave., Vasey 5, Villanova, PA 19085
Elisa Loprete Hibbs, Business Production Manager
Tel: (610) 519-4897
Fax:(610) 519-6803
theatre.villanova.edu
  Submission Materials: See website. Fee: Yes.

**Virginia Tech (VT)**
250 E. Henderson Hall, Blacksburg, VA 24061
Patricia Raun, Chair, Theater Dept.
Tel: (540) 231-5335
Fax:(540) 231-7321
praun@vt.edu
www.theatre.vt.edu
  Degrees offered: BA, MFA. Submission Materials: See website. Fee: Yes.

**Wayne State University**
4841 Cass Ave., Detroit, MI 48201
David S. Magidson
Tel: (313) 577-6508
d_magidson@wayne.edu
www.wayne.edu
  Degrees offered: BA, BFA, MFA, MFA, PhD. Submission Materials: See website. Fee: Yes.

**Yale University School of Drama**
Box 208325, New Haven, CT 6520
Paula Vogel, Chair, Playwriting
Tel: (203) 432-0254
www.drama.yale.edu
  Est. 1924. Degree offered: MFA. Submission Materials: See website. Fee: Yes. Deadline(s): Fe. 1, 2011

## Workshops

**Academy for New Musical Theatre (ANMT)**
5628 Vineland Ave., B9, North
Hollywood CA 91601
Elise Dewsberry, Executive Director
Tel: (818) 506-8500
Fax:(818) 506-8500
academy@anmt.org
www.anmt.org
Est. 1981.Commercial development
(readings, workshops, contest) of new
musicals. Submit via website. Preferred
Genre(s): Musical theatre. Preferred
Length: Any length. Submission
Materials: Query letter only. Fee: Yes.

**ASCAP Musical Theatre Workshop [NY]**
1 Lincoln Plaza, Fl. 7, B9, New York NY
10023
Michael A. Kerker, Director Musical
Theatre
Tel: (212) 621-6234
Fax:(212) 621-6558
mkerker@ascap.com
www.ascap.com
Directed by Stephen Schwartz,
program of 50-min from works-in-
progress before a panel of professional
directors, musical directors, producers,
critics and fellow writers. All sessions
begin 7pm, May-Jun. Preferred
Genre(s): Musical theatre. Preferred
Length: 50-60 min.. Submission
Materials: Synopsis, audio (4 songs),
bio, song descriptions.

**ASCAP/Disney Musical Theatre Workshop [CA]**
7920 W. Sunset Blvd., Fl. 3, B9, Los
Angeles CA 90046
Michael Kerker, Director Musical Theatre
Tel: (323) 883-1000
Fax:(323) 883-1049
mkerker@ascap.com
www.ascap.com
Directed by Stephen Schwartz, 50-min
presentation of works-in-development
before a professional panel. All
sessions begin 7pm, Jan-Feb. Preferred
Genre(s): Musical theatre. Preferred
Length: 50-60 min.. Submission
Materials: Synopsis, audio (4 songs),
bio, song descriptions.

**BMI Lehman Engel Musical Theatre Workshop - Librettists Work**
BMI, B97 World Trade Center, 250
Greenwich Street, New York NY
10007
Jean Banks, Sr. Director Musical Theater
Tel: (212) 830-2508
Fax:(212) 262-2508
jbanks@bmi.com
www.bmi.com
Weekly 2-hr sessions (Monday eves,
Sep-May) in NYC. Occasional special
events. housing available. Download
application from website. Preferred
Genre(s): Musical theatre. Preferred
Length: Any length. Submission
Materials: Application, sample . Fee:
Yes. Deadline(s): 5/15/2011 postmark

**BMI Lehman Engel Musical Theatre Workshop - Songwriters Work**
BMI, B97 World Trade Center, 250 Greenwich Street, New York NY 10007
Jean Banks, Sr. Director Musical Theatre
Tel: (212) 586-2000
Fax:(212) 262-2508
jbanks@bmi.com
www.bmi.com/genres/theatre
    Weekly 2-hr sessions (Sept - May) Monday evenings (First Year) or Tuesday evenings (Second Year) in NYC. Housing available. Preferred Genre(s): Musical theatre. Preferred Length: Any length. Submission Materials: Application, sample audio. Fee: Yes. Deadline(s): 8/1/2011

**Broadway Tomorrow Musical Theatre**
191 Claremont Ave., #53, B9, New York NY 10027
Elyse Curtis, Artistic Director
Tel: (212) 531-2447
Fax:(212) 532-2447
solministry@earthlink.net
www.solministry.com/bway_tom.html
    Est. 1983. New musicals w/new age, transformative, spiritual themes. Concert readings with writer/composer involvement. Response time: 6 mos. Preferred Genre(s): Adaptation. Preferred Length: Any length. Submission Materials: Synopsis, audio (3 songs), SASE.

**Cherry Lane Theatre Mentor Project**
38 Commerce St., B9, New York NY 10014
James King, Managing Director
Tel: (212) 989-2020
Fax:(212) 989-2867
company@cherrylanetheatre.org
www.cherrylanetheatre.org
    Est. 1997. Pairs young writers by professional recommendation with master to work on scripts for full season, ending with Equity Showcase. Production: medium cast size, orchestra. Submissions not returned. Preferred Genre(s): All genres. Preferred Length: Any length. Submission Materials: See website.

**Chesterfield Writer's Film Project**
1158 26th St., Box 544, B9, Santa Monica CA 90401
Tel: (213) 683-3977
Fax:(310) 260-6116
www.chesterfield-co.com
    Based at Paramount Pictures, WFP began with support of Steven Spielberg's Amblin Entertainment. It is currently ON HIATUS.

**Colorado New Play Summit**
1101 13th St., B9, Denver CO 80204
Douglas Langworthy, Literary Manager
Tel: (303) 893-4000
Fax:(303) 825-2117
bsevy@dcpa.org
www.dcpa.org
    Est. 1979. Offering unproduced/uptioned rehearsed reading for industry and general audience. Must be resident of AZ, CO, ID, MT, NM, UT, WY. Response time: 6 mos. Preferred Genre(s): Plays. Preferred Length: Full-length. Submission Materials: Agent only submissions.

**David Henry Hwang Writers Institute**
120 N. Judge John Aiso St., B9, Los Angeles CA 90012
Jeff Liu, Literary Manager
Tel: (213) 625-7000
Fax:(213) 625-7111
jliu@eastwestplayers.org
www.eastwestplayers.org
    Est. 1991. 2 workshops per yr (fall, spring). Submission Materials: Query letter only. Fee: Yes.

**Florida Playwrights' Process**
736 Scotland St., B9, Dunedin FL 34698
Elizabeth Brincklow, Artistic Director
Tel: (727) 734-0880
Fax:(727) 734-0880
flplaypro@yahoo.com
    Unproduced/uptioned musical development w/tech support. Request application via email. Production: cast up to 6, simple set, simple props & costumes. Response: 3 mos. Preferred Genre(s): Musical theatre. Preferred Length: One-act or Full-length. Submission Materials: Sypsis, 30pg sample, full script, SASE.

**Frank Silvera Writers' Workshop**
P.O. Box 1791, B9 Manhattanville
Station, New York NY 10027
Garland Lee Thompson, Founding
Executive Director
Tel: (212) 281-8832
Fax:(212) 281-8839
playrite@earthlink.net
www.fsww.org
Est. 1973. Playwright development
program. Submit via US mail or hand
deliver. Work must be
unoptioned/unproduced/unpublished.
Preferred Genre(s): All genres.
Submission Materials: Complete script
& SASE.

**Frederick Douglass Creative Arts
Center Writing Workshops**
270 W. 96th St., B9, New York NY
10025
Kermit Frazier, Acting President
Tel: (212) 864-3375
Fax:(212) 864-3474
fdcac@aol.com
www.fdcac.org
Submission Materials: See website.

**Hangar Theatre Lab Company
Playwriting Residencies**
Box 205, B9, Ithaca NY 14851
Hangar Theatre Literary Assistant
Tel: (607) 273-8588
literary@hangartheatre.org
www.hangartheatre.org
4 playwrights offered 2-3 wk residency
in Jul-Aug. Full production by Lab
Company. The Hangar solicits full-
lengths from former winners. Email
submissions only. Preferred Genre(s):
All genres. Preferred Length: Any
length. Submission Materials: See
website. Fee: Yes. Deadline(s):
3/8/2011

**Harold Prince Musical Theatre
Program**
311 W. 43rd St., #307, B9, New York NY
10036
Tel: (212) 246-5877
Fax:(212) 246-5882
www.thedirectorscompany.org

Preferred Genre(s): Musical theatre.
Preferred Length: Full-length.
Submission Materials: See website.
Fee: Yes.

**Manhattan Playwrights Unit (MPU)**
338 W. 19th St., #6-B, B9, New York,
NY 10011
Saul Zachary, Artistic Director
Tel: (212) 989-0948
Fax:(212) 823-0084
saulzachary@yahoo.com
Est. 1979. Ongoing biweekly in-house
workshop for professional-level
playwrights and screenwriters. Informal
and intense. Submissions not returned.
Preferred Genre(s): All genres.
Preferred Length: Any length.
Submission Materials: Query, resume.

**Missouri Playwrights Workshop
(MPW)**
129 Fine Arts Bldg., B9, Columbia MO
65211
David Crespy, Artistic Director
Tel: (573) 882-0535
Fax:(573) 884-4034
crespyd@missouri.edu
theatre.missouri.edu/mpw/index.htm
Est. 1998. Weekly salon for developing
work by playwrights residing in
Missouri who can attend workshop.
Submissions not returned. Preferred
Genre(s): All genres. Preferred Length:
Any length. Submission Materials:
Query and synopsis only.

**New Directors/New Works (ND/NW)**
Drama League, B9520 8th Ave., #320,
New York NY 10018
Roger Danforth, Artistic Director
Tel: (212) 244-9494
Fax:(212) 244-9191
www.dramaleague.org
Directors Project program to support
new works by directors and
collaborating artists. Preferred
Genre(s): Plays or Musicals. Preferred
Length: One-act or Full-length.
Submission Materials: See website.
Deadline(s): 2/1/2011

## Pataphysics
41 White St., B9, New York NY 10013
The Flea
Tel: (212) 226-0051
Fax:(212) 965-1808
garyw@theflea.org
www.theflea.org
   Pataphysics workshops are scheduled
   sporadically and occur unexpectedly.
   To receive notification of upcoming
   classes, please email. Submission
   Materials: See website.

## Playwrights' Center of San Francisco Staged Readings
588 Sutter St., #403, B9, San Francisco
   CA 94102
Tel: (415) 820-3206
playwrightscentersf.org
   Preferred Genre(s): All genres.
   Preferred Length: Any length.
   Submission Materials: See website.
   Deadline(s): 4/30/2011, 11/30/2011

## Playwrights' Platform
398 Columbus Ave #604, B9, Boston,
   MA 02116-6008
Kelly DuMar, Artistic Director
Tel: (781) 894-0081
membership@playwrightsplatform.org
www.playwrightsplatform.org
   Est. 1976. Monthly developmental
   readings in Boston area and annual
   festival in Boston, MA. Response: 3
   mos. Preferred Genre(s): All genres.
   Preferred Length: Any length.
   Submission Materials: See website.
   Fee: Yes.

## Primary Stages Playwriting Workshops
307 W. 38th St., #1510, B9, New York
   NY 10018
Michelle Bossy, Assoc Artistic Director
Tel: (212) 840-9705
Fax:(212) 840-9725
www.primarystages.org
   Est. 2002. Each wk, 8 writers bring
   10-15 pgs for instructor feedback and
   group discussion, completing first draft
   of new full-length in 10 wks. Preferred
   Genre(s): Plays. Preferred Length:
   Full-length. Submission Materials:
   Application. Fee: Yes.

## Remembrance Through the Performing Arts New Play Development
P.O. Box 162446, B9, Austin TX 78716
Rosalyn Rosen, Artistic Director
Tel: (512) 329-9118
Fax:(512) 329-9118
remperarts@aol.com
   Est. 1988. New plays
   (unoptioned/unproduced/unpublished)
   in workshop. Production: cast limit 8.
   Response: 2 mos. Preferred Genre(s):
   Plays. Preferred Length: One-act or
   Full-length. Submission Materials:
   Query, synopsis, 10-pg sample &
   SASE.

## Sewanee Writers' Conference
735 University Ave., 123-D Gailor H, B9,
   Sewanee TN 37383
Cheri B. Peters, Mgr, Creative Writing
   Programs
Tel: (931) 598-1141
Fax:(931) 598-1145
cpeters@sewanee.edu
www.sewaneewriters.org
   Est. 1990. Workshop in late July led by
   two noted playwrights. Limited number
   of scholarships and fellowships
   available on a competitive basis.
   Preferred Genre(s): All genres.
   Preferred Length: Any length.
   Submission Materials: See website.
   Fee: Yes. Deadline(s): See website

## Soho Rep's Writer/Director Lab
Soho Repertory, B986 Franklin St., Fl. 5,
   New York NY 10013
Daniel Manley, Co-Chair
Tel: (212) 941-8632
Fax:(212) 941-7148
writerdirector@sohorep.org
www.sohorep.org
   Est. 1998. Writers and directors are
   paired for the workshop. Meet
   bimonthly Oct-April to read plays
   aloud and discuss. Each writers brings
   work in 3 times during workshop.
   Preferred Genre(s): Plays. Preferred
   Length: One-act or Full-length.
   Submission Materials: Application,
   sample.

**Southern Writers Project (SWP)**
1 Festival Dr., B9, Montgomery AL
  36117
Nancy Rominger, Artistic Associate
Tel: (334) 271-5342
Fax:(334) 271-5348
swp@asf.net
www.southernwritersproject.net
  Est. 1991. Prefer Southern or African
  American themed work or from a
  Southern writer. Develop unproduced
  scripts in weeklong workshop w/
  possible production. Response: 6 mos.
  Preferred Genre(s): Plays. Preferred
  Length: Full-length. Submission
  Materials: Complete script, SASE.

**Sundance Institute Theatre Program**
180 Varick St. , B9 Suite 1330, New
  York NY 10014
Ignacia Delgado, Coordinator
Tel: (646) 822-9564
Fax:(310) 360-1975
theatre@sundance.org
www.sundance.org/theatreapp
  Est. 1981. Developmental July
  workshops for directors and
  playwrights in Sundance, UT. Can be
  plays, musicals, solo work, devised
  work. Response: 4 mos. Preferred
  Genre(s): All genres. Preferred Length:
  Any length. Submission Materials:
  Application, full script, audio, video,
  SASE. Fee: Yes. Deadline(s): Oct. 1
  2011

**The Kennedy Center New Visions/New
Voices Festival (NVNV)**
Kennedy Center, B9P.O. Box 101510,
  Arlington VA 22210
Kim Peter Kovac, Director, TYA
Tel: (202) 416-8830
Fax:(202) 416-8297
kctya@kennedy-center.org
www.kennedy-
  center.org/education/nvnv.html
  Est. 1991. Biennial (even yrs)
  weeklong residency in May to
  encourage and support creation of new
  plays and musicals for young people
  and families. Preferred Genre(s): Plays
  or Musicals. Special Interest: Theatre

for Young Audiences. Preferred
Length: One-Act. Submission
Materials: See website. Deadline(s):
See website

**The New Harmony Project**
Box 441062, B9, Indianapolis IN 46244
Joel Grynheim, Project Director
Tel: (317) 464-1103
Fax:(317) 464-1103
jgrynheim@newharmonyproject.org
www.newharmonyproject.org
  Est. 1986. Development thru rehearsals
  and readings in 14 day conference of
  scripts that explore the human journey
  by offering hope and showing respect
  for the positive values of life. Preferred
  Length: Full-length. Submission
  Materials: See website. Deadline(s):
  Oct 1, 2011

**Theatre Building Chicago Musical
Theatre Writers' Workshop**
1225 W. Belmont Ave., B9, Chicago IL
  60657
Allan Chambers, Artistic Director
Tel: (773) 929-7367
Fax:(773) 327-1404
jsparks@theatrebuildingchicago.org
www.theatrebuildingchicago.org
  Est. 1984. 3-tiered workshop: Intro (1st
  yr), Intermediate (2nd yr), Advanced
  (ongoing). Preferred Genre(s): Musical
  theatre. Preferred Length: Any length.
  Submission Materials: Application.
  Fee: Yes. Deadline(s): Sep 1, 2011

**Urban Retreat**
Young Playwrights Inc, B9P.O. Box
  5134, New York NY 10185
Tel: (212) 594-5440
Fax:(212) 684-4902
www.youngplaywrights.org
  July workshop: authors age 14-21
  collaborate with professional
  dramaturgs, directors, and actors on
  staged reading of a new play to be
  presented in an Off-Broadway theater.
  Preferred Genre(s): Plays. Special
  Interest: Theatre for Young Audiences.
  Submission Materials: Application,
  sample . Fee: Yes. Deadline(s):
  3/1/2011 , 5/1/2011

**Waldo M. & Grace C. Bonderman Playwriting for Youth National**
140 W. Washington Street, B9,
  Indianapolis IN 46204
Dorothy Webb
Tel: (317) 506-4566
Fax:(317) 278-1025
dwebb@iupui.edu
www.indianarep.com/Bonderman
  1 week of development and staged
  readings for young auds grades 3 - 12.
  Work must be unpublished, unproduced
  (professionally). Preferred Genre(s):
  Musical theatre. Special Interest:
  Theatre for Young Audiences. Preferred
  Length: One-act or Full-length.
  Submission Materials: Application, full
  script (3 copies). Deadline(s): See
  website

**Young Playwrights Inc. Advanced Playwriting Workshop**
PO Box 5134, B9, New York NY 10185
Amanda Junco, Exec. Associate
Tel: (212) 594-5440
Fax:(212) 684-4902
www.youngplaywrights.org
  Advanced Playwriting Workshop meets
  for 18 or younger in midtown
  Manhattan every Tue, 4:30-7:00pm,
  October - May. Exercises help
  members develop and revise new
  plays. Preferred Genre(s): Plays.
  Preferred Length: Any length.
  Submission Materials: See website.
  Fee: Yes. Deadline(s): 9/20/2011

# Writer Resources

## Emergency Funds

**Authors League Fund**
31 E. 32nd St., Fl. 7, New York, NY
10016
Isabel Howe, Administrator
Tel: (212) 568-1208
Fax:(212) 564-5363
staff@authorsguild.org
www.authorsleaguefund.org
Interest-free loans for personal
emergencies of immediate need (rent,
medical, etc.).

**Mary Mason Memorial Lemonade
Fund**
1663 Mission Street, #525, San
Francisco, CA 94103
Tel: (415) 430-1140
Fax:(415) 430-1145
dale@theatrebayarea.org
www.theatrebayarea.org/programs/lemonade.jsp

Mail application through US mail.
Submission Materials: Application.

**PEN Writers Fund**
588 Broadway, #303, New York, NY
10012
Lara Tobin, Coordinator
Tel: (212) 334-1660
Fax:(212) 334-2181
lara@pen.org
www.pen.org
Est. 1921. Emergency fund for
professional writers with serious
financial difficulties. Assistance: $2,000
limit. Response Time: 2 mos
Submission Materials: See website.

## Membership & Service Organizations

**Actors' Fund of America**
729 7th Ave., Fl. 10, New York, NY
10019
Barbara Davis, Chief Program Officer
Tel: (212) 221-7300
info@actorsfund.org
www.actorsfund.org
Est. 1882. Human services org for all
entertainment professionals. Also
makes emergency grants for essential
needs. Fee: No.

**ACTS Institute Inc.**
Box 30854, Palm Beach Gardens, FL
33420
Charlotte Plotsky, Exec Dir
Tel: (561) 625-2273
Fax:(561) 625-6010
actsinstitute@bellsouth.net

Est. 1981. Nonprofit foundation for
developing artists. Submission
Materials: Query letter and S.A.S.E..
Fee: No.

**Alliance of Artists Communities (AAC)**
255 South Main St., Providence, RI
02903
Tel: (401) 351-4320
Fax:(401) 351-4507
aac@artistcommunities.org
www.artistcommunities.org
Fee: No.

**Alliance of Los Angeles Playwrights
(ALAP)**
7510 Sunset Blvd., #1050, Los Angeles,
CA 90046
Dan Berkowitz, Jonathan Dorf, Co-Chairs
Tel: (323) 957-4752
info@laplaywrights.org
www.laplaywrights.org
Service and support org for
professional needs of LA playwrights.
Submission Materials: Application.
Fee: Yes.

**Alternate ROOTS Inc.**
1083 Austin Ave., NE, Atlanta, GA 30307
Shannon Turner, Manager of Programs &
Services
Tel: (404) 577-1079
Fax:(404) 577-7991
shannon@alternateroots.org
www.alternateroots.org
Service org for resident Southern
playwrights, directors &
choreographers creating original,
community-based projects. Submission
Materials: Application. Fee: Yes.

**American Association of Community
Theatre (AACT)**
1300 Gendy St., Fort Worth, TX 76107
Rod McCullough, President
Tel: (817) 732-3177
Fax:(817) 732-3178
www.aact.org
Est. 1986. Non-producing company.
Submission Materials: See website.
Fee: No.

**Around the Block Urban Dramatic
Literature Workgroup**
5 E. 22nd St., #9-K, New York, NY
10010
Carlos Jerome, Leader
Tel: (212) 673-9187
info@aroundtheblock.org
www.aroundtheblock.org
Est. 2001. Focusing on urban life.
Committed to color blind casting.
Contact to participate. Response time:
2 wks. Preferred Genre(s): All genres.
Submission Materials: See website.
Fee: No.

**ASCAP (American Society of
Composers, Authors & Publishers)**
1 Lincoln Plaza, New York, NY 10023
Tel: (212) 621-6234
Fax:(212) 621-6558
mkerker@ascap.com
www.ascap.com
Preferred Genre(s): Musical theatre.
Submission Materials: Application.
Fee: No.

**Association for Jewish Theatre (AJT)**
444 W. Camelback Rd., #208, Phoenix,
AZ 85013
Edward Einhorn, Executive Director
Tel: (602) 264-0402
Fax:(602) 264-7131
utc61@aol.com
www.afjt.com
Info on international network of Jewish
theater. Annual newsletter, website,
member pages, annual conf, submission
guide on website. Submission
Materials: See website. Fee: No.

**Association for Theatre in Higher
Education (ATHE)**
Box 1290, Boulder, CO 80306
Nancy Erickson, Administrative Director
Tel: (888) 284-3737
Fax:(303) 530-2168
info@athe.org
www.athe.org
Promoting excellence in theater
education thru publications,
conferences, advocacy, projects and
collaborative efforts with other
organizations. Preferred Genre(s):
Educational. Submission Materials:
Application. Fee: Yes.

**Association of Authors'
Representatives, Inc.**
676A 9th Avenue, #312, New York, NY
10036
Emily Cullings
arinc@mindspring.com
www.aar-online.org
Fee: Yes.

**Black Theatre Network**
2609 Douglass Rd., SE, #102,
Washington, DC 20020
Luther Wells, President
Tel: (850) 656-9061
luther.wells@famu.edu
www.blacktheatrenetwork.org
Special Interest: African-American.
Submission Materials: See website.
Fee: No.

**Chicago Dramatists**
1105 W. Chicago Ave., Chicago, IL
60642
Russ Tutterow, Artistic Director
Tel: (312) 633-0630
newplays@chicagodramatists.org
www.chicagodramatists.org
Est. 1979. Developmental theater and
playwright workshop. See "Programs"
chapter on website for details.
Preferred Genre(s): All genres.
Submission Materials: See website.
Fee: Yes.

**Circus Theatricals**
Hayworth Theatre Center, 2511 Wilsh,
Los Angeles, CA 90057
Jeannine Stehlin, Producing Director
Tel: (310) 701-0788
www.circustheatricals.com
Est. 1983. Membership company of
actors, directors and writers. Preferred
Genre(s): All genres. Preferred Length:
Any length. Submission Materials: See
website. Fee: Yes.

**Dramatists Guild of America Inc.**
1501 Broadway, #701, New York, NY
10036
Rebecca Stump
Fax:(212) 944-0420
rstump@dramatistsguild.com
www.dramatistsguild.com
Est. 1920. Works for the professional
rights of writers of stage works and the
conditions under which those works are
created and produced. Also fights to
secure fair royalties and protect
subsidiary rights, artistic control, and
copyright ownership. Preferred
Genre(s): All genres. Preferred Length:
Any length. Submission Materials:
Application, full script. Fee: Yes.

**Educational Theatre Association**
2343 Auburn Ave., Cincinnati, OH 45219
David LaFleche, Director Membership
Tel: (513) 421-3900
Fax:(513) 421-7077
dlafleche@edta.org
www.edta.org
Submission Materials: See website.
Fee: Yes.

**FirstStage [CA]**
Box 38280, Los Angeles, CA 90038
Dennis Safren, Literary Manager
Tel: (323) 850-6271
Fax:(323) 850-6271
firststagela@aol.com
www.firststagela.org
Est. 1983. Develops new, unproduced
work (30 min or less) for stage and
screen. Response: 6 mos. Preferred
Genre(s): Plays. Preferred Length: 10-
30 min.. Submission Materials:
Complete script & SASE. Fee: Yes.

**Fractured Atlas**
248 W. 35th St., 10th Floor, New York,
NY 10001
Adam J. Natale, Director Member
Services
Tel: (888) 692-7878
Fax:(212) 277-8025
support@fracturedatlas.org
www.fracturedatlas.org
Est. 2002. Microgrants for creative and
organizational development.
Submission Materials: See website.
Fee: Yes. Deadline(s): June 30th, 2011,
December 31st, 2011

**Greensboro Playwrights' Forum**
200 N. Davie St., #2, Greensboro, NC
27401
Stephen D. Hyers, Director
Tel: (336) 335-6426
Fax:(336) 373-2659
stephen.hyers@greensboro-nc.gov
www.playwrightsforum.org
Est. 1993. Aids area dramatists in
publishing, producing, and learning
theater writing with monthly meetings
& workshops, staged readings,
newsletter, and studio space. Preferred
Genre(s): All genres. Preferred Length:

Any length. Submission Materials: Application. Fee: Yes.

**Helen Hayes Awards**
2233 Wisconsin Ave., NW, #300, Washington, DC 20007
Tel: (202) 337-4572
Fax:(202) 625-1238
www.helenhayes.org
  Est. 1984. Submission Materials: See website. Fee: No.

**Hispanic Organization of Latin Actors (HOLA)**
107 Suffolk St., #302, New York, NY 10002
Manuel Alfaro, Executive Director
Tel: (212) 253-1015
Fax:(212) 253-9651
holagram@hellohola.org
www.hellohola.org
  Submission Materials: See website. Fee: No.

**Inside Broadway**
630 9th Ave., #802, New York, NY 10036
Michael Presser, Executive Director
Tel: (212) 245-0710
Fax:(212) 245-3018
mpresser@insidebroadway.org
www.insidebroadway.org
  Professional children's theater producing classic musicals in NYC public schools. Also offer hands-on, in-school residencies that enrich core curriculum through drama, dance, and music. Preferred Genre(s): Musical theatre. Special Interest: Theatre for Young Audiences. Preferred Length: Any length. Submission Materials: See website. Fee: No.

**International Theatre Institute US Center (ITI/US)**
520 8th Ave., Fl. 24, New York, NY 10018
Emilya Cachapero, Director
Tel: (212) 609-5900
Fax:(212) 609-5901
iti@tcg.org
www.tcg.org Fee: No.

**LA Stage Alliance**
644 S. Figueroa St., Los Angeles, CA 90017
Douglas Clayton, Membership Manager
Tel: (213) 614-0556
Fax:(213) 614-0561
info@lastagealliance.com
www.lastagealliance.com
  Est. 1975. Nonprofit service org of groups /individuals providing L.A. Stage magazine, networking opportunities, half-price tix, Ovation Awards, cooperative ads, info, referrals. Submission Materials: Application. Fee: No.

**League of Chicago Theatres/Foundation**
228 South Wabash #200, Chicago, IL 60604
Tel: (312) 554-9800
Fax:(312) 922-7202
info@chicagoplays.com
www.chicagoplays.com
  Est. 1979. Submission Materials: See website. Fee: Yes.

**League of Professional Theatre Women**
12 Stuyvesant Oval, apt 8-D, New York, NY 10009
Linda S. Chapman, Vice President,, Membership
Tel: (212) 414-8048
Fax:(212) 225-2378
lindanyc@rcn.com
www.theatrewomen.org
  Nonprofit advocacy organization promoting visibility and increasing opportunities for women in the professional theater. Fee: Yes.

**Literary Managers & Dramaturgs of the Americas (LMDA)**
P.O.Box 36. 20985, P.A.C.C., New York, NY 10129
Danielle Carroll, Admin Director
Tel: (800) 680-2148
lmdanyc@gmail.com
www.lmda.org
  Est. 1985. Volunteer membership org w/conferences, quarterly journal, newsletter, advocacy caucuses,

dramaturgy prize and more.
Submission Materials: Application.
Fee: No.

**New Dramatists**
424 W. 44th St., New York, NY 10036
Emily Morse, Director, Artistic
   Development
Tel: (212) 757-6960
Fax:(212) 265-4738
newdramatists@newdramatists.org
www.newdramatists.org
   Est. 1949. New Dramatists is dedicated
   to identifying gifted playwrights and
   giving them the time/tools/space to
   develop their craft. For emerging and
   mid-career writers. Submission
   Materials: See website. Fee: No.
   Deadline(s): between July 15 and
   September 15 annually

**New Playwrights Foundation**
608 San Vicente Blvd., #18, Santa
   Monica, CA 90402
Jeffrey Bergquist, Artistic Director
Tel: (310) 393-3682
dialogue@newplaywrights.org
www.newplaywrights.org
   Est. 1969. Meets every other Thursday
   in Santa Monica. NPF has produced
   works for stage, film and video by
   NPF members. Accepts material from
   members only. Guests free. Preferred
   Genre(s): All genres. Preferred Length:
   Any length. Submission Materials:
   Application. Fee: Yes. Deadline(s):
   Ongoing

**North Carolina Writers' Network
(NCWN)**
P.O. Box 21591, Winston-Salem, NC
   27120
Ed Southern
Tel: (336) 293-8844
ed@ncwriters.org
www.ncwriters.org
   Nonprofit to connect, promote and lead
   NC writers thru conferences, contests,
   newsletter, website, member pages,
   member book catalog, critique and
   consultation, etc. Submission Materials:
   Application. Fee: Yes.

**OPERA America**
330 7th Ave., Fl. 16, New York, NY
   10001
Tel: (212) 796-8620
Fax:(212) 796-8631
www.operaamerica.org
   National service org promoting
   creation, presentation and enjoyment of
   opera. Provides professional
   development resources for composers,
   librettists, educators, etc. Preferred
   Genre(s): Opera. Submission Materials:
   Application. Fee: Yes.

**Orange County Playwrights Alliance
(OCPA)**
21112 Indigo Circle, Huntington Beach,
   CA 92646
Eric Eberwein, Director
Tel: (714) 962-7686
firenbones@aol.com
www.ocplaywrights.org
   Est. 1995. Member org. workshop of
   Orange Co. dramatists. Develops new
   works, staged readings, occasional
   productions. Submission Materials: See
   website. Fee: Yes.

**Pacific Northwest Writers Assn.**
PMB 2717, 1420 NW Gilman Blvd, St 2,
   Issaquah, WA 98027
Dana Murphy-Love, Executive Director
Tel: (425) 673-2665
pnwa@pnwa.org
www.pnwa.org
   Est. 1956. Submission Materials:
   Application. Fee: No. Deadline(s): Fall

**Philadelphia Dramatists Center (PDC)**
P.O. 22666, Philadelphia, PA 19110-2666
Wally Zialcita, Executive Director
director@pdc1.org
www.pdc1.org
   Membership org for improving the
   craft, opportunities and conditions of
   dramatic writers. Members/non-
   members can sign up for e-mailing list.
   Submission Materials: Application.
   Fee: Yes.

**Playformers**
30 Waterside Plaza, #7D, New York, NY 10010
Joann Lee
Tel: (917) 825-2663
playformers@earthlink.net
> Est. 1987. Playwright Group. Monthy meetings (Sep-May) to read new work by members. Response: 2 mos. Preferred Genre(s): All genres. Preferred Length: Any length. Submission Materials: Complete script & SASE. Fee: Yes.

**Playwrights' Forum [MD]**
Box 5322, Rockville, MD 20848
Ernie Joselovitz, President
Tel: (301) 816-0569
Fax:(301) 816-0569
www.playwrightsforum.org
> Est. 1991. Author must be a Mid-Atlantic resident. Submission Materials: Application. Fee: Yes. Deadline(s): Jan. 15, 2011 , May 15, 2011, Sept 15, 2011

**Playwrights Guild of Canada (PGC)**
215 Spadina Ave. Suite 210, Toronto, ON M5T-2C7 Canada
Kevin Gojmerac, Manager, Membership
Tel: (416) 703-0201
Fax:(416) 703-0059
info@playwrightsguild.ca
www.playwrightsguild.ca
> Est. 1972. National nonprofit offering triannual directory of Canadian plays/playwrights and quarterly magazine. Response: 3 wks. Submission Materials: Application and resume. Fee: Yes.

**Saskatchewan Writers Guild (SWG)**
Box 3986, Regina, SK S4P 3R9 Canada
Judith Silverthorne
Tel: (306) 757-6310
info@skwriter.com
www.skwriter.com
> Est. 1969. Membership is open to all writers, teachers, librarians, publishers, booksellers, students and others interested in Saskatchewan writing. Submission Materials: See website. Fee: Yes. Deadline(s): Last working day of June annually

**The Field**
161 6th Ave., Fl. 14, New York, NY 10013
Michael Helland, Marketing Associate
Tel: (212) 691-6969
Fax:(212) 255-2053
michael@thefield.org
www.thefield.org
> Est. 1986. The Field has been dedicated to providing impactful and supportive programs to thousands of performing artists in a variety of areas of the performing arts. Preferred Genre(s): All genres. Preferred Length: Any length. Submission Materials: Application. Fee: Yes.

**The Playwrights' Center (MN)**
2301 Franklin Ave. E., Minneapolis, MN 55406
Kevin McLaughlin
Tel: (612) 332-7481
Fax:(612) 332-6037
annap@pwcenter.org
www.pwcenter.org
> Provides services that support playwrights and playwriting. Programs incl. listed submission opportunities, fellowships, workshops, readings, classes, and online member-to-member networking services. Submission Materials: Application. Fee: Yes.

**The Purple Circuit**
921 N. Naomi St., Burbank, CA 91505
Bill Kaiser, Co-founder/Editor
Tel: (818) 953-5096
purplecir@aol.com
www.buddybuddy.com/pc.html
> Service group to promote GLBT performing arts worldwide. Maintains Calif. show listings hotline (818-953-5072), directory of GLBT-friendly venues, and freelisting of playwrights. Special Interest: GLBT. Fee: No.

**The Theatre Museum**
40 Worth Street, Suite 824, New York, NY 10013
Helen M. Guditis
Tel: (212) 764-4112
information@thetheatremuseum.org

Est. 2003. The only nonprofit museum in America with the mission to preserve, perpetuate and protect the legacy of the theatre. Fee: No.

## The Writers' Guild of Great Britain
40 Rosebery Avenue, London, United Kingdom
Anne Hogben, Asst. General Secretary
Tel: (442) 078-3307 Ext 77
Fax:(442) 078-3347 Ext 77
anne@writersguild.org.uk
www.writersguild.org.uk
TUC-affiliated union for professional writers living or working in UK. Submission Materials: See website. Fee: Yes.

## The Writers Room
740 Broadway, Fl. 12, New York, NY 10003
Donna Brodie, Executive Director
Tel: (212) 254-6995
Fax:(212) 533-6059
writersroom@writersroom.org
www.writersroom.org
Est. 1978. Large loft with 44 work stations, library, storage area, kitchen/lounge and phone room. Open 24/7. 1 month list for full-time membership; no wait list for part-time. Submission Materials: See website. Fee: Yes.

## Theatre Bay Area (TBA)
1663 Mission Street #525, San Francisco, CA 94103
Brad Erickson, Executive Director
Tel: (415) 430-1140
Fax:(415) 430-1145
tba@theatrebayarea.org
www.theatrebayarea.org
Nonprofit org of individuals and theater companies for Bay Area resident authors offering grants, publication and more. Submission Materials: Application. Fee: Yes.

## Theatre Communications Group (TCG)
520 8th Ave., Fl. 24, New York, NY 10018
Teresa Eyring, Executive Director
Tel: (212) 609-5900
Fax:(212) 609-5901
tcg@tcg.org
www.tcg.org
National service org for nonprofit US professional theater. Services incl grants, fellowships, workshops, conferences, advocacy, research, ticket discounts. Submission Materials: Application. Fee: Yes.

## Theatre Development Fund (TDF)
520 8th Ave. #801, New York, NY 10018
David LeShay, Director of Communications
Tel: (212) 917-9770
Fax:(212) 768-1563
dleshay@tdf.org
www.tdf.org
Est. 1968. Enabling a diverse audience to attend live theatre and dance through discount ticket booths, memberships. Submission Materials: Application. Fee: Yes.

## Theatre West
3333 Cahuenga Blvd. W., Hollywood, CA 90068
John Gallogly, Executive Director
Tel: (323) 851-4839
Fax:(323) 851-5286
theatrewest@theatrewest.org
www.theatrewest.org
Est. 1962. Member org. Author must be a resident of So. Cal. Mandatory 6 hrs/mo volunteering in 1st year of membership. Preferred Genre(s): Plays. Preferred Length: Full-length. Submission Materials: Complete script. Fee: Yes.

## TRU (Theater Resources Unlimited)
115 MacDougal Street, New York, NY 10012
Bob Ost, President
Tel: (212) 714-7628
Fax:(212) 864-6301
trunltd@aol.com
www.truonline.org

Est. 1992. Support and educational services for producers, theater companies, and self-producing artists, emphasizing the business side of the arts. Preferred Genre(s): Plays or Musicals. Preferred Length: One-act or Full-length. Submission Materials: See website. Fee: Yes. Deadline(s): 1/7/2011 , 8/22/2011

**United States Copyright Office**
101 Independence Ave., SE, Washington, DC 20003
Tel: (202) 707-3000
www.copyright.gov
Though registration isn't required for protection, copyright law provides several advantages to registration. Submission Materials: See website. Fee: Yes.

**V&A Theatre and Performance Department**
Blythe House, 23 Blythe Road, London, W14 OQX United Kingdom
Beverley Hart, Librarian
Tel: 0 (207) 942-2697
tmenquiries@vam.ac.uk
www.vam.ac.uk/collections/
  theatre_performance
Submission Materials: See website. Fee: No.

**Waterfront Ensemble & New Jersey Dramatists**
Box 1486, Hoboken, NJ 7030
Pete Ernst, Artistic Director
Tel: (201) 708-6535
njdramatists@hotmail.com
www.waterfrontensemble.org
Nonprofit organization dedicated to new workshop/reading/production of new plays. **Please note, at press

time, group on hiatus. Check website for details** Preferred Genre(s): Plays. Preferred Length: One-Act. Submission Materials: 30pg writing sample. Fee: Yes.

**Writers Guild of America, East (WGAE)**
555 W. 57th St., #1230, New York, NY 10019
Tel: (212) 767-7800
Fax:(212) 582-1909
www.wgae.org
Est. 1954. Submission Materials: See website. Fee: Yes.

**Writers Guild of America, West (WGAW)**
7000 W. 3rd St., Los Angeles, CA 90048
Corinne Tippin, Membership Admin.
Tel: (323) 782-4532
Fax:(323) 782-4800
www.wga.org
Submission Materials: See website. Fee: Yes.

**Young Playwrights Inc. (YPI)**
P.O. Box 5134, New York, NY 10185
Sheri Goldhirsch, Artistic Director
Tel: (212) 594-5440
Fax:(212) 684-4902
admin@youngplaywrights.org
www.youngplaywrights.org
Est. 1981. YPI identifies and develops young (18 and younger) US playwrights by involving them as active participants in the highest quality professional productions of their plays. Preferred Genre(s): Plays. Submission Materials: See website. Fee: Yes. Deadline(s): See website

# Special Interests

## TEN-MINUTE AND SHORT PLAY OPPORTUNITIES

In recent years, the ten-minute play has blossomed into a genre all its own, affording playwrights myriad opportunities for exposure to new and diverse audiences. The following list is by no means completely comprehensive. This chapter is meant as a supplement to the general listings in the directory. Consider this a place to start your journey on the path toward production of your ten-minute. plays. As always, we strongly recommend that you take the time to consult websites, as deadlines and guidelines frequently change.

### General Sites
http://www.burryman.com/submissions.html#sub
http://www.aact.org/cgi-bin/webdata_contests.pl?cgifunction=Search
http://enavantplaywrights.yuku.com/forums/3/t/Opportunities-10-Minute-amp-Other-Short-Plays.html

### Publishers Of Ten-Minute Plays

**Brooklyn Publishers** - www.brookpub.com "We highly encourage you to send your submission via our Web site at www.brookpub.com, by clicking on Submit a Play in the Author's Corner on the left border. You may also submit a play by e-mail with attachment at editor@brookpub.com or by snail-mail with a complete manuscript to me at: Brooklyn Publishers, Attn: Editor, 5213 New Orleans Drive, Odessa, Texas 79762. When you submit a play, please include the following: short synopsis of the work; the play's genre, duration, and cast size; character list; production history (if any - not required); short bio of the playwright; contact information, including e-mail address, phone number, and mailing address."

**Big Dog Plays** - www.bigdogplays.com "We welcome submissions from new and established playwrights. If you would like to submit a play, please send a printed copy of your script and a self-addressed stamped envelope to our mailing address. Be sure to include a cover letter, a production history and/or a list of awards (if applicable), and a cast list and character breakdown. Because we give each script careful consideration, please allow 8 weeks for response. We look forward to reading your work. Sorry, we do not accept submissions via e-mail."

**Meriweather** – www.meriwetherpublishing.com/school.aspx -A query letter is suggested, but ten-minute plays should be appropriate for the school or church market and most should be in a collection of plays. Production tested plays are encouraged. Editor, Contemporary Drama Service, 885 Elkton Drive, Colorado Springs, CO 80907. Or e-mail query letters (no attachments) to: editor@meriwether.com

**Dramatic Publishing** - http://www.dramaticpublishing.com/submissions.php
Due to the large number of scripts we receive, our current response time is 4 to 6 months. Unless we have requested additional manuscripts from you, please submit only one or two at a time. More than that causes backups for everyone. Please use the

136

guidelines from the website when submitting a script. Linda Habjan, Submissions Editor. 311 Washington St. Woodstock, IL 60098  Ph: (800)448-7469 Fax: (800)334-5302.

**Pioneer Drama Service** - www.pioneerdrama.com/playwrights/submit.asp -A query letter or email is suggested: http://www.pioneerdrama.com//contactus.asp?ID=5 Plays must be accompanied by a Synopsis/Description, Cast List and Breakdown (i.e. 5M, 6W), Running Time, Set Design, Prop List, Recording of Music (when applicable). All plays received will be considered for publication and will usually be accepted or rejected within four months. Send submissions to: Editor Pioneer Drama Service, Post Office Box 4267, Englewood, CO 80155-4267

## LISTINGS

### 10 by 10 in the Triangle
The Arts Center
300-G East Main Street
Carrboro, NC 27510
(919) 929-2787
www.artscenterlive.org
info@artscenterlive.org

Remuneration. $100 plus travel stipend. Preference. 10-minute plays. No 10-minute monologues. Musicals accepted. **Application.** For each play, send two separate emails to theatre@artscenterlive.org.  The first e-mail regards playwright contact information, and the second regards contents of the play.  E-mail 1 – the subject line and the attached file retain the same name, which is the title of the play followed by the phrase "contact info."  For example, if the name of the play is Poker Face, the subject line and attached file would read "Poker Face contact info". The attached file only contains the title page with contact information.  Please use the full title of the play as numerous plays with similar titles are often received. Email 2 – the subject line and the attached file retain the same name, which is the title of the play. For example, the subject line of this email is Poker Face and the attached file is Poker Face.  This file contains cast, set requirements, and script. No contact information, please.  If you are submitting two scripts, please send four separate emails.  Please do not zip the files. **Deadline:** January 10-February 11.

### 10-Minute International Play Competition
10-Minute Play Competition
Fire Rose Productions
11246 Magnolia Blvd.
NoHo Theatre & Arts District, CA 91601
818.766.3691
www.fireroseproductions.com
info@fireroseproductions.com

Consideration. Fees: $5 each play. Remuneration. production, $200. Youth Award: $100 gift certificate. Preference. Length: 8-12 minutes. **Application.** Submit unbound play, fee, and application form (see website) to 10-Minute Play Competition, Fire Rose Productions, 11246 Magnolia Blvd., NoHo Theatre & Arts District, CA 91601. **Deadline:** March 30, postmarked

**6 Women Play Festival**
6 Women Play Festival
c/o Pikes Peak Arts Council
PO Box 1073
Colorado Springs, CO 80901
www.sixwomenplayfestival.com
http://www.sixwomenplayfestival.com/guidelines.html
> Remuneration. $100.00 and a travel stipend to attend the festival. Preference. Length: 10 pages. Content/Subject Matter: See website for theme. Author Must Be: female. Material Must Be: unpublished, unproduced. **Application:** Submit three copies of play (bound with staple only) with title only. Include one unbound sheet which includes title of play, author's name and address, email, and phone number. **Deadline:** see website.

**Annual Jersey Voices Festival**
Chatham Playhouse
23 North Passaic Avenue
Chatham, New Jersey 07928
973-635-7363
www.chathamplayers.org/jerseyvoices.html
jerseyvoices@chathamplayers.org
> Preference. Length: 20 minute or less. Musicals accepted. Author Must Be: New Jersey playwright. **Application.** Submit play to Jersey Voices c/o CCP, P.O. Box 234, Chatham, NJ 07928 or email (in Word of PDF format) to jerseyvoices@chathamplayers.org. **Deadline:** see website.

**Chester Horn Short Play Festival**
TheatreRats
www.theatrerats.com
Remuneration. Production. Preference. Length: no more than 15 pages. Any style/genre accepted. **Application.** Submit script (PDF or Word) to scripts@theatrerats.com. **Deadline:** see website.

**EATfest**
EATheatre, Emerging Artists Theatre
464 W. 25th St. #4
New York, NY 10001-6501
(212) 247-2429
EATheatre.org
EATheatre.org/submissions.php
> Remuneration. Production. Preferences. No monologues. Length: 10 to 50 minutes. Material Must Be: unproduced in NYC, unpublished. **Application.** Submit online via website (preferred), or send play to Emerging Artists Theatre, Attention: Playwrights Manager, 464 W. 25th St. #4, New York, NY 10001-6501. Include play and a letter including your name, telephone number, address and e-mail address. **Deadline:** January 7.

**Estrogenius Short Play Showcase**
EstroGenius/Manhattan Theatre Source
177 MacDougal Street
New York, NY 10011
212.260.4698
www.estrogenius.org
estrogenius.festival@gmail.com
> **Preferences.** Only new short plays about women, no monologues. Female writer preferred but not required. Length: 10-15 minutes. Simple production values. **Application:** see website for "cover sheet." Submit play, completed cover sheet, and character breakdown to Manhattan Theatre Source, Attn: ESTROGENIUS SHORT PLAY SHOWCASE - play selection, 177 MacDougal Street, NY, NY 10011. **Deadline:** see website.

**Festival of One-Act Plays**
Theatre Three
P.O. Box 512
Port Jefferson, NY 11777-0512
631.928.9202
www.theatrethree.com
http://www.theatrethree.com/oneactsubmissionguidelines.htm
> **Remuneration.** Small stipend, production. **Preference.** Length: 40 minutes maximum. Simple set, 8 actors or less. **Material Must Be:** unproduced, no adaptations, musicals, or children's plays. **Application.** Submit a cover letter, a synopsis, and a resume along with one copy of the play. Cover sheet of play should have title, author, author's address, author's telephone number, and author's email address (if available). Plays should be neatly bound or stapled on the left-hand corner. (No loose pages and no binders, please.) All submissions must include a standard SASE for correspondence. Submit to The 13th Annual Festival of One-Act Plays, Attn: Jeffrey Sanzel, Artistic Director, THEATRE THREE, P.O. Box 512, Port Jefferson, NY 11777-0512. **Deadline:** see website.

**Festival of Originals**
Theatre Southwest
944 Clarkcrest,
Houston, Texas 77063
www.theatresouthwest.org
http://www.theatresouthwest.org/foorules.html
> **Remuneration.** Production, $100. **Preference.** No Monologues. Length: 20 minutes. **Material Must Be:** unproduced. **Application.** Submit script, fee, plot summary to Theatre Southwest, 944 Clarkcrest, Houston, Texas 77063, Attention: Festival Submissions; or email mimi@theatresouthwest.org. **Deadline:** March 15 at 3 PM.

**Future 10**
Future Tenant
Stacey Vespaziani
Future 10 Play Submissions
3251 Pinehurst Ave.
Pittsburgh, PA 15216
svespaz@mac.com
http://www.futuretenant.org/
    Production. Preference. Length: approx 10 pages. Theme: "Life in Pittsburgh."
    Production: Cast size 2-6, limited set/prop requirements. **Application.** Submit four
    copies of play, plus a cover letter with all contact info and title of play. No contact
    info or name should be on submitted scripts. **Deadline:** see website.

**Inspirato Festival, Toronto Ten Minute Play Festival**
Inspirato Festival
www.inspiratofestival.ca
http://www.inspiratofestival.ca/write-a-play.php
    Remuneration. $100, production. Preference. Length: 10 minutes. Content/Subject
    Matter: Sense of touch must be an important element in the play (see website).
    **Application.** See website for online submission. **Deadline:** see website.

**Kansas City Women's Playwriting Festival**
Potluck Productions
7338 Belleview
Kansas City, MO 64114
www.kcpotluckproductions.com
    Remuneration. Production. Preference. Length: 10-20 minutes. Author Must Be:
    female. Material Must Be: unpublished. **Application.** Send two (2) paper copies of
    your script (bound), a show synopsis, resume, and cover letter. Enclose two (2) SASE
    envelopes or postcards. Submit to: Potluck Productions, 7338 Belleview, Kansas City,
    MO 64114. **Deadline:** see website.

**National Ten-Minute Play Contest**
Actors Theatre of Louisville
www.actorstheatre.org
www.actorstheatre.org/humana_contest.htm
    Remuneration. $1000, production. Preference. Length: 10 pages or less. Author
    Must Be: US citizen. Material Must Be: unproduced, not previously submitted.
    **Application.** Submit play with contact info to: National Ten-Minute Play Contest,
    Actors Theatre of Louisville, 316 West Main Street, Louisville, KY 40202-4218.
    **Deadline:** November 1.

**One Act Play Festival**
Circus Theatricals
info@circustheatricals.com
310 226-6144 ext. 1
www.circustheatricals.com/playwrights.html
www.circustheatricals.com
    Preference. Length: 15 pages or less, simple production value. **Application.** Submit
    three copies of full script, typed and securely bound. No contact info on script/
    separate title page with contact info. Short bio. Previous productions must not have
    been in L.A. or Southern CA. Submit to: Circus Theatricals, Attn: One Act Plays
    Festival 2008, PO Box 586, Culver City , CA 90232. **Deadline:** see website.

**Pick of the Vine**
Little Fish Theatre
www.littlefishtheatre.org
> Preference. Minimal set requirements, 6 or fewer characters. **Application.** Email script with contact info to melanie@littlefishtheatre.org or mail hard copy to: Melanie Jones , Little Fish Theatre, 619 West 38th St, San Pedro CA 90731. **Deadline:** August 1.

**Premiere One-Act Competition**
Moving Arts
www.movingarts.org/submission_guidelines.html
> Consideration. $10 entry fee per script (made out to Moving Arts). Remuneration: $200. Preferences: One-Acts, unproduced in L.A. **Application.** Submit script, cover letter, SASE to Moving Arts, Premiere One-Act Competition, P.O. BOX 481145, Los Angeles, CA 90048. Playwright's name should appear only on the cover letter and nowhere on the script. Scripts must be three-hole punched, preferably with a cover–please do not send loose sheets or spiral bound scripts. **Deadline:** see website.

**Queer Shorts**
StageQ
Queer Shorts, c/o StageQ
PO Box 8876
Madison, WI. 53708-8876
www.stageq.com
> Preference. Length: 5-15 minutes. Content/Subject Matter: queer lifestyle
> **Application.** Email play, paragraph synopsis, production requirements, cast breakdown, and if there are any queer characters or nudity, to QueerShorts@stageq. com, or mail to: Queer Shorts, c/o StageQ, PO Box 8876, Madison, WI. 53708-8876. **Deadline:** see website.

**Quickies - the annual festival of shorts**
Live Girls! Theater
www.livegirlstheater.org
> Consideration: Production or reading. Preferences. Small cast and low production requirements. Length: 10-minute. Author Must Be: Female. **Application.** Email plays and include your bio\resume, production history for plays submitted to: submissions@livegirlstheater.org. Attach plays as Word docs. **Deadline:** see website.

**Reader's Theatre**
Theatre Southwest
944 Clarkcrest
Houston, Texas 77063
www.theatresouthwest.org
http://www.theatresouthwest.org/rfrules.html
> Preference. Length: 5-15 minutes. Material Must be: unpublished. **Application.** Submit up to 3 plays with character breakdown and one paragraph play summary (not required) to Theatre Southwest, 944 Clarkcrest, Houston, Texas 77063, Attention: Festival Submissions; or email mimi@theatresouthwest.org. **Deadline:** see website.

**Salute UR Shorts New Play Festival**
Rapscallion Theatre Collective
2064 46th St 2nd Floor
Astoria, NY 11105
www.rapscalliontheatrecollective.com
rapscalliontheatre@gmail.com
>   Consideration. Production. Preference. Length: 10-15 minutes. **Application.** Submit
>   play to rapscalliontheatre@gmail.com (preferred method), or mail to Reynold
>   Malcolm Hewitt, Rapscallion Theatre Collective, 2064 46th St 2nd Floor, Astoria,
>   NY 11105. **Deadline:** see website.

**ShowOff! Camino Real International Playwriting Festival**
Camino Real Playhouse
ShowOff!
Camino Real Playhouse
31776 El Camino Real
San Juan Capistrano, CA 92675
www.caminorealplayhouse.org/ShowOffs.html
info@city-theater.org, pantheater@comcast.net
>   Consideration. Contest, production. Fees: $10.00 per play. Disclosure: for use as
>   winner stipends. Remuneration: not specified. Preference. Length: 10 minutes.
>   Comedy or drama. **Application.** Submit plays unbound (stapled is OK) with your full
>   contact info on the cover or title page to: ShowOff!, Camino Real Playhouse, 31776
>   El Camino Real, San Juan Capistrano, CA 92675. **Deadline:** see website.

**Snowdance 10 Minute Comedy Festival**
Over Our Head Players
SNOWDANCE
c/o Sixth Street Theatre
318 6th St.
Racine, WI, 53403
www.overourheadplayers.org
>   Consideration. Production, prize. Remuneration: A cash award of $300.00, $100.00
>   to second and third place. Preference. Length: 10 minutes. Content/Subject Matter:
>   comedy. Material Must Be: unpublished. **Application.** Submit play with contact
>   info to: SNOWDANCE, c/o Sixth Street Theatre, 318 6th St., Racine, WI, 53403.
>   **Deadline:** see website

**Source Festival**
1835 14th St., NW
Washington, DC 20009
http://www.sourcedc.org/
202-315-1305
>   Remuneration. Production. Preference. Length: 10 minutes. Material Must Be:
>   unpublished. **Application.** Submit play online at theatre's website. Include contact
>   info on title page and submission form found on website. Plays only accepted in
>   following formats: .doc, .pdf, or .rtf. All pages must have number and include title of
>   play and name of playwright. One submission per applicant. **Deadline:** see website.

**Ten-Minute Play Contest**
Lakeshore Players
Outreach Committee
4820 Stewart Ave
White Bear Lake, MN  55110
www.lakeshoreplayers.com
> Remuneration. Production, $10 per performance. Preference. Length: 10 minutes.
> High school students also encouraged to submit. Production: 5 or fewer characters
> **Application.** Submit two copies of script (One with contact information, one with
> title only) to: Lakeshore Players Outreach Committee, 4820 Stewart Ave. White Bear
> Lake, MN  55110. **Deadline:** see website.

**Ten-Minute Play Contest**
Princeton University Ten-Minute Play Contest
Theater and Dance Program
185 Nassau Street
Princeton University
Princeton NJ 08544
http://www.princeton.edu/arts/lewis_center/high-school-contests/ten-minute-play-contest/
(609) 258-8562
> Consideration. Juniors in high school only. Remuneration: First Prize: $500.00;
> Second Prize: $250.00; Third Prize: $100.00. Preference. Length: 10-Minute. Author
> Must Be: Any student who is in the eleventh grade. **Application.** Submit one copy
> of play, include name, address, and phone number on submission and online form.
> Submit to: Princeton Ten-Minute Play Contest, Theater and Dance Program, 185
> Nassau Street, Princeton University, Princeton NJ 08544. **Deadline:** see website.

**The Actors' Theatre 15th Annual Ten-Minute Play Contest**
The Actors' Theatre
1001 Center St., Suite 12
Santa Cruz, CA 95060
831.425.1003
www.actorssc.org
www.actorssc.org/contests.php#810s
> Consideration. Fees: $10 per play. Preference. Length: 10 pages maximum. Minimal
> set requirements. Material Must Be: unproduced, unpublished. **Application.** Submit
> 5 copies of your play (securely bound, preferably in a soft cover). Two types of cover
> pages: 1) a separate cover letter, which includes your name, address, phone number,
> e-mail and the play title. 2) the play title on each copy. No identifying information on
> the script other than the title.  Submission: mail five hard copies (see address above)
> to Ten-Minute Play Contest. **Deadline:** see website.

**The Seven: New Works Fest**
FUSION Theatre
700 1st Street NW
Albuquerque, New Mexico 87102
http://www.fusionabq.org/theseven.htm
jeng@fusionabq.org
>    Consideration. Production, award. Fees: $5. Disclosure: offset printing costs,
>    Remuneration: jury prize. Preference. Length: 10 pages or less, Content/Subject
>    Matter: see website. Material Must Be: unproduced, not previously submitted.
>    **Application.** Play with title page and contact info, fee with e-submission at: http://
>    thecell.fatcow.com/store/page6.html, or mail to: FUSION Theatre Co., Attn: Jen
>    Grigg, 700 1st Street NW, Albuquerque, New Mexico 87102. Theme announced in
>    February. **Deadline:** see website.

**Theatre Oxford 10-Minute Play Contest**
Theatre Oxford
10 Minute Play Contest
P. O. Box 1321; Oxford, MS 38655
Dinah Swan, Contest Director: 662-236-5052,
www.10minuteplays.com
>    Consideration. Production, contest. Fees: $10 made out to Theatre Oxford.
>    Remuneration: $1000 prize. Preference. Length: max 10 pages. Material Must
>    Be: unproduced. **Application.** Assemble script as follows: Optional cover letter;
>    a title page with the play's title, author's name, address, phone number, and email
>    address. (This is the only place the author's name should appear.) The second page
>    should contain a cast of characters list and time and place information. The third
>    page will be the first page of the script. The other pages of the play follow. Name of
>    play and page numbers on every page. Do NOT use binders or folders of any kind.
>    Plays cannot be returned. Enclose a SASP if you want assurance that your play was
>    received. Submit to: Theatre Oxford 10 Minute Play Contest, P. O. Box 1321, Oxford,
>    MS 38655. **Deadline:** see website.

## VOLUNTEER OPPORTUNITIES FOR DRAMATISTS GUILD MEMBERS

Volunteering can be far more than simply doing a good deed. Volunteering is a great way to develop new skill sets, make friends, garner new professional contacts, get exercise, spend time outdoors, and spend time with the elderly, animals or children. Volunteering is also an excellent routine breaker. Finding the right volunteer opportunity for your lifestyle is extremely important. This list simply seeks to be a springboard for your own exploration into the world of volunteering. Many of you may already volunteer on a regular basis. But how often do you use your skills as a writer when volunteering? Based on an idea from *The Dramatist's* "From the Desk of Gary Garrison," we've created a brief list of opportunities where you, as a writer, can use your talents to support all sorts of exciting organizations. Use your skills in requesting grants for your theatre companies to request grants for other organizations in need, use your wit and charm to write thank you letters, or holiday cards. I challenge you to find new ways to incorporate your artistic skills into volunteering.

**Rebecca Stump**, Membership Assistant, The Dramatists Guild of America

## Atlanta

### The Orion School

We need someone to help our development professional to write small grants to help support and expand the specialized programs we have in place including the Orton Gillingham method for reading, Handwriting Without Tears, Drumming Circle, Yoga, Dance, Art, Photography, Occupational Therapy, Club Orion after school program, Camp Orion, A parent Support Series, and physical activities such as swimming, fencing, rock climbing, and recreational hiking. The Orion School is a small, non-profit, alternative school located in Midtown Atlanta. We specialize in educating students who have complex ADHD and co-occurring conditions such as dyslexia and OCD. All our students struggle to regulate their behavior in more traditional schools. Our school is designed to ensure success for students who are impulsive, hyperactive, inattentive, and highly distractible. We value our student's individuality and use their strengths to help them learn strategies to live successfully with ADHD.

   Website: http://www.theorionschool.org/
   Email: Director@theorionschool.org
   Phone: 404-551-2574

## Boston

### Make-A-Wish Foundation of Massachusetts and Rhode Island

Volunteer Creative Writers Needed for "Wish Stories": Creative writers are needed in our Boston location to produce heartfelt "Wish Stories" that will be used in thank you letters, newsletter articles and other Foundation publications. These two to three paragraph stories are written from the information that is gathered about our Wish children and their experiences on their Wish. This opportunity is open to someone who can come into our Boston office on a weekly basis between the hours of 9am-5pm. The Make-A-Wish Foundation of Massachusetts and Rhode Island grants the wishes of children with life-threatening medical conditions to enrich the human experience with hope, strength, and joy. We strive to create uplifting, meaningful, and empowering experiences for our wish children, and a much-needed respite for families during a difficult time.

> Website: http://www.massri.wish.org
> Email: kbishop@massri.wish.org
> Phone: 617-367-1054

### Alliance for Cultural & Economic Exchange, Inc

Our mission is to provide rainforest children with educational opportunities. We do this by bringing together people from a wide range of backgrounds to partner for economic development and cultural sustainability at the community level. At the root is our desire to help prepare the next generation for their work – to be stewards of their Kishwa culture and their Amazonian rainforest environment. Seeking a  volunteer Grant Writer: Description: Researches and identifies viable grant opportunities for Alliance Exchange as well as prepares and submits grant applications, letters of inquiry and formal proposals accordingly. Works in collaboration with the Team Leader Volunteers.

> Website: http://www.alliancexchange.org/
> Email: madsen@alliancexchange.org
> Phone: 617-628-9297

### Newton Senior Center

Creative Writing Group Leader: This group needs a new leader. They meet weekly on Mondays at 1:30 and share their work, gently critique and encourage each other. Knowledge of writing techniques and ability to work with a group a plus. Other creative opportunities available as well. Confidence and humor helpful!

> Website: http://www.newtonseniors.org/
> Email: jfisher@newtonma.gov
> Phone: 617-796-1660

## Houston

### Homeless Pet Placement League

The Homeless Pet Placement League has many opportunities for volunteers to help raise much needed funds for their four-legged ones. HPPL was founded in 1989 by a group of individuals who were concerned about the plight of homeless dogs and cats in the Houston area; specifically, animals that would not usually be put up for adoption by the local animal shelters. These include animals with skin problems such as mange, heartworm positive dogs, broken bones and injured or seriously malnourished strays. Opportunities range anywhere from 'hands on' at adoptions sites, to planning, grant writing, organizing, mail-outs and golf tournaments.

> Website: http://www.hppl.org/
> Email: hppl@hppl.org
> Phone: 713-862-7386

**Sarah's House**

Sarah's House seeks to provide emergency shelter, meals, clothing and basic necessities for homeless women and their children. Our daily goals are to assist in providing these families with stability, education, life-skills to improve employment opportunities and achieve self-sufficiency. Sarah's House is looking for a volunteer Grant Writer to successfully write grants for our organization. Experience with Grant Writing, references.

Website: http://www.sarahshousetx.org/
Email: info@sarahshousetx.org
Phone: 713-475-1480

## Los Angeles

**826LA**

826LA is a non-profit organization dedicated to supporting students ages 6 to 18 with their creative and expository writing skills, and to helping teachers inspire their students to write. Our services are structured around the understanding that great leaps in learning can happen with one-on-one attention, and that strong writing skills are fundamental to future success. With this in mind, we provide after-school tutoring, evening and weekend workshops, in-school tutoring, field trips, help for English language learners, and assistance with student publications. All of our programs are challenging and enjoyable, and ultimately strengthen each student's power to express ideas effectively, creatively, confidently, and in his or her individual voice.

Website: http://www.826la.org/
Email: iwanttohelp@826la.org
Phone: (310) 305-8418

**The Young Storytellers Foundation**

Volunteer Mentors: The Young Storytellers Foundation offers a uniquely engaging and effective arts education program to targeted public schools in Los Angeles, where students are at-risk and have little or no access to the arts. Our program pairs adult mentors from the entertainment industry with students from arts-poor public schools. The mentors volunteer one lunch hour a week for eight weeks to guide and encourage the students as they imagine and develop their own short screenplay. In the ninth week, professional Hollywood actors perform the students' scripts for a live audience. We call these performances the "Big Show" because for the students watching their creation come to life, it is a very big moment. For kids who normally receive little individualized attention and support, working one-on-one with an adult to create their own story, and seeing actors like Zachary Levi (Chuck), Ben McKenzie (Southland), Josh Radnor (How I Met Your Mother), and Raven Symone (That's So Raven) not only take it seriously, but bring it brilliantly to life for everyone they know, is transformative. From this experience, children learn that they matter. They see that people value what they have to say. Their communication skills improve. And they discover that attending school and studying can be enjoyable and immensely rewarding.

Website: http://youngstorytellers.com/
Email: writeus@youngstorytellers.com
Phone: (323) 962- 4500

**FACES: Family Assessment, Counseling & Education Services**
>Volunteer Grant Writer: Join our active development team. Help us prevent family violence by partnering with donors and foundations in the community. FACES is conducting interviews with interested volunteers who would like to be trained and who will assist with grant research, donor files, thank you notes, outreach opportunities, board development, and capital campaign. This is a wonderful opportunity to learn about non profit work from the inside out! FACES Family Services would not be so successful if it were not for the dedication of our strong volunteer programs. Each program focuses on bringing professional services, given with care and compassion. Our mission is to provide strategies and solutions to families stressed out by separation and divorce. We seek to strengthen the single parent family and increase kids' self esteem and feelings of safety and security. Your letters and proposals will connect generous donors and encourage them to support our wonderful programs. If you feel you have the motivation and commitment to help an agency that serves over 3000 children and families on a very low budget, join us!
>     Website: http://www.facescal.org/
>     Email: facesoc@yahoo.com
>     Phone: 714-993-2237 ext. 14

## Miami

**StandUp For Kids**
>Grant Writer: StandUp For Kids is committed to the help and rescue of homeless and street kids. We do this, every day, in cities across America. We carry out our mission through our volunteers who go to the streets in order to find, stabilize and otherwise help homeless and street kids improve their lives. We have been on the streets since January 1990 and continue to grow our organization to help America's homeless youth. We are looking for volunteers to lead and assist in the grant application process including grant writing and research of grant opportunities.
>     Website: http://www.standupforkids.org/local/florida/Miami/
>     Email: Miami@StandUpForKids.org
>     Phone: 786-371-1980

## New York

**Medwiser**
>Medwiser is devoted to stopping the spread of HIV in youth. We are different from almost every other nonprofit organization. We have no paid staff. Medwiser's content is free to use by anyone or any organization. We are driven by a global community of volunteers, all dedicated to stopping the spread of HIV/AIDS. Currently, we are working relentlessly to form an online grassroots movement that empowers individuals from around the globe to stop HIV. Candidates should have good communication and organization skills, and be proficient with word processing & internet. Experience with grant writing, public administration or public health is ideal.
>Website: http://medwiser.org/Medwiser/
>Email: medwiservolunteers@gmail.com
>Phone: (646) 872-2747

### Citymeals-on-Wheels

Every week, Citymeals receives letters of appreciation from our elderly meal recipients. These letters often include touching, heartfelt stories about their lives. Through the Senior Script program, volunteers write back to our clients with a warm personalized response.

Website: http://www.citymeals.org/
Email: vivienne@citymeals.org or sheila@citymeals.org
Phone: 212-687-1234

## Philadelphia

### Lower Bucks County Chapter American Red Cross

Communications/PR Volunteer: Write press releases on behalf of the local chapter for submission to local newspapers, speak at local events.

Website: http://www.redcrosslbcc.org/
Phone: (215) 946-4870 ext. 103

### American INSIGHT

Volunteer Grant Writer: As a multigenerational organization created to bring the stories of our past to the screen, American INSIGHT counts on experienced adults who have the desire and patience needed to learn the production process. We are looking for independent, self-motivated individuals who respect the priceless value of storytelling, and the patience to conduct historical research. Please request further information on how to volunteer with American INSIGHT by sending your name, resume and contact information to

Website: http://www.americaninsight.org/
Email: Outreach@AmericanINSIGHT.org
Phone: 610-617-9919

## Phoenix

### International Cancer Advocacy Network

Volunteer Thank-you note writer: Excellent penmanship; nothing too scrolly. It must be very easy to read. The ability to pick up work and return within a day or two. We provide the note cards and the stamps and the template or draft for the thank you notes. It would make sense for the person taking on this position to live in or near North Central Phoenix as pick-ups and drop offs would be in North Central Phoenix, specifically the 85021 zip code area.

Website: http://www.askican.org/volunteer.html
Email: volunteer@askican.org
Phone: (602) 861-9642

## Twin Cities

### Lift Kids

Volunteer Grant Writer: Lift Kids is in need of volunteers to join our grant writing team. Please email or call us if you can help us help children here and around the world! Work can be done virtually. Writing experience preferred, but we are willing to train and provide templates.
Website: http://liftkids.org/builds/
Email: jbarrett@liftkids.org
Phone: 651-298-9200

### Be The Match

Volunteer Grant Writer: The Volunteer Grant Writer will research and evaluate potential foundation matches, write grant letters and submit applications. The Grant Writing can be done remotely, as well as at our office. Volunteers should be located in the Greater Minneapolis MN Area Thousands of patients with leukemia and other life-threatening diseases depend on Be The Match to raise funds to help make bone marrow and umbilical cord blood transplants possible. Be The Match Foundation® and its partner, the National Marrow Donor Program® (NMDP), work to ensure that patients in need of a life-saving marrow or umbilical cord blood transplant get the treatment and support they so desperately need. 70% of patients diagnosed with leukemia, lymphoma and other life-threatening blood diseases do not have a matching marrow donor in their family. These patients turn to Be The Match Foundation and the NMDP for help securing an unrelated marrow donor and a second chance at life. Since 1987, we have facilitated more than 45,000 transplants.
Website: http://www.marrow.org/index.html
Email: outreach@nmdp.org
Phone: (800) 507-5427

## Salt Lake City

### SLCC Community Writing Center

Volunteer Writing Coach: The SLCC Community Writing Center supports, motivates and educates people of all abilities and educational backgrounds who want to use writing for practical needs, civic engagement and personal expression. CWC volunteer Writing Coaches provide collaborative writing assistance and feedback, both online and at libraries and community centers throughout the Salt Lake Valley. Volunteer writing coaches typically volunteer two hours every other week and assist writers who have a range of backgrounds and abilities. Volunteers interested in becoming a Writing Coach typically provide a six-month commitment to the program.
Website: http://www.slcc.edu/cwc/index.asp
Email: cwc@slcc.edu
Phone: (801) 957-4992

## San Francisco

### Streetside Stories
Storytelling Exchange program: Storytelling Exchange volunteers inspire students to write the stories of their lives. They offer writing help one on one and facilitate small group discussions. Bilingual Spanish and Chinese speakers are especially welcome to help with our ESL classes. Help kids create mini-movies: Share your tech expertise in our Tech Tales program. During the Tech Tales program, students write stories about their lives and turn them into short movies using our mobile digital media lab. Tech Tales volunteers help students one on one with writing, storyboarding and basic film editing. If you have used editing programs like iMovie or pick up new tech skills quickly, Tech Tales is the program for you. Edit student stories: Help copy edit student stories for publication in our Storytelling Exchange anthology and our Streetside After School zines. Editing is our most popular volunteer option, and volunteer positions are competitive.

Website: http://www.streetside.org/index.htm
Email: outreach@streetside.org
Phone: (415) 864-5221

## Seattle

### VIBES: Volunteers in Bellevue's Education System
VIBES is an in-school volunteer program, supporting students of all needs in Bellevue School District. Some volunteers prefer to be matched with one student, while others choose to work with small groups assisting the teacher in specific academic subjects. The VIBES program places volunteers in schools as one-on-one mentors, literacy/math tutors, classroom assistants and story sharers. There are also opportunities to volunteer in supervised before and after school programs and technology/computer/language classes. There are opportunities available in all elementary, middle and high schools throughout the district. Volunteer commitment is one hour per week through the end of the current school year. Volunteers are positive, dependable role models. They support students' academic and enrichment needs, encourage development of social skills and motivate students to become lifelong learners. Volunteers work in the school setting in partnership with the school staff. Our volunteers routinely state that they "get more than they give" and learn firsthand the challenges facing students and educators today. Take a break from your busy day and join us!!

Website: http://www.bsd405.org/vibes
Email: vibes@bsd405.org
Phone: (425) 456-4154

## Washington D.C.

### Literacy Volunteers of America-Prince William

Literacy Volunteers of America-Prince William has volunteer opportunities to help adults within our county improve their reading, writing skills. We have a variety of students seeking our services. They are Americans or people who are learning English as their second language. The typical tutor-student session is two hours per week. The day and time are whatever is most convenient for you both. If you are an adult and are interested in becoming a tutor volunteer, please contact us! Prior experience is not necessary. We will train you at our quarterly tutor training workshops. There is a one-time $35 fee which covers the cost of your textbook and other printed materials. We look forward to hearing from you. Only the desire to help another adult read and write is needed.

Website: http://www.lvapw.org/default.htm
Email: lvapw@aol.com
Phone: 703-670-5702

### Empowered Women International Inc.

We are looking for someone to help us publicize and promote the success stories of our clients by interviewing and writing feature stories about 10 chosen artists. This is a wonderful opportunity to speak with immigrant and refugee women artists in the DC metro and hear the incredible stories they have to share about their lives and their work, as well as to use your writing talent for a terrific cause. The stories will be sent out through our newsletter, posted on our website and various social networking sites, and featured in the EWI office. Whether you are interested in writing one of the stories or have the time to do all 10, please contact us and include a short writing sample. Writing and journalistic ability: Experience with writing, interviewing, capturing people's stories, etc. Need to have excellent English writing skills and be able to talk comfortably with people of different cultures and backgrounds.

Website: http://ewint.org/
Email: cfripp@aol.com
Phone: 571-366-7724

## National Opportunities

### Make A Wish Foundation

Since 1980, the Make-A-Wish Foundation® has enriched the lives of children with life-threatening medical conditions through its wish-granting work. The Foundation's mission reflects the life-changing impact that a Make-A-Wish® experience has on children, families, referral sources, donors, sponsors, and entire communities.

Website: http://www.wish.org/
Phone: 602-279-9474

### The Posse Foundation

Founded in 1989, Posse identifies public high school students with extraordinary academic and leadership potential who may be overlooked by traditional college selection processes. Posse extends to these students the opportunity to pursue personal and academic excellence by placing them in supportive, multicultural teams—Posses—of 10 students. Posse partner colleges and universities award Posse Scholars four-year, full-tuition leadership scholarships. Help recruit the next class of Posse Scholars or work directly with Scholars during their senior year of high school as a writing coach. Writing coaches help Posse Scholars transition from high school-to college-level writing during the Pre-Collegiate Training Program. Individuals with experience teaching writing and working with young people are preferred.

Website: http://www.possefoundation.org
Email: info@possefoundation.org
Phone: (212) 405-1691

### Stand Up For Kids

The mission of STAND UP FORKIDS is to help homeless and at-risk youth. Everyday homeless youth face obstacles that most of us cannot comprehend. Where will I have my next meal? When can I shower? Where will I sleep tonight? STAND UP FOR KIDS helps homeless youth tackle some of their everyday obstacles and work towards a life off the streets. From basic necessities such as food, clothing, and hygiene to resources for housing, employment, and education, STAND UP FOR KIDS counselors use an open, straightforward and caring counseling approach to help kids reach their full potential. Grant Research/Writer: We are looking for volunteers to lead and assist in the grant application process including grant writing and research of grant opportunities. Experience in grant writing for non-profit organizations would be preferable; however, we welcome volunteers that are looking to gain experience as well.

Website: http://www.standupforkids.org/
Email: Staff@standupforkids.org
Phone: 1- 800.365.4KID

## LGBTQ-FRIENDLY THEATRES AND FESTIVALS

In the past few years, the amount of opportunities available to LGBTQ writers and dramatists has soared. The following list includes theatres and festivals that only accept LGBTQ-specific themes and content; theatres – many avant-garde – that encourage LGBTQ submissions; and theatres that welcome LGBTQ writing. Some theatres have been included that do not accept unsolicited submissions, and those are noted. From Diversionary Theatre to the Dixon Place HOT! Festival, the opportunities in this list are meant to represent a vast and rapidly growing LGBT and Queer presence in the theatre world. While the list is by no means comprehensive, we hope we have found some new and innovative theatres and production companies that you haven't yet discovered. Good luck!

**Emma DeGrand**, Intern, The Dramatists Guild of America

## THEATRES

**Abingdon Theatre Company**
www.abingdontheatre.org
312 W. 36th Street, Sixth Floor
New York, NY 10018-7570
T: 212-868-2055
F: 212-868-2056
> Produces new work from American playwrights who have not been produced in the New York metropolitan area. Submit your full-length script to Kim T. Sharp, Literary Manager, at the above address.

**About Face Theatre**
1222 West Wilson Avenue
2nd Floor West
Chicago, IL 60640
T: 773.784.8565
F: 773.784.8557
Bonnie Metzgar – Artistic Director
http://aboutfacetheatre.com/index.php
> About Face is interested in producing full-length plays, musicals and performance art. Scripts and artists are of particular interest. Looking for material that challenges expectations and ideas about gender and sexuality in historical or contemporary contexts. Interested in scripts that break traditional ideas about dramatic form, structure and presentation. Please include in your letter how your play/project relates specifically to our mission at About Face. Will consider second productions. Adaptations accepted. Agent submissions are encouraged.
> To submit, contact literary@aboutfacetheatre.com. No unsolicited scripts. Send query letter with synopsis, cast list, resume, and relevant production history. Only electronic submissions accepted.

**Alliance Theatre**
www.alliancetheatre.org
1280 Peachtree Street NE
Atlanta, GA 30309
T: 404-733-4650
F: 404-733-4625
allianceinfo@woodruffcenter.org
> As the premier theatre of the Southeast, the Alliance Theatre sets the highest artistic standards, creating the powerful experience of shared theatre for diverse people. Accepts scripts from Georgia residents and professional representatives. Hosts the Kendada Graduate Playwriting Competition for student playwrights.

**Alternative Theatre Company**
www.alternativetheatreco.org
PO Box 846
New York, NY 10163
212-464-8875
altrcompany@aol.com
> Produces plays specific to the LGBT community.

**And Toto too Theatre Company**
http://andtototoo.org
P.O. Box 12192
Denver, CO 80212
720-280-7058
Executive Director: susanlyles@andtototoo.org
Submissions: submissions@andtototoo.org
General information: info@andtototoo.org
> And Toto too Theatre Company is made up of dedicated artists and business people who recognize the importance of the contributions of women in the arts. And Toto too strives to remove assumptions and generalizations, presenting to audiences thought-provoking new works written by women. Women playwrights who have never been produced in Colorado can submit full-length plays. Submissions should be full-length plays with minimal set requirements and 6 characters or less. And Toto too does not produce musicals or plays for children. Send synopsis, character outline, first ten pages, and playwright bio/production history. Send submissions only by e-mail to submissions@andtototoo.org.

**Arizona Women's Theatre Company**
www.azwtc.org
6501 E. Greenway Parkway
Suite 103, PMB 338
Scottsdale, AZ 85024
480-422-5386
info@azwtc.org
> The Arizona Women's Theatre Company produces contemporary, provocative, thought-provoking plays written by women. Provides an innovative forum for women's voices. The Arizona Women's Theatre is the only theatre in Arizona to focus on women playwrights and directors. Founded in 2003 as a non-profit corporation, the Women's Theatre produces work that reveals women's lives and documents women's experiences. Hosts the annual Pandora Festival, which is now making a national call for women playwrights outside of Arizona, in addition to Arizona playwrights. Send 3 copies of your unpublished full-length, one-act, or ten-minute play to the address above.

**Ars Nova**
www.arsnovanyc.com
511 West 54th Street
New York, NY 10019
T: 212-489-9800
F: 212-489-1908
contact@arsnovanyc.com
> A not-for-profit supporting theatre, comedy, and music artists early in their career.
> Has programs such as Showgasm and ANT FEST which accept unsolicited
> submissions. To send work, see http://www.arsnovanyc.com/get-involved.html for
> program opportunities.

**Artistic New Directions**
www.artisticnewdirections.org
250 West 90th St #15-G
New York, NY 10024
212-875-1857
info@artisticnewdirections.org
> Seeks new work and works-in-progress at its weekly Anything Goes, an open-to-all
> developmental lab program that moves plays from inception to production (see the website
> for more information). New work is only accepted via Anything Goes and specific Calls for
> Entries. AND presents its annual Eclectic Evening of Shorts in the spring.

**Bailiwick Chicago Theatre Company**
www.bailiwickchicago.com
Mailing address: 6201 N Hermitage
Chicago, IL 60660
General Information: 773-969-6201
info@bailiwickchicago.com
> Mission: "We tell stories that stimulate our audience and celebrate our diverse
> community, enhancing our understanding of ourselves and others."
> Not currently reading scripts, but is trying to gather the resources to be able to
> read unsolicited work, and encourages playwrights to send their work via email to:
> newworks@bailiwickchicago.com. For info about what to send, see their website:
> http://www.bailiwickchicago.com/playwrights.

**BAX/Brooklyn Arts Exchange**
www.bax.org
421 Fifth Avenue
Brooklyn, NY 11215
Adm/Office/Reservations: 718-832-0018
F: 718-832-9189
info@bax.org
Contact: Marya Warshaw, director
> 75-seat theater. Presents dance, theater, performance, and video. Hosts an Artists
> in Residency program which offers space grants to develop new work for Brooklyn
> based artists. Also offers professional workshops to artists as well as to the general
> public. Occasionally sponsors visiting performers.

**Bloody Unicorn Theatre**
www.bloodyunicorn.com
514 N 2nd Avenue
Tucson, AZ 85705
520-990-3628
tyraroc@yahoo.com
Ry Herman, artistic director
> Not currently accepting submissions, but operates with the goal of producing exciting
> new work. Recently hosted "Lesbian Shorts IV," a festival "with a Sapphic slant."

**Bread & Water Theatre**
http://www.breadandwatertheatre.org/
7 Bly Street
Rochester, New York 14620
585-271-5523
info@breadandwatertheatre.org
J.R. Teeter, artistic director
> Produces new works and revivals of classic plays. Founded in 2000, Bread & Water
> Theatre is committed to making the arts accessible and affordable to a broad-
> based audience and acting as a positive agent of change in its community. Provides
> audiences with challenging contemporary drama and innovative community outreach
> programs. Has produced plays such as *My Gay Family* by Nancy Agabian. To submit,
> send a cover letter and script to Play Development at the above address. Due to limited
> funding, plays without elaborate design requirements are preferred. For more details:
> http://www.breadandwatertheatre.org/getinvolved/new_play_development.htm.

**Brooklyn Academy of Music (BAM)**
www.bam.org
30 Lafayette Avenue
Brooklyn, NY 11217-1486
info@bam.org
718-636-4100
Contact: Joseph V. Melilo, executive producer
> BAM's mission is to be the preeminent progressive performing and cinema arts
> center of the twenty-first century, engaging both global and local communities. BAM
> strives to create a distinctive environment for an inspirational and transformative
> aesthetic experience. Hosts the Next Wave Festival, a festival of theater, dance, and
> music. To request that BAM consider your work for presentation, send a videotape,
> promotional materials, or a performance invitation by mail to Joseph V. Melilo,
> executive producer, at the above address. E-mail programming@bam.org.

**Buddies in Bad Times Theatre**
www.buddiesinbadtimestheatre.com
12 Alexander Street
Toronto, ON, M4Y 1B4 Canada
T: 416-975-9130
F: 416-975-9293
info@buddiesinbadtimes.com
Contacts: Brendan Healy, artistic director
> Founded in 1979, Buddies in Bad Times Theatre is a not-for-profit professional theater
> dedicated to the promotion of queer theatrical expression. It offers special events, youth
> initiatives, play development programs, and late night weekend cabarets. Unsolicited scripts

accepted year-round; call or email in advance. Sponsors visiting performers and events. Send outline.

## Cabaret Company

Home.istar.ca/~anita
P.O. Box 306
31 Adelaide St E
Toronto, ON, Canada M5C 2J4
905-522-7584
anita@istar.ca
Contact: Sky Gilbert, artistic director and literary manager
A theatre company dedicated to engaging queer-themed work. No unsolicited scripts.

## Cherry Lane Theatre

www.cherrylanetheatre.org
38 Commerce Street
New York, NY 10014
T: 212-989-2020
F: 212-989-2867
company@cherrylanetheatre.org

## Cleveland Public Theatre

www.cptonline.org
6415 Detroit Avenue
Cleveland, OH 44102
T: 216-631-2727
F: 216-631-2575
info@cptonline.org
A theatre as committed to producing new work as it is to supporting the community. Especially interested in work by women, minorities, and local writers. CPT develops new work through two programs, Big Box and the Dark Room. To inquire, email artistic@cptonline.org.

## Co-Op Theatre East

www.cooptheatreeast.org
cooptheatreeast@gmail.com for info
cotesubmissions@gmail.com for playwrights
Contact: Casey Cleverly
Co-Op Theatre East believes in the power of art to foster a dialogue for social change, providing an entertaining performance forum in which to ask evocative, challenging questions of artists and audiences on our way to creating collaborative answers. Co-Op Theatre East has an open submission policy and welcomes all playwrights to submit work. Accepts all types of submissions, including solo pieces, one-act plays, musicals, and full-length plays. Reads every submission.

**Diversionary Theatre**
diversionary.org
4545 Park Blvd., #101, San Diego, CA 92116
619-220-6830; Box office 619-220-0097; fax 619-220-0148
Contact: Dan Kirsch, executive and artistic dir.
    3rd-oldest continuously producing GLQBT theatre in the US. Play submissions
    accepted year-round.

**Dixon Place**
http://www.dixonplace.org/index2.html
161A Chrystie Street
New York, NY, 10002
T: (212) 219-0736
F: (212) 219-0761
contact@dixonplace.org
submissions@dixonplace.org
    Accepts scripts only from artists based in NYC. Looking for works of performance
    and theater in new forms. Especially encourage women and minorities to submit.
    Send script and/or video with SASE and a brief letter. Allow 8-10 weeks for reply.
    Submission information page: http://dixonplace.org/html/submissions.php

**Dobama Theatre**
www.dobama.org
2340 Lee Road
Cleveland Heights, OH 44118
Admin: 216-932-6838
Box office: 216-932-3396
dobama@dobama.org
    Produces premier plays by emerging and established playwrights. Accepts unsolicited
    scripts, but has no formal reporting process on plays. Hosts the writing group,
    "Playwrights' Gym," which is for local playwrights.

**Electric Pear Productions**
www.electricpear.org
917-202-4481
info@electricpear.org
literary@electricpear.org
Contacts: Melanie Sylvan, executive producer; Julie Haverkate, literary director
    A theatre that explores where the mainstream meets the avant-garde. Send
    submissions to Julie Haverkate, Literary Director, at literary@electricpear.org in PDF
    or word format. Submissions should include resume, synopsis, and first 10-20 pages.

**Elixir Productions**
www.elixirproductions.org
154 Kensington Avenue, #205
Jersey City, NJ 07304
201-918-2242
info@elixirproductions.org
    Based in New York/New Jersey and producing off off Broadway since 1999, Elixir
    Productions Theatre Company is committed to developing plays and performances
    about gender, sexuality, and the impact of sexual identity on society, human
    relationships, and ourselves. Aims to create a uniquely queer experience where our
    voices can reach new possibilities and summon new power in shaping our culture.

**Evolution Theatre Company**
http://evolutiontheatre.org
Mailing address: c/o Paul Lockwood
1610 Holland Drive
Hilliard, OH 43026
614-256-1223
info@evolutiontheatre.org
Contac Paul Lockwood, artistic director
    Accepts unsolicited play submissions; e-mail attachments preferred.

**EXIT Theatre**
www.theexit.org
156 Eddy Street
San Francisco, CA 94102
mail@theexit.org
415-931-1094
    An independent theatre in downtown San Francisco. LGBT-welcoming; hosts the San Francisco Fringe Festival.

**Freedom Train Productions**
www.freedomtrainproductions.org
138 South Oxford Street
Brooklyn, NY 11217
info@freedomtrainproductions.org
    Freedom Train Productions is a black queer theater company dedicated to political art and social activism that engages artists and audiences. Develops and stages challenging and controversial narratives about the universal struggle for freedom and transformation through the lens of black queer protagonists. Not currently accepting unsolicited manuscripts, but send an introductory letter with an invitation to an open rehearsal, reading, or performance of your work to work@freedomtrainproductions. org.

**Ganymedearts: DC's GLBT Arts Company**
www.ganymedearts.org
1708 Euclid Street NW
Washington, DC 20009
202-709-3698
ganymedeinfo@gmail.com
    A theatre company dedicated to the LGBTQ experience. Mission is to provide high-quality, professional theatre and art (dance and musical performances, poetry readings, and art shows) that foster social and cultural awareness of and for the GLBT community. Accepts unsolicited scripts.

**Here Theatre**
www.here.org
145 6th Avenue
New York, NY 10013-1548
T: 212-647-0202
F: 212-647-0257
info@here.org
    HERE builds a community that nurtures career artists as they create innovative hybrid live performance in theatre, dance, music, puppetry, media and visual

art. Their artist residencies support the singular vision of the lead artist through commissions, long-term development, and production support. HERE's programs and performances promote relationships among local, national, and international artists. Their space is a destination for audiences who are passionate about ground-breaking contemporary work and the creative process behind it. HERE does not accept unsolicited scripts, but has a program called HARP (HERE Artist Residency Program) for artists to curate their own pieces over a long period of time. As part of HARP, artist residents show works-in-progress, develop workshop productions, and mount full-scale productions. Accepting applications through January 3. For application and more info: http://here.org/programs/harp.

**Highways Performance Space**
www.highwaysperformance.org
1651-18th St
Santa Monica, CA 90404
310-453-1755
res. 310-315-1459
leogarcia@highwaysperformance.org
Contact: Leo Garcia, executive and artistic director
    Primarily a performance art space for LA Artists.

**Horse Trade Theater Group**
Currently managing Kraine Theater and The Red Room
www.horsetrade.info
85 East 4th Street
New York, NY 10003
 212-777-6088
office@horsetrade.info
Also managing: UNDER St. Marks
94 St. Marks Place
New York, NY 10009
    A self-sustaining independent theatre group that focuses on new work. Send submissions by mail or to submissions@horsetrade.info.

**Human Race Theatre**
www.humanracetheatre.org
126 North Main Street, Suite 300
Dayton, OH 45402
T: 937-461-3823
F: 937-461-7223
    Dayton's only professional, not-for-profit theatre. Provides an alternative to mainstream theatre with thought-provoking productions that challenge and enlighten audiences. As our name suggests, we present universal themes that explore the human condition and startle us all into a renewed awareness of ourselves. Has a musical theatre workshops program that produces new musicals. To submit, send an introductory letter with information about your show. Response time: 6-10 months. Accepts unsolicited scripts, but currently has no formal reading process.

## Intar Theatre
www.intartheatre.org
P.O. Box 756
New York, NY 10108
212-695-6134
intar@intartheatre.org
> Focuses on bold new work from Latino artists in English. Send submissions to: INTAR Theatre, Attn: Literary Department, and the address above, or: submissions@ intartheatre.org.

## The Ivy Theatre
www.theivytheatre.org
14501 Debba Drive
Austin, Texas 78734
tuiejones@aol.com
Contact: Marian Jones, producing artistic director
> The Ivy is a non-profit organization founded to foster the understanding and acceptance of diverse persons through education, activism, visual and performing arts. Diversity includes ethnicity, socio-economic status, and sexual orientation.

## Jump-Start Performance Company
www.jump-start.org
108 Blue Star
San Antonio, TX 78204
Fax 210-222-2231
info@jump-start.org
Contacts: S.T. Shimi, artistic director; Lisa Suarez, guest artists program director.
> Jump-Start is dedicated to the discovery and support of new ideas in the arts and arts education. By encouraging visionary thought and non-traditional approaches, Jump-Start is committed to the creation of art that is a lasting voice of diverse cultures and communities. No unsolicited scripts. Inquiries regarding the Company's original works go to shimi@jump-start.org.

## La MaMa E.T.C.
www.lamama.org
74A East 4th St
New York, NY 10003
212-475-7710
web@lamama.org
> Looking for new work of all backgrounds; LGBTQ friendly. Also offers exhibition space in their art gallery, La Galleria.

## Legion Arts
www.legionarts.org
1103 Third Street, SE
Cedar Rapids, IA 52401-2305
T: 319-364-1580
F: 319-362-9156
info@legionarts.org
> Visual and performing arts presenter based at CSPS, a community arts center in a landmark, century-old building. Committed to diversity, regularly presents solo performers, small companies, and musicians. Rarely produces outside work. E-mail or call to inquire.

**The Los Angeles Women's Theatre Project**
www.lawomenstheatreproject.com
10061 Riverside Dr.#528
Toluca Lake, CA 91602
818-471-9100
deejaecox@lawomenstheatreproject.com
Contact: Dee Jae Cox, co-founder, artistic director
    The Los Angeles Women's Theatre Project is a 501(c) nonprofit organization that
    supports and creates opportunities for women in the performing arts. Not lesbian-
    exclusive, but definitely lesbian-inclusive. Accept scripts: contact them first by e-mail.

**Manbites Dog Theatre**
manbitesdogtheater.org
P.O. Box 402
Durham, NC 27702
919-682-4974; reservations 919-682-3343
manbitesdogtheater@gmail.com
Contact: Edward Hunt, managing director
    Mission is to produce new and challenging work, as well as support new playwrights.
    Not currently accepting submissions or proposals.

**Manhattan Class Company**
www.mcctheater.org
MCC Theater Offices
311 W 43rd Street #302
New York, NY 10036
212-727-7722
    Mission is to produce works that force us to reexamine the world we live in through
    the unique perspectives of extraordinary writers. LGBT-friendly. Has a Playlab
    program in which plays written by members of their Playwrights' Coalition are
    read, rehearsed, and selected for the Main Stage. MCC does not accept unsolicited
    manuscripts, but will read synopsis and 10-page dialogue sample. For more info:
    http://www.mcctheater.org/literary/submissions.html

**Manhattan Theatre Source**
www.theatresource.org
177 MacDougal Street
New York, NY 10011
Reservations: 212-260-4111
Business: 212-260-4698
F: 212-260-4697
managersource@gmail.com
    A theatre committed to linking together disparate communities within New York's
    off-off Broadway theatre scene, and also to supporting independent theatre artists.
    Hosts several "Genius" festivals, each focusing on a different broad group of writers
    (men, women, youth, etc).

**Mauckingbird Theatre Company**
www.mauckingbirdtheatreco.org
mauckingbird@mac.com
    Mauckingbird Theatre Company is committed to producing professional gay-themed
    theatre, while also exploring classic literature and musical genres and providing
    affordable productions of infrequently produced works.

**Naked Angels**
www.nakedangels.com
191 7th Avenue, Suite 2-S
New York, NY 10011
212-343-7394
> Focused on new work; does not accept unsolicited full-length scripts, but has a Tuesdays at Nine Series (T@9) featuring cold readings of new work with an open submission policy. Bring a 10-page sample. For more info, http://www.nakedangels. com/development-programs/get-involved/).

**NativeAliens Theatre**
www.nativealiens.org
nativealiens@gmail.com
212-726-8891
140 Seventh Avenue, #2K
New York, NY 10011
> The NativeAliens Theatre Collective is a developmental theatre company dedicated to exploring the commonalities among all communities while celebrating the rich diversities that make us all unique. Operating under the belief that society is comprised of dynamic and diverse communities that are often under-represented in mass culture, NATC is dedicated to offering provocative theatre that entertains, challenges and enlightens. Submission policy varies every year; updated submission information posted on their website by January 15th of each year.

**New Conservatory Theatre Center**
www.nctcsf.org
25 Van Ness Avenue, Lower Lobby
San Francisco, CA 94102
T: 415-861-4914
F: 415-861-6988
email@nctcsf.org
for writers: ED@nctcsf.org
Contact: Ed Decker, artistic and executive director
> Mission: to champion innovative, high-quality theatre experiences for youth, adults, and artists to effect personal and societal growth, enlightenment, and change. Hosts the series Pride Season Plays, which presents work by and for the LGBT community. Also has two programs for emerging writers: Playwrights' Corner, which develops new LGBT work, and Emerging Artists, which provides stipends to support local queer actors, singers, and writers. For more info, see the programs section of their website. Check website frequently for updated information regarding when and where to send work.

**New Georges**
www.newgeorges.org
109 W. 27th Street, Suite 9A
New York, NY 10001
info@newgeorges.org
Contact: Susan Bernfield, artistic director
> New Georges, in business since 1992, is an award-winning nonprofit theater which produces ambitiously theatrical new plays downtown; and is a play and artist development organization, providing essential resources to a community of venturesome artists (who are women). New Georges is about sparking opportunities

and relationships that push adventurous artists (who are women) and their work into the world. A New Georges play is structurally or otherwise idiosyncratic. But it tells a good story, has a strong emotional core, and is at least a little funny. New Georges is devoted to the process of developing plays over a long period of time. To get involved, send your resume to Susan Bernfield, and/or your play to Kara-Lynn Vaeni, literary manager, at the above address.

## New Line Theatre
newlinetheatre.com
3802-A Keokuk Street
St. Louis, MO 63116
Info: 314-773-6526
Reservations: 314-534-1111
newchaz64@aol.com
Contact: Scott Miller, artistic director
  Called "The Bad Boy of Musical Theatre," New Line's mission is to create and explore provocative, alternative, politically, and socially relevant works of musical theatre. Accepts scripts for issue-oriented, full-length, small cast musicals. To submit, first send inquiry to info@newlinetheatre.com. Time for reply varies. No visiting performers.

## New York Theatre Workshop
www.nytw.org
79 E 4th Street
New York, NY 10003
T: 212-780-9037
F: 212-460-8996
nytw@aol.com
Contacts: Jerry Manning, artistic associate; Jim Nicola, artistic director; Mandy Hackett, literary manager. Accept scripts. Send a 10-page synopsis and writing sample with SASE.

## Out North
www.outnorth.org
3800 DeBarr Road
Anchorage, AK 99508
907-279-8099
res. 907-279-3800
art@outnorth.org
Contacts: Scott Turner Schofield, executive artistic director, and Jonathan Minton, literary coordinator for Brand Spankin' Drama
  Mission is to find and share cultural explorers whose ideas challenge and inspire our lives; to raise up creative space where people of all cultures, generations, and abilities gather and learn; and to champion, through the arts and humanities, people marginalized in our times. Out North doesn't accept unsolicited scripts for its main stage, but is starting a new play series called Brand Spankin' Drama which workshops unpublished, unproduced plays through a talkback process. To submit a play, e-mail scott@outnorth.org or jonathan@outnorth.org with a paragraph explaining why your play meets Out North's mission, and what you are looking for from a talkback process. Underrepresented artists and plays with disability and other social issue themes are encouraged. Out North also sponsors visiting performers. Send an e-mail about upcoming engagements in US and abroad.

**Out Productions/Les Productions Out**
www.out.ca
Studio 303-372 St. Catherine St. W.
Montreal QC H3B 1A2 Canada
in@out.ca
Contacts: David Allan King, artistic director; Miriam Ginestier, associate artistic
director
  Not accepting unsolicited scripts at this time. Interested in sponsoring visiting
  performers. Out Production's Pink Network links Canadian producers of GLBT
  performing arts together for visibility, mutual support and pride in our arts and
  communities. The Network's Québéçois home also taps into producers of French-
  language performing arts. Out provides the network free of charge to Canadian
  companies and individuals involved in queer creation in the performing arts.

**Performance Space 122**
www.ps122.org
150 First Avenue
New York, NY 10009
T: 212-477-5829
F: 212-353-1315
ps122@ps122.org
Contact: Gallejo Gantner, artistic director
  A space that seeks the intersections among dance, music, theatre, and performance.
  Encourages and supports artists from diverse cultural backgrounds. P.S. 122 does not
  accept unsolicited submissions; call to inquire.

**Pride Films and Plays**
www.pridefilmsandplays.com
3023 N Clark 327
Chicago, IL 60657
773-250-3112
pridefilmsandplays@gmail.com
  From their website: Pride Films and Plays, based in Chicago, links an international
  network of writers with professionals working in film and theater. Through readings,
  contests, classes, screenings and full theater productions, Pride Films and Plays
  engages artists and audiences in the full developmental process needed to make great
  artistic experiences. Submit unsolicited work to reading series and contests at www.
  pridefilmsandplays.com.

**Queer Cultural Center**
www.queerculturalcenter.org
934 Brannan Street
San Francisco, CA 94103
Pamela S. Peniston, Executive Director
director@queerculturalcenter.org
  An organization that supports queer artists and artistic events. Does not have a
  physical theatre of their own, but showcases staged readings and co-sponsors full
  productions. Hosts the annual National Queer Arts Festival, a month-long event
  that documents and presents queer artists. Another QCC program, Creating Queer
  Community, commissions LGBT artists to create new work.

**Ragged Blade Productions**
raggedblade.com
St. Louis, MO
314-280-1035
ragdblade@aol.com
Contacts: Jerry Rabushka, artistic director; Skip Hardesty, managing director
No scripts; occasional visiting performers.

**Rattlestick Playwrights Theatre**
www.rattlestick.org
224 Waverly Place
New York, NY 10014
212-627-2556
info@rattlestick.org
Rattlestick is focused on supporting new playwrights. Accepts full, unsolicited
scripts, and gives each script thorough consideration. For submission information:
http://rattlestick.org/content/getinvolvedSubmissions

**Richmond Triangle Players**
www.rtriangle.org/home.html
804-346-8113
Contact: John Knapp, artistic director
rolfesdad@aol.com
Specializes in LGBT content and themes. Venue: a small, 75-80-seat cabaret theatre.
Richmond Triangle puts on 4 or 5 mainstage shows per year, and occasionally
sponsors other cabaret acts, comedy skits, etc. Generally prefers plays with small
casts; everything from drama to comics to musicals. Accepts unsolicited scripts;
inquiry with synopsis preferred.

**Soho Playhouse**
www.sohoplayhouse.com
15 Vandam Street
New York, NY 10013
212-691-1555
Contact: Darren Lee Cole
info@sohoplayhouse.org
Submit unsolicited scripts only electronically.

**Stage Left Theatre**
www.stagelefttheatre.com
3408 N. Sheffield Avenue
Chicago, IL 60657
Resident at Theatre Wit
1229 West Belmont
Chicago, IL 60657
773-883-8830
Contact: Vance Smith, artistic director; Laura Blegen, managing director scripts@
stagelefttheatre.com
Stage Left's mission is to develop and produce plays that raise debate and challenge
perspectives on political and social issues. To submit your script, send a cover letter,
resume, production/development history, 1-page synopsis, 10-page excerpt, and any
other helpful materials to scripts@stagelefttheatre.com or to Literary Department at
the above address. In addition to the main stage, Stage Left hosts an annual festival of
new work, Leapfest, in which five new scripts are presented in workshop productions.

**StageQ, inc.**
stageq.com
P.O. Box 8876
Madison, WI 53708-8876
608-661-9696, ext 3
stageq@stageq.com
Contact: Tara Ayres, artistic director, artisticdirector@stageq.com
 Produces work with LGBT themes, and promotes "out" actors, writers, artists, and
 musicians. Resident company at the Bartell Theatre, 113 E. Mifflin Street, Madison
 WI. Occasionally produce visiting LGBT performers. To submit a script, send
 synopsis electronically first to artisticdirector@stageq.com.

**Studio 303**
www.studio303.ca (the website is in French; for an English translation, click on
"English" near the bottom of the page)
372 Ste-Catherine West
Montreal QC, H3B1A2 Canada
514-393-3771
info@studio303.ca
 Concentrating on the physical body, Studio 303 is a unique resource centre which
 offers cutting edge workshops, innovative administrative services and a flexible,
 intimate studio laboratory where new works may be created and presented. Studio
 303's programming aims to stimulate enriching exchanges between a variety of
 artists, art forms and the public. In concert with its presenting events, Studio 303
 offers a network of intersecting support and resource activities, providing a nurturing
 home base for independent artists. All the info about our calls for submissions are at
 http://www.studio303.ca/en/calls-for-submissions/. Offers various opportunities to
 submit unsolicited scripts throughout the year: from the Edgy Women Festival (see
 Festivals) to In the Round, performed for an audience surrounded by stage on all
 sides.

**Subjective Theatre**
www.subjectivetheatre.org
info@subjectivetheatre.org
 Dedicated to producing politically and socially relevant work.

**Tapit/New Works, Ensemble Theatre**
www.tapitnewworks.org
1957 Winnebago Street
Madison, WI 53704
Adm./reservations 608-244-2938
info@tapitnewworks.org
Contacts: Donna Peckett and Danielle Dresden, producing artistic directors
Etta Gasport, tour coordinator
 Produces theatre, dance, music, and visual art. No unsolicited scripts.

**Theatre Askew**
theatreaskew.com
P.O Box 1603 Cooper Station
New York, NY 10276-1603
646-338-3057
theatreaskew@yahoo.com
Contact: Tim Cusack, artistic director; Jason Jacobs, artistic director, Theatre Askew
Youth Performance Experience (TAYPE)

Describes itself as "NYC's premier producer of queer theatre." From the theatre: "Theatre Askew views the world through a queer eye in order to create bold and innovative theatrical events for viewers of all orientations. Through productions and outreach, Theatre Askew strives to make work of social impact and spiritual consequence. All projects originated by the artistic directors." No scripts or synopses accepted. No visiting artists. Notices of NYC-area productions or readings are welcome.

## Theater for the New City
www.theaterforthenewcity.net
155 First Avenue
New York, NY 10003
T: 212-254-1109
F: 212-979-6570
info@theaterforthenewcity.net

A community cultural center with the goal of supporting a diverse group of artists and audiences. TNC's mission includes discovering relevant new writing and nurturing new playwrights; being a bridge between playwright, experimental theater artist, and the ever-growing audiences in the community; and creating space where a new vision can breathe and be nourished by a working process not subject to commercial constraints and pressures. To submit a script, send ten pages, a brief synopsis, and a letter of introduction to the theatre (address above) to the attention of Michael Scott-Price, Literary Manager.

## Theatre Rhinoceros
http://www.therhino.org/
1360 Mission Street
Suite #200
San Francisco, CA 94103
Contact: John Fisher, Executive Director
415-552-4100
jfisher@therhino.org

Theatre Rhinoceros develops and produces works of theatre that enlighten, enrich, and explore both the ordinary and extraordinary aspects of our queer community. Theatre Rhinoceros does not accept unsolicited manuscripts.

## The Flea Theater
www.theflea.org
411 White Street
New York, NY 10013
Admin: 212-226-0051
Box Office: 212-226-2407
Fax: 212-965-1808
Contact: Jim Simpson, Artistic Director, jims@theflea.org

Produces 4-6 new plays per year through their resident acting company, The Bats. To submit a play, fill out the questionnaire (includes synopsis and your contact info) on their website.

## The Living Theatre
www.livingtheatre.org
21 Clinton Street
New York, NY 10002
Contact: Brad Burghess
Birdsy18@gmail.com
978-273-9443
> Send submissions by mail.

## The Public Theater
www.publictheater.org
425 Lafayette Street
New York, NY 10003
212-539-8500
marketing@publictheater.org
> As the nation's foremost theatrical producer of Shakespeare and new work, The
> Public Theater is dedicated to achieving artistic excellence while developing an
> American theater that is accessible and relevant to all people through productions of
> challenging new plays, musicals and innovative stagings of the classics. The Public
> does not accept unsolicited scripts, but will read a synopsis and sample dialogue. For
> musicals, sample songs are also welcome.

## The Theater Offensive
www.theateroffensive.org
29 Elm St #2
Cambridge, MA 02139
Abe Rybeck, Artistic Director
T: 617.661.1600
F: 617.661.1610
> Mission: Grounded in our commitment to build an activist-based artistic forum,
> our groundbreaking programming has become a vital arena for the unique voices
> of diverse queer cultures, and has led to lasting coalitions between the varied
> communities under the queer umbrella. The Theatre Offensive puts on the Out On
> The Edge: Annual Queer Theatre Festival, as well as OUT in Your Neighborhood,
> a series of performances in various neighborhoods in Greater Boston. Accepts
> unsolicited scripts, but has no formal reading process.

## Theatre Out
www.theatreout.com
P.O. Box 2989
Anaheim, CA 92814
714-826-8700
info@theatreout.com
Contact: Darcy Hogan, literary director, darcy@theatreout.com
> Calling itself "Orange County's gay and lesbian theatre," Theatre Out strives "to
> tell our stories by presenting classic pieces that helped to form our identity, and new
> works that continue to redefine our community." Accepts scripts. Submission may be
> sent to Darcy Hogan, literary director, at darcy@theatreout.com and should include
> production history synopsis and brief biography of the playwright, including other
> works. Full-length and one-acts welcome. Visiting performers welcome in the future.

**Theatre Q**
www.theatreq.org
c/o Dragon Productions
535 Alma Street
Palo Alto, CA 94301
650-493-2006
infotheatreq@aol.com
> Theatre Q exists to portray the evolving images of gays and lesbians throughout
> the Bay Area. Accepts unsolicited scripts with LGBT themes. All types of plays
> are welcome; Theatre Q produces musicals only rarely. Scripts should call no more
> than 7 actors. Submissions by mail preferred. Those wishing to submit scripts
> electronically should contact us first at infotheatreq@aol.com.

**The Weird Sisters Women's Theater Collective**
http://weirdsisterscollective.com
> The Weird Sisters Women's Theater Collective is a group of women in Austin, Texas
> dedicated to promoting women in the arts. The Collective embraces the feminist
> ideology of collaboration; each participant is encouraged to use her voice. The Weird
> Sisters does not promote any narrow feminist agenda, but one that is encompassing.
> All feminists are welcome here – many waves, various sexualities, diverse cultures,
> numerous backgrounds, and an array of beliefs.

**TotoToo: Ottawa's Gay and Lesbian Community Theatre**
www.tototoo.ca
472 O'Connor Street
Ottawa, ON, K1S 3P4 Canada
613-237-4834
board@tototoo.ca
> TotoToo Theatre's mandate is to stage live theatre performances of plays written by
> Canadian playwrights for the national capital region's gay and lesbian community.
> Selects plays that may not otherwise be produced in Ottawa by other community
> and professional theatre companies because of their gay and/or lesbian themes and/
> or content. Well-crafted plays that will hold the attention of TotoToo's audience and
> reflect the many facets of GLBT life. Submissions may be made electronically to
> board@tototoo.ca.

**TOSOS (The Other Side of Silence)**
tosos2.org
506 Ninth Avenue., 3FN
New York, NY 10018
212-563-2218
tosos2@nyc.rr.com
Contacts: Doric Wilson, general director, founder;
Mark Finley, Artistic Director; Barry Childs, administrative director; Chesley Chambers
Playwrights Project leader Cathleen Warnock
> Revival of TOSOS, the world's pioneer professional gay theater company. Dedicated
> to an honest and open exploration of the life experience and cultural sensibility of the
> GLBT community and to preserving and promoting our literary past in a determined
> effort to keep our theatrical heritage alive. Does not accept unsolicited scripts. Hosts
> a once-a-month (except for summer) play reading series, the Chesley Chambers
> Playwrights Project, which produces revivals and new works.

**Triangle Productions!**
www.tripro.org
8420 SW Canyon Lane, #13
Portland, OR 97225-3968
503-239-5919
trianglepro@juno.com
Contact: Donald I. Horn, artistic director
 Produces shows at several venues in the Portland area. Accepts scripts. Allow 3-6
 months for reply. Sponsors visiting performers. Send video, script, and press packet.

**The Village**
1125 N. McCadden Pl.
Los Angeles, CA 90038
Wheelie accessed
T: 323-860-7393
F: 323-308-4090
Contact: Matt Walker, coordinator
Jon Imparato, cultural arts dir.
 Identity: GLQBT Accept scripts. Info: 323-860-7336 (Sue). Interested in sponsoring
 visiting performers.

**Turtle Lane Playhouse**
www.turtlelane.org
283 Melrose Street
Auburndale, MA 02466
T: 617-244-0169
F: 617-607-6101
boxoffice@turtlelane.org
Other inquiries: turtelanesoup@comcast.net
 A non-profit corporation that produces full-length musicals and original works. Also
 provides educational programs and community services. Accepts unsolicited scripts,
 but has no formal reading process; occasionally produces new works in festivals or
 on their main stage.

**Village Playwrights**
New York's Gay Playwrights Collective
villageplaywrights.googlepages.com
LGBT Community Center
208 West 13th Street
New York, NY 10011-7702
Adm./Tickets: 212-645-1514
villageplaywrights@gmail.com
Contact: Emanuel Gavales
 New and developing plays read on the 2nd and 4th Wednesdays. Playwrights have
 opportunity to self-produce post-workshop plays at economical cost.

**Who Wants Cake? @ The Ringwald Theatre**
22742 Woodward Avenue
Ferndale, MI 48220
248-545-5545
joebailey@whowantscaketheatre.com
Contact: Joe Bailey, Artistic Director
 Who Wants Cake? is dedicated to providing a creative environment for local artists
 to produce works that challenge, confront, and entertain. Who Wants Cake? is known

primarily for staging works that are of the indie/alternative bent. Accepts submissions (looking for new, edgier works) but can't promise a quick response. GLBT plays are very welcome. Playwrights can either send hard copies to the theatre or sent query to info@whowantscaketheatre.com.

**Women's Project**
www.womensproject.org
Administrative Offices: 55 West End Avenue
New York, NY 10023
T: 212-765-1706
F: 212-765-2024
info@womensproject.org
A theater devoted to supporting and promoting woman theater artists. Provides women's perspectives on a wide variety of political, social, international, religious, and cultural topics; mentors exceptional writers, directors, and producers through WP's Lab; develops new works and classic plays by women in readings and workshops; advocates on behalf of women theater artists within the national and international professional theater. Accepts scripts through an agent. If unrepresented, send cover letter, brief synopsis, and ten-page dialogue sample to the Playwrights Lab (www.womensproject.org/labs.htm).

**Wow Café Theater**
wowcafetheater@gmail.com
info@wowcafe.org
www.hypergender.com
Wow Café focuses on work by women and transgender writers. Produces work by active members of the Collective, a writing group at the theatre that meets weekly. To join, simply show up. The Collective has an annual retreat in July, during which they decide what to produce that year.

# FESTIVALS

All of the festivals in this section accept work with LGBTQ content and/or themes. Many of them are annual, and a good many take place around Pride Festival (usually June and July). For festivals beyond those in this list, keep an eye on the theatres mentioned above; almost all of them have their own Pride festival during those summer months, and many theatres that don't usually cater to LGBTQ writers have a Pride festival as well.

**BAAD – Out Like That Festival**
www.bronxacademyofartsanddance.org
841 Barretto Street
Bronx, NY 10474
718-842-5223
The Bronx Academy of Arts and Dance is a 70-seat performance and workshop space dedicated to presenting challenging works of established and emerging choreographers, dancers, playwrights, musicians, visual artists, poets, writers, and directors. Their summer Out Like That Festival celebrates gay pride in the Bronx; call for more info. Out Like That produces anything from ten-minute plays to full-lengths. To submit to the festival, e-mail ric-gonzalez@usa.net with a proposal.

**Dixon Place's HOT! Festival of Queer Performance and Culture**
www.hotfestival.org
> Using Penny Arcade's definition of queer as "anyone who has ever experienced a period of isolation and exclusion so profound they could never exclude anyone else," this festival takes place at the Dixon Place Theatre on Chrystie Street, with the goal of being a place where queer and minority voices can influence social change. To submit, contact Dixon Place (see above).

**Conn Artist Performance Event, Inc. Presents the Provincetown Fringe Festival**
ptownfringe.org
Ocean Grove and Asbury Park, NJ
Adm./fax 732-807-4052; cell 617-512-6066
Contact: Marjorie Conn, Artistic Director
> In the spirit of giving everyone a chance, Conn Artist has an open door policy. Presents the year-round Provincetown Fringe Festival in Asbury Park, N.J.

**The Columbus National Gay and Lesbian Theatre Festival**
www.columbustheatrefestival.com
Act Out Productions
2517 N. 4th Street
Columbus, OH 43202
614-263-9448
fabact1@aol.com
> Mission: to celebrate and examine our lives through all aspects of theatre. Looking for polished pieces – from solo performances to full-length productions – that are able to move into a venue with a minimum of rehearsal time.

**Gayfest NYC**
http://www.sunnyspotproductions.com/currentprojects.html
One River Place, Suite 917
New York, NY 10036
212-868-5570
Bruce Robert Harris
212-868-5570
gayfestnyc@aol.com
> An annual festival for work centering on LGBT characters or issues. Produces 3-5 new works (plays or musicals) on their Main Stage, as well as additional pieces presented in studio readings.

**Glasgay! Festival**
www.glasgay.co.uk
Q! Gallery and Studio
87-91 Saltmarket
Glasgow G1 5LE Scotland
+44(0)141 552 7575
info@glasgay.com
> Scotland's annual celebration of queer culture. Presented annually from mid-October to mid-November. Presents top acts from around the world, spanning comedy, music, theatre, performance art, and more. Send submissions by mail or e-mail; for what to send, see www.glasgay.co.uk/submissions.

**Out on the Edge Festival**
www.thetheateroffensive.org/oote_09
29 Elm Street #2
Cambridge, MA 02139
T: 617-661-1600
F: 617-661-1610
info@theateroffensive.org
    22 performances and 17 Festival Institute offerings, all performed in intimate cabaret settings.

**SNAP!fest**
www.snapproductions.com
PO Box 8464
Omaha, NE 68108
402-341-2757
Contact: Michael Simpson, artistic director
artistic@snapproductions.com

**Stage Left – Left Out Festival**
www.leftoutfestival.xbuild.com
www.stagelefttheatre.com
3408 N. Sheffield Avenue.
Chicago, IL 60657
773-883-8830
Contact: Kein Heckman and Zev Valancy, co-literary managers, scripts@
stagelefttheatre.com
    A celebration of gay performance art.

**Studio 303 – Edgy Women Festival**
www.studio303.ca (the website is in French; for an English translation, click on
"English" near the bottom of the page)
372 Ste-Catherine West
Montreal QC, H3B1A2 Canada
514-393-3771
info@studio303.ca
    Presented by Studio 303, Edgy Women has blossomed from a 4-day event into a
    full-blown international festival, featuring a plethora of neophyte and experienced
    artists in a diverse programme of cutting edge work which is both experimental
    AND entertaining. Through its performance series, artist talks, and professional
    workshops, Edgy Women creates a forum for cultural exchange through a thematic
    context, providing an excellent opportunity for audiences to experience content-
    driven artwork by women.

**Queer Shorts Festival**
stageq.com
P.O. Box 8876
Madison, WI 53708-8876
608-661-9696, ext 3
stageq@stageq.com
Contact: Tara Ayres, artistic director, artisticdirector@stageq.com
    An annual festival produced by StageQ. 12 shows in one night; runs two weekends
    only. Looking for short plays with queer content. Plays for this year's festival are due

October 30, 2010. They should be no longer than 12 minutes in length and include a précis with a description of the play and its needs (for more info, see ). Send script and précis to queershorts@stageq.com.

**XYZ FESTIVAL OF NEW WORKS**
http://aboutfacetheatre.com/index.php
For contact info, see About Face Theatre
literary@aboutfacetheatre.com
Looking for material that challenges expectations and ideas about gender and sexuality in historical or contemporary contexts; scripts that break traditional ideas about dramatic form, structure, and presentation. Accepts full-length scripts at any stage of development, but must be a new work that has not seen full production (readings and workshops okay). Send submission electronically; see website for details about formatting.

## BOOKS ON WRITING FOR THE STAGE: ART, CRAFT, THEORY, AND BUSINESS

The following list was designed to aid writers in selecting the scriptwriting craft and business books that best fit their individual needs. Readers can generally assume that playwriting craft books will explore action, character, and dialogue. Specific aspects of craft that are emphasized by the author are listed under Features. Chapter or section titles that suggest further distinguishing features are listed in quotes.

**The 2009 Screenwriter's and Playwright's Market**
By Chuck Sambuchino
Publisher: Writers Digest Books (January 7, 2009)
ISBN-13: 9781582975528
    Features: Business strategies, Business resources

**The Art and Craft of Playwriting**
By Jeffrey Hatcher
Publisher: Story Press (March 1, 2000)
ISBN-13: 9781884910463
    Features: Aristotle's theories, Interviews, "Space, Time, and Causality," Structure

**The Art of Dramatic Writing**
By Lajos Egri
Publisher: Simon and Schuster (June 1, 1960)
ISBN-13: 9780671213329
    Features: Character behavior, Dialectics, "Orchestration," Premise, "Unity of Opposites"

**The Art of the Playwright - Creating the Magic of Theatre**
By William Packard
Publisher: Thunder's Mouth Press; 2nd edition (May 5, 1997)
ISBN-13: 9781560251170
    Features: Business resources, "Contemporary and Avant Garde Playwrights," "Dramatic Versus Narrative"

**The Art of Writing Drama**
By Michelene Wandor
Publisher: A&C Black (September 2008)
ISBN-13: 9780413775863

**An Artist's Guide to the Law: Law and Legal Concepts Every Artist, Performer and Writer Ought to Know**
By Rich Amada
Publisher: Focus Publishing (March 1, 2010)
ISBN-13: 9781585103560
    Features: Copyright, Licensing, Fair Use, "First Amendment Protections", Protecting Intellectual Property

**Backwards & Forwards: A Technical Manual for Reading Plays**
By David Ball
Publisher: Southern Illinois University Press; 1st edition (July 7, 1983)
ISBN-13: 9780809311101

**Blunt Playwright: An Introduction to Playwriting**
By Clem Martini
Publisher: Consortium Books (September 30, 2007)
ISBN-13: 9780887548949
    Features: Exercises, Play Analyses, Rewriting, Workshopping

**Collaborative Playwright: Practical Advice for Getting Your Play Written**
By Bruce Graham, Michele Volansky
Publisher: Heinemann (March 30, 2007)
ISBN-13: 9780325009957
    Features: Collaboration, Interviews, "Prewriting and outlines," Rewriting

**The Crafty Art of Playmaking**
By Alan Ayckbourn
Publisher: Palgrave Macmillan (September 30th, 2008)
ISBN-13: 9780230614888
    Features: Directorial perspectives

**Creating Unforgettable Characters**
By Linda Seger
Publisher: Henry Holt (July 1, 1990)
ISBN-13: 9780805011715
Features: Character psychology, "Creating Nonrealistic Characters," Research

**Developing Story Ideas**
By Michael Rabiger
Publisher: Elsevier Science (October 21, 2005)
ISBN-13: 9780240807362
    Features: Artistic Identity, Exercises, Generating ideas

**Dramatic Writer's Companion: Tools to Develop Characters, Cause Scenes and Build Stories**
By Will Dunne
Publisher: University of Chicago Press (April 15, 2009)
ISBN-13: 9780226172538
    Features: Character development, Structure

**Dramatists Toolkit: The Craft of the Working Playwright**
By Jeffrey Sweet
Publisher: Heinemann (November 1, 1993)
ISBN-13: 9780435086299
    Features: "Negotiations," "Violating Rituals"

**The Elements of Playwriting**
By Louis E. Catron
Publisher: Waveland Press (November 1, 2001)
ISBN-13: 9781577662273

**A More Perfect 10: Writing and Producing the Ten-Minute Play**
By Gary Garrison
Publisher: Focus Publishing (December 1, 2008)
ISBN-13: 9781585103270
    Features: Ten-Minute Plays

**Musical Theatre Writer's Survival Guide**
By David Spencer
Publisher: Heinemann
ISBN-13: 9780325007861 (July 1, 2005)
    Features: Musical Writing, Collaboration, Business Strategies, "Presentation,
    Formatting and Packaging," "The Spirit of the Thing, or: Adaptation"

**Naked Playwriting: The Art, the Craft, and the Life Laid Bare**
By Robin U. Russin and William M. Downs
Publisher: Silman-James Press (December 15, 2004)
ISBN-13: 9781879505766
    Features: Business strategies, Generating ideas, Rewriting

**New Playwriting Strategies: A Language-Based Approach to Playwriting**
By Paul C. Castagno
Publisher: Theatre Arts Book (2001)
ISBN-13: 9780878301362
    Features: "On Multivocality and Speech Genres," Play analyses

**New Tax Guide for Writers, Artists, Performers and Other Creative People**
By Peter Jason Riley
Publisher: Focus Publishing (February 1, 2009)
ISBN-13: 9781585103799
    Features: Record Keeping, Tax Planning, "Setting up a Business Entity", the Audit
    Process

**Notes from a Practicing Writer: The Craft, Career, and Aesthetic of Playwriting**
By Ed Shockley
Publisher: Hopewell Publications (January 30, 2007)
ISBN-13: 9780972690638
    Features: Business strategies, "Compression," "The Magic What-If," "Projection,"
    Play analyses, "Reduction"

**Playwright's Guidebook**
By Stuart Spencer
Publisher: Farrar Straus and Giroux (April 1, 2002)
ISBN-13: 9780571199914
    Features: Exercises, Generating ideas, Rewriting, Structure, "High Stakes and High
    Hopes," "Writing from an Image"

**The Playwright's Handbook**
By Frank Pike, Thomas G. Dunn
Publisher: Plume; Rev Upd Su edition (April 1, 1996)
ISBN-13: 9780452275881
    Features: Rewriting, Business Strategies, Workshops, "Sight, Hearing, Touch, Taste,
    Smell," "Understanding the Relationship of Ritual and Drama"

**The Playwright's Workbook**
By Jean-Claude Van Itallie
Publisher: Applause (1997)
ISBN: 1557833028
  Features: Exercises, Play analyses, Images, Various forms and genres

**The Playwright's Workout**
By Liz Engelman, Michael Bigelow Dixon
Publisher: Smith and Krause Publishers (April 1, 2009)
ISBN-13: 9781575256177
  Features: Exercises

**The Playwright's Process - Learning the Craft from Today's Leading Dramatists**
By Buzz McLaughlin
Publisher: Back Stage Books (May 1, 1997)
ISBN-13: 9780823088331
  Features: Interviews, Rewriting, Development, "The Play Idea Worksheet," "The
  Short-form Biography," "The Long-form Biography"

**Playwriting in Process: Thinking and Working Theatrically (2nd ed.)**
By Michael Wright
Publisher: Focus Publishing (August 1, 2009)
ISBN-13: 9781585103409

**Playwrights Teach Playwriting**
By Joan Harrington (editor) and Brian Crystal (editor)
Publisher: Smith & Kraus (September 30, 2006)
ISBN-13: 9781575254234
  Features: Essays, Interviews, Teaching methods

**Playwriting: A Practical Guide**
By Noel Greig
Publisher: Routledge (February 28, 2005)
ISBN-13: 9780415310444
  Features: Generating ideas, Rewriting

**Playwriting, Brief and Brilliant**
By Julie Jensen
Publisher: Smith & Kraus (October 30, 2007)
ISBN-13: 9781575255705

**Playwriting in Process: Thinking and Working Theatrically (2nd ed.)**
By Michael Wright
Publisher: Focus Publishing (August 1, 2009)
ISBN-13: 9781585103409
  Features: Exercises, Process, Writer's Block

**Playwriting Master Class: The Personality of Process and the Art of Rewriting
(2nd ed.)**
By Michael Wright
Publisher: Focus Publishing (October 1, 2010)
ISBN-13: 9781585103423

**Playwriting : The Structure of Action**
By Norman A. Bert, Sam Smiley
Publisher: Yale University Press (October 30, 2005)
ISBN-13: 9780300107241
    Features: Aristotle's principles, Generating ideas

**Playwriting: Writing, Producing and Selling Your Play**
By Louis E. Catron
Publisher: Waveland Press (July 1990)
ISBN-13: 9780881335644
    Features: Business strategies, Aristotle's principals, Workshops

**The Power of the Playwright's Vision: Blueprints for the Working Writer**
By Gordon Farrell
Publisher: Heinemann Drama (September 6, 2001)
ISBN-13: 9780325002422

**Reminiscence Theatre : Making Theatre from Memories**
By Glenda Jackson, Pam Schweitzer
Publisher: Jessica Kingsley Publishers (January 15, 2006)
ISBN-13: 9781843104308
    Features: Community building, Documentary, Teaching methods, Therapy

**Script is Finished, Now What Do I Do: The Scriptwriter's Resource Book and Agent Guide**
By K. Callan
Publisher: SCB Distributors (January 15, 2007)
ISBN-13: 9781878355188
    Features: Business resources, Business strategies

**Solving Your Script : Tools and Techniques for the Playwright**
By Jeffrey Sweet
Publisher: Heinemann (February 15, 2001)
ISBN-13: 9780325000534
    Table of Contents: "Negotiation Over Objects," "Different Relationships, Different Roles," "Disruption of a Ritual"

**So You Want to Be a Playwright? : How to Write a Play and Get It Produced**
By Tim Fountain
Publisher: Nick Hern Books (April 1, 2008)
ISBN-13: 9781854597168

**Stage Writers Handbook: A Complete Business Guide for Playwrights, Composers, Lyricists and** Librettists
By Dana Singer
Publisher: Theatre Communications Group (May 1, 1996)
ISBN-13: 9781559361163
    Features: Business resources, Business strategies

**Strategies for Playbuilding: Helping Groups Translate Issues into Theater**
By Will Weigler
Publisher: Heinemann (March 15, 2001)
ISBN-13: 9780325003405
    Features: Community building, Documentary, Teaching methods

**Teaching Young Playwrights**
By Gerald Chapman, Lisa A Barnett
Publisher: Heinemann (November 26, 1990)
ISBN-13: 9780435082123
    Features: Exercises, Teaching methods

**Teach Yourself Writing a Play**
By Ann Gawthorpe, Lesley Brown
Publisher: McGraw-Hill (October 26, 2007)
ISBN-13: 9780071496971
    Features: Business strategies, Generating ideas, Genres, Rewriting

**To Be a Playwright**
By Janet Neipris
Publisher: Theatre Arts Book; New edition (September 28, 2005)
ISBN-13: 9780878301881
    Features: "Twelve Habits of Successful Playwrights," "Adapting from Fact and
    Fiction," "Critics"

**The Way of Story: The Craft & Soul of Writing**
By Catherine Ann Jones
Publisher: Ingram Publisher Services (August 1, 2007)
ISBN-13: 9781932907322
    Features: Dialogue Structure, Rewriting, Generating ideas,

**"Writer's Block" Busters : 101 Exercises to Clear the Deadwood and Make Room
for Flights of Fancy**
By Velina Hasu Houston
Publisher: Smith & Kraus (September 16, 2008)
ISBN-13: 9781575255972
    Features: Exercises

**Writing For The Stage: A Practical Playwriting Guide**
By Leroy Clark
Publisher: Allyn & Bacon (September 23, 2005)
ISBN-13: 9780205412976

**The Writer Got Screwed (but didn't have to): Guide to the Legal and Business
Practices of Writing for the Entertainment Industry**
By Brooke A. Wharton
Publisher: Harper Paperbacks (March 14, 1997)
ISBN-13: 9780062732361
    Features: Business strategies

**The Writer's Journey: Mythic Structure for Writers**
By Christopher Vogler
Publisher: Ingram Publisher Services (November 1, 2007)
ISBN-13: 9781932907360
    Features: Mythic Structure, Mythic Characters

# Index of Special Interests

# Submission Calendar

These opportunities accept submissions year-round. Consult the company website for the most up-to-date information. Also, consult the Dramatists Guild website for new opportunities, changes in rules and deadlines, and for ongoing opportunities not listed in this year's directory.

## January

| | | |
|---|---|---|
| 1/1/2011 | Kitchen Dog Theater (KDT) New Works Festival | 45 |
| 1/1/2011 | WordBRIDGE Playwrights Laboratory | 58 |
| 1/3/2011 | Young Playwrights Inc. National Playwriting Competition | 58 |
| 1/7/2011 | Theater Resources Unlimited (TRU)/TRU Voices | 50 |
| 1/7/2011 | TRU (Theater Resources Unlimited) | 134 |
| 1/12/2011 | Camargo Foundation | 37 |
| 1/15/2011 | Ashland New Plays Festival | 42 |
| 1/15/2011 | Playwrights' Forum [MD] | 133 |
| 1/15/2011 | Premiere Stages Play Festival | 47 |
| 1/15/2011 | Summerfield G. Roberts Award | 57 |
| 1/15/2011 | Virginia Center for the Creative Arts (VCCA) | 40 |
| 1/16/2011 | PEN/Laura Pels Foundation Awards for Drama | 55 |
| 1/18/2011 | Helene Wurlitzer Foundation of New Mexico | 38 |
| 1/18/2011 | Sundog Theatre | 105 |
| 1/30/2011 | Baker's Plays High School Playwriting Contest | 51 |
| 1/31/2011 | Dubuque Fine Arts Players One Act Play Contest | 59 |
| 1/31/2011 | Lionheart Theatre's Make the House Roar Prize | 61 |

## February

| | | |
|---|---|---|
| 2/1/2011 | Centre Stage New Play Festival | 42 |
| 2/1/2011 | New Directors/New Works (ND/NW) | 124 |
| 2/1/2011 | U.S./Japan Creative Artists' Program | 40 |
| 2/1/2011 | Vermont Playwrights Award | 58 |
| 2/1/2011 | Yale University School of Drama | 121 |
| 2/14/2011 | Penobscot Theatre | 46 |
| 2/14/2011 | The Present Company | 113 |
| 2/15/2011 | Fresh Fruit Festival | 43 |
| 2/15/2011 | Jane Chambers Playwriting Award | 53 |
| 2/15/2011 | Jane Chambers Student Playwriting Award | 53 |
| 2/15/2011 | North Dakota Council on the Arts | 68 |
| 2/15/2011 | Theatre Oxford 10-Minute Play Contest | 63 |
| 2/28/2011 | Attic Theatre One-Act Marathon | 42 |
| 2/28/2011 | McLaren Memorial Comedy Playwriting Competition | 61 |
| 2/28/2011 | Missouri Arts Council | 67 |

## March

| | | |
|---|---|---|
| 3/1/2011 | Alabama State Council on the Arts | 64 |
| 3/1/2011 | Byrdcliffe Arts Colony Artist-in-Residence (AIR) | 37 |
| 3/1/2011 | Clauder Competition for New England Playwrights | 52 |
| 3/1/2011 | Dorland Mountain Arts Colony | 38 |
| 3/1/2011 | Edward Albee Foundation | 38 |
| 3/1/2011 | North Carolina Arts Council | 68 |
| 3/1/2011 | Old Opera House Theatre Company New Voice Play Festival | 50 |
| 3/1/2011 | South Dakota Arts Council | 69 |
| 3/1/2011 | U.S. Dept. of State Fulbright Program for US Students | 70 |
| 3/1/2011 | Ucross Foundation Residency Program | 40 |
| 3/1/2011 | Urban Retreat | 126 |

## April

## May

## June

## July

## August

| | | |
|---|---|---|
| 8/1/2011 | Aurora Theatre Company: Global Age Project | 59 |
| 8/1/2011 | BMI Lehman Engel Musical Theatre Workshop - Songwriters Work | 123 |
| 8/1/2011 | Indo-American Arts Council Inc. (IACC) | 44 |
| 8/1/2011 | Jewish Ensemble Theater Festival of New Plays | 44 |
| 8/1/2011 | Little Fish Theatre (LFT) | 91 |
| 8/1/2011 | Playfest - Harriett Lake Festival of New Plays | 46 |
| 8/1/2011 | Yaddo | 41 |
| 8/2/2011 | Delaware Division of the Arts | 65 |
| 8/15/2011 | Altos de Chavon | 37 |
| 8/15/2011 | David C. Horn Prize | 52 |
| 8/15/2011 | North Carolina New Play Project (NCNPP) | 55 |
| 8/31/2011 | Fulbright Program for US Scholars | 65 |
| 8/31/2011 | The Ten Minute Musicals Project | 62 |

## September

| | | |
|---|---|---|
| 9/1/2011 | Electric Theatre Company | 83 |
| 9/1/2011 | Mississippi Theatre Association | 54 |
| 9/1/2011 | Theatre Building Chicago Musical Theatre Writers' Workshop | 126 |
| 9/10/2011 | Year-End Series (YES) New Play Festival | 48 |
| 9/14/2011 | Jonathan Larson Performing Arts Foundation | 66 |
| 9/15/2011 | John Simon Guggenheim Memorial Foundation | 66 |
| 9/15/2011 | Kleban Award | 66 |
| 9/15/2011 | New Dramatists | 132 |
| 9/15/2011 | Playwrights First Award | 56 |
| 9/15/2011 | Susan Smith Blackburn Prize | 57 |
| 9/15/2011 | Teatro del Pueblo | 47 |
| 9/17/2011 | Wisconsin Arts Board | 70 |
| 9/20/2011 | Young Playwrights Inc. Advanced Playwriting Workshop | 127 |
| 9/24/2011 | Hedgebrook | 38 |
| 9/30/2011 | Actors Collective | 72 |
| 9/30/2011 | Boomerang Theatre Company | 42 |
| 9/30/2011 | Long Beach Playhouse New Works Festival | 49 |
| 9/30/2011 | Theatre Three [NY] One-Act Play Festival | 48 |

## October

| | | |
|---|---|---|
| 10/1/2011 | Latino Playwriting Award | 61 |
| 10/1/2011 | Lorraine Hansberry Playwriting Award | 61 |
| 10/1/2011 | Millay Colony for the Arts | 39 |
| 10/1/2011 | Musical Theater Award | 61 |
| 10/1/2011 | National Student Playwriting Award | 62 |
| 10/1/2011 | Paula Vogel Award for Playwriting | 62 |
| 10/1/2011 | Radcliffe Institute Fellowships | 69 |
| 10/1/2011 | Rhode Island State Council on the Arts | 69 |
| 10/1/2011 | Stanley Drama Award | 62 |
| 10/1/2011 | Sundance Institute Theatre Program | 126 |
| 10/1/2011 | The New Harmony Project | 126 |
| 10/1/2011 | Theatre Building Chicago | 48 |
| 10/15/2011 | ShowOff! Ten-Minute Playwriting Festival | 50 |
| 10/20/2011 | Ledig House Writers Residency Program | 39 |
| 10/31/2011 | Cultural Conversations | 43 |
| 10/31/2011 | FutureFest | 43 |
| 10/31/2011 | International Mystery Writers' Festival | 44 |
| 10/31/2011 | Southern Appalachian Playwrights' Conference | 47 |

## November

| | | |
|---|---|---|
| 11/1/2011 | American-Scandinavian Foundation (ASF) | 51 |
| 11/1/2011 | Hodder Fellowship | 65 |

| | | |
|---|---|---|
| 11/1/2011 | Lost Nation Theater | 91 |
| 11/1/2011 | National Ten-Minute Play Contest | 55 |
| 11/1/2011 | Summer Play Festival (SPF) | 47 |
| 11/1/2011 | Tennessee Williams/New Orleans Literary Festival | 47 |
| 11/2/2011 | Richard Rodgers Awards for Musical Theater | 56 |
| 11/15/2011 | Boston Theater Marathon | 42 |
| 11/15/2011 | Lark Play Development Center: Playwrights' Week | 44 |
| 11/15/2011 | Seven Devils Playwrights Conference | 47 |
| 11/15/2011 | Theater of the First Amendment, First Light Discovery Progra | 108 |
| 11/25/2011 | FirstStage One-Act Play Contest | 59 |
| 11/30/2011 | Bay Area Playwrights Festival (BAPF) | 42 |
| 11/30/2011 | Edgar Allan Poe Award for Best Play | 53 |
| 11/30/2011 | Poems & Plays | 35 |
| 11/30/2011 | Raymond J. Flores Short Play Festival (Around the Block) | 50 |

## December

| | | |
|---|---|---|
| 12/1/2011 | American College Theater Festival (ACTF) | 41 |
| 12/1/2011 | David Mark Cohen Playwriting Award | 59 |
| 12/1/2011 | Georgia College and State University | 60 |
| 12/1/2011 | Jean Kennedy Smith Playwriting Award | 60 |
| 12/1/2011 | John Cauble Short Play Awards Program | 60 |
| 12/1/2011 | Lavender Footlights Festival | 45 |
| 12/1/2011 | National Latino Playwriting Award | 54 |
| 12/1/2011 | One-Act Playwriting Competition | 55 |
| 12/1/2011 | SETC High School New Play Award | 62 |
| 12/1/2011 | Ten-Minute Play Festival | 62 |
| 12/1/2011 | Utah Shakespearean Festival: New American Playwrights Projec | 50 |
| 12/6/2011 | TeCo Theatrical Productions New Play Competition | 57 |
| 12/15/2011 | Collaboraction: Sketchbook Festival | 43 |
| 12/15/2011 | Dorothy Silver Playwriting Competition | 52 |
| 12/15/2011 | Genesis Festival | 44 |
| 12/15/2011 | Goshen College Peace Playwriting Contest | 53 |
| 12/15/2011 | Michener Center for Writers | 67 |
| 12/15/2011 | New York City 15-Minute Play Fest | 46 |
| 12/15/2011 | Reverie Productions | 62 |
| 12/15/2011 | Robert J. Pickering Award for Playwriting Excellence | 56 |
| 12/15/2011 | Teatro Dallas | 113 |
| 12/15/2011 | Theatre in the Raw Play Writing Contest | 63 |
| 12/16/2011 | Burning Coal Theatre Company | 77 |
| 12/20/2011 | Last Frontier Theatre Conference | 45 |
| 12/30/2011 | Cincinnati Fringe Festival | 49 |
| 12/31/2011 | Inspirato Festival | 44 |
| 12/31/2011 | Ohioana Career Award | 55 |
| 12/31/2011 | Ohioana Citations | 55 |
| 12/31/2011 | Ohioana Pegasus Award | 55 |
| 12/1/2012 | Ruby Lloyd Apsey Award | 56 |

# INDEX

189

# M

# N

# O

# P

# Q

# R

# S